Secrets

BY THE SAME AUTHOR

Secrets

BOYHOOD IN A JEWISH HOTEL

1932–1954

Ronald Hayman

PETER OWEN · LONDON

ISBN 0 7206 0642 X

PETER OWEN LIMITED
73 Kenway Road London SW5 0RE

First published 1985
© Ronald Hayman 1985

Photoset and printed in Great Britain by
Photobooks (Bristol) Ltd

For Imogen and Sorrel

Contents

All fiction is partly autobiography, all autobiography partly fiction.

1

Grannie's Place

It was Grannie's place. Linen table-cloths and napkins, gold-embroidered blue curtains, a blue carpet with a whirly pattern. From the head of the family table in the corner, her pale grey spectacled eyes moved as if the glinting lenses could send out rays to make the waiters bustle faster down the runways, black coat-tails flapping, trays crammed with steaming silver dishes. It was all hers, the long mahogany sideboard, the mirrored walls that made the room look even bigger, the blurred hum of a hundred mealtime conversations, the non-stop chinking and clinking of knives and forks and spoons on plates, the soft satisfaction of soundless swallowing, the distant shouts of orders for more food from the kitchen and the swishing of the swing doors as waiters hurried out with an empty tray in one hand while other waiters hurried in with a loaded tray in both hands.

'Madam' they all called her. When Mummy, who sat next to her, ordered 'A baked apple for Madam', the waiter would respectfully repeat 'A baked apple for Madam' before he disappeared through the swishing door to shout 'Baked apple for Madam', as if that apple had to be bigger and better baked than the others, with a thicker crust of sugar scorched on to its skin.

The visitors all spoke to Grannie first. Some of them kissed her and called her Annie. Even the ones who didn't know her knew who she was. 'You must be Mrs Morris.' She smiled and shook hands, waiting for Mummy to tell her their name, which Mummy always knew because she worked in the reception. 'This is Mr and Mrs Abel.'

'Nice to see you, Mr and Mrs Gabel. I hope you have a nice holiday.'

11

'I'm Mrs Hayman, and this is my husband Jack, and these are my sons, Ronnie and Teddy.'

We stood up to shake hands. Grannie never stood, but Mummy did. Most of the visitors told me: 'I remember you when you weren't any taller than he is.' Patting Teddy on the head.

Soon Grannie would shout 'Tonks', and the head waiter, who could carry four plates of fried fish in each hand, would whirl round like a ballroom dancer, probably sidestep to let another waiter pass him with a loaded tray, deposit his fried fish on one of the high serving tables and glide over to greet the newcomers. 'Good evening, sir. Good evening, madam.' Bowing, and never quite straightening his back afterwards. 'I've got a nice window table for you.' And lead them off. Another waiter would pull out their chairs and Tonks, with a flap and a flourish, would unfurl the starched linen napkins and flaunt them towards the newcomers' knees.

Everything about Tonks was creased, from his voice and his smile to his trousers and his patent-leather shoes. His long, arched back came into its own when he was leaning forward to accept a discreetly palmed tip or if he was playing ping-pong. When Teddy and I were in the games room he often appeared in the doorway, and if he joined in a game of doubles his shoulders loomed unfairly close to the net, while every stroke he played put a spin on the ball. But if Daddy came in, he'd say 'Just going, sir' as if he'd been trying all along to get away.

When I did wee-wee in my cot it was nice for a moment and then nasty when the warm wetness against my tummy quickly got cold and clammy, making me smell the nasty hard rubber sheet under the nice soft white sheet, and there was nothing for it but to cry. Nanny would come in and lift me gently out of the cot and wrap me in something warm and put me to sit by myself in the armchair while she changed the sheet, but it didn't take long before the cot was ready for me to be settled back into it with my cuggie in my hand – the silk-bordered shawl I needed for comfort when I was sad or sleepy. Then I'd get a hug and a kiss and a touch on the hair and she'd tuck me up tight under the blankets. After she'd gone there was still the crack of light under the door and there were beams of light sweeping round the ceiling from the headlights of cars down in the drive.

Sometimes I woke up screaming about the hole in the ground. It was a big black gaping hole with rough crumbly sides. It was there because of the road-drill. Road-drills were terrifying. The noise came from the big, ugly machines that made the single giant metal tooth quiver fiercely as it bit into the road, spurting crumbs of stone and gravel upwards and showering dust on the strong, bare, hairy arms of the men who held the drills. The hole in the ground was waiting for me. While I was in the nursery I was safe, but sooner or later I was going to be in the hole, and then the rough, crumbly sides would gradually tighten around my defenceless body, squashing into me until there was no sky left above.

I'd want the rest of the night to hurry towards the moment I could never quite catch when there'd be nothing but vague warm dreams drifting past till Nanny was there shaking my shoulder and I'd know that time had gone by. In the dark each minute blurred into the next because there was nothing except the light under the door and the beams on the ceiling and whatever it was in my head and the knowledge that sooner or later everything would tumble softly over the edge. The more cunningly you tried to lie in wait for that moment, the more cunningly it slid away from you. But when you stopped waiting for it, it caught you unawares and the next thing you knew was that you were blinking at the sunlight streaming past Nanny's dressing-table mirror, and if it was the first day of a new month she'd remind you to say 'Rabbits' before you spoke any other word so that you could be sure of getting a present. The way to be sure of getting a letter was to catch a falling leaf before it touched the ground.

On the wall in the nursery was an oblong mirror in a wooden frame that Mummy's fair-haired friend Clarice had painted for me. It was white with an elephant, a ballerina, two clowns doing the splits and a red passenger train running all along the bottom, puffing out a long cloud of blue smoke. I've still got it. Nanny took the mirror off the wall when Gilly came to the nursery and we played hairdressers, using my toy scissors with blunt blades and handles like silver sticks of twisty barley sugar. Gilly had long golden curls and a very fair skin. Of all the children who came to the hotel as visitors, she was the one I most pined for. Her little sister Patricia had long fair hair too, but she was a cry-baby. Their big brother, Justin, also had fair curly hair, but he was nasty. Nanny told him off one day for throwing stones at the geraniums and he said: 'Why shouldn't I? My father's paying for them.'

Shiny cars parked all along the drive and there were bushes that Grannie called rhodedandrums. One obstacle to objectivity is the illusion of closeness: childhood seems less like an irretrievable time than an inaccessible place. Images I recall have an insidious animal attractiveness and a fierce territorial acquisitiveness. I acknowledge that the space they occupy is imaginary, but I can't accept the impossibility of clambering back into it. If a Wellsian time machine were invented, and if I had use of it for a limited time, how much of this would I squander on my childhood instead of exploring Jacobean London?

When I was being psychoanalysed, there was nothing I enjoyed talking about more than the Bournemouth hotel, and I was quite pleased when the analyst, invisible behind me with her soft German voice, said: 'You were like a crown prince.' It sounded both accurate and complimentary. Months passed before I understood that it was intended critically, and as a warning.

The lino on the day-nursery floor was blue and you could see the sea if you stood on my wooden stool and held on to the metal bars that had been put across the windows to stop me from falling out. The night nursery was next door, and once I bolted both the interconnecting door and the door to the corridor. It was my place. No one else was allowed in the sea that was the blue lino. Then Nanny spoke to me through the door and soon Mummy's voice came. I nearly managed to turn the knob of the bolt, but not quite. I went on crying till the moustached face of the garage-man appeared outside the window. He was on a long ladder. He forced the window open, jumped down into my world and walked over it to open the door. 'Now promise you'll never do that again,' Mummy said.

Most of the day she worked in the reception office at her desk which was tucked around a corner so that visitors at the polished wooden counter couldn't see whether she was there or not. She could hear all the conversations they had with the receptionists and could poke her head round if she wanted to join in. Sometimes, when she kept out of sight, she must have overheard remarks that visitors wouldn't have made if they'd known she was there, but the receptionists would have to carry on the conversation as if she weren't.

When she came up to the day nursery, she'd grumble. There isn't enough fresh air. Open the window. Is he eating his puréed spinach? A sieve was kept in the white cupboard under the wash-basin. The floor waiter brought up the cooked spinach and the strong smell got stronger as Nanny used a spoon to push it through the sieve. Dark flecks of nasty green on the side of the bowl under the steam. It wasn't very hot by the time she fed it to me with the same spoon. Sometimes Mummy did it herself. 'One for Mummy,' she said. If Daddy was there he talked about Popeye the sailor-man, but I didn't want my muscles to stick out like that anyway.

Grannie called me 'Skinnamalinks' and said I should always eat up all my food and leave a nice clean plate. I had a special hot-plate with a thick bottom and a little spout where Nanny poured in hot water to keep the food warm, and as it was slowly spooned up there was a picture that gradually came into view of Peter Rabbit being kicked through a window by Mr McGregor's enormous boot. Grannie never fed me in the day nursery, but she gave me chocolate when I went to her bedroom, sometimes from a big box with dark, crinkly paper around each chocolate. Otherwise there'd be two pieces broken off from a Cadbury's milk bar, nestling in silver paper between the scent and the enamel-backed hairbrushes on her glass-topped dressing-table. I watched myself eating them in the triple mirror. There was a Ronnie in each mirror, and if I tilted the side-mirrors enough to make them look at each other, there were so many Ronnies in both that I couldn't even count them.

She had a mole the size of a farthing on her left shoulder and one day I asked if I could touch it. 'No,' said Mummy, 'it's not for touching.' 'Of course he can, why not?' said Gran, and I ran

timidly forward to put my finger on it, relieved it didn't feel
nastier. She had a rest after lunch every day, for which she
would only half undress. If you went into the room at tea-time
you'd find her stiff, pink corsets on the back of the armchair. She
would be half sitting, half lying on three pillows, with a pink
shawl loosely around her bulky shoulders and pink underwear
showing between the white sheets. 'You're my nice Ron-boy,'
she said as she hugged me. Her soft, sagging flesh smelled of
talcum powder and eau-de-Cologne. Her false teeth were in a
glass on the bedside table next to her small tin of Carnation milk
with thick blobs congealing around the two holes gashed into
the metal. It was a big and sunny room. I liked being in it. You
could see the sea and she was always cheerful, even if she did talk
to you as if you were still a baby. She was the one who liked
kissing most, but her skin wasn't as soft as Mummy's, and Daddy
was the nicest one to kiss. I liked the smell of his brilliantine
better than the smell of Mummy's scent, and I liked his voice.

You could hear seagulls in all the rooms, but the day and
night nurseries both faced west and the 'flat' faced east. There
were three rooms and a little corridor in the flat – the bedroom,
the bathroom and Daddy's dressing-room. Mummy kept her
clothes in the polished walnut wardrobe in the bedroom. There
was a sofa with a koala bear that Daddy's friend, Mr Reuben
Cohen, had sent from South Africa, and there was an electric
fire with imitation coal and a wheel that turned round inside to
produce an artificial flicker. In the bathroom the walls, the lino,
the bath and the wash-stand were all green. I was allowed in
when Daddy was shaving and sometimes I put the lather on with
his shaving-brush. The bubbly white beard would disappear
gradually under the clean strokes of the Gillette razor-blade,
and I could kiss him afterwards when his cheek wasn't prickly
any more. I liked everything on the wide shiny black shelf except
Mummy's glass of water with senna pods in it. They both used
laxatives every day, but Daddy used one which fizzed when you
poured water on it. Sometimes he let me have a little sip and I
liked it when the spicy bubbles went up my nose. There was a big
jar of bath salts, green crystals that looked like sweets. There was
a box with a big mirror in the lid, an empty round tin with silver
lettering on the black lid saying NOS SOURCES SONT CELLES

DU BONHEUR. And at first I thought all the scent and powder had been brought from Paris too. It all said 'Bourjois' on it and there were line drawings of the Eiffel Tower and the outlines of a tall man and woman dancing in elegant evening clothes.

Daddy's dressing-room smelt of shoe leather and lavender brilliantine. There was a pile of letters and bills on top of the narrow dressing-table, which had a special compartment for the stiff white round collars that fitted on top of each other like the jelly-moulds I used for making shapes in the sand. He folded his trousers round frame-like trouser-presses with slats of wood that slotted in to keep them in place. All his suits were dark blue or dark grey, but some had chalk-like stripes or a faint pattern. When he opened the big wardrobe a smell of cloth came out. The jackets and waistcoats were kept on hangers that lived on a sliding rail. There was only one chair with a wicker seat. I would choose a clean pair of socks for him from the little drawer in the dressing-table, and he'd sit down in his Viyella underclothes to adjust his sock suspenders, while I sat on the floor next to a row of shoes. The elastic made marks on his legs. He used to have curly hair like mine when he was a little boy, he said, but when he was a young man he'd used butter to keep it flat, so now he hadn't got much left. I decided never to use butter on mine.

When he was in the bathroom, I stayed in the dressing-room, talking to him through the locked door. I could hear the scraping noise he made in his throat to dislodge the yellowish gobs he spat into the lavatory. When I stood next to him in a gentlemen's lavatory, he'd look downwards to spit, but normally he'd look upwards as if he had nothing to do with whatever it was that made the splashy noise. I imitated this stance. Afterwards we washed our hands together. You always had to wash your hands after touching an unclean part of your body.

He smoked a lot, which yellowed his thumb, two finger-tips on his right hand and the corner of his lip just in front of his gold tooth. He told me that each time you coughed you shortened your life by a day. I resolved never to cough again, but it seemed a pity he was shortening his life so much by smoking, and it was awful when I coughed absent-mindedly. 'Oh dear, that's another two days gone.' When I found what it was like when you wanted to cough and didn't let yourself, I wondered how much fun you could have as an old man of ninety and whether it would really make up for the feeling in my throat. I wondered how long he'd live and how long we could all have lived if nobody coughed. It was a nuisance that we weren't told what our full ration of life would have been, but it was good to know we were being watched all the time. God wouldn't have time to count coughs himself, but there were lots of angels.

It was important not to eat chocolate or anything with milk in it for four hours after eating meat. On Friday evening and Shabbos I mustn't write or draw or paint or tear paper or cut anything with scissors or touch money or ride on a trolley bus or in the lift or play records on my gramophone or switch on an electric light. It was all right if Nanny switched it on for me as long as I didn't ask her to. I could drop hints. 'Nan, isn't it getting dark in here?' You were supposed to enjoy Shabbos, but the part I enjoyed most was the *Havdallah* service that meant it was all over. You couldn't say *Havdallah* until it was dark enough for three stars to have come out, but you didn't have to watch the sky – you could look the time up in the *Jewish Chronicle*. For *Havdallah* there was a big silver spice-pot we all sniffed, a big silver cup of wine we all sipped, and a special candle with red, blue and yellow plaited together, and the flames from the separate wicks joining into one wide flame. Shabbos had to have gone out before you could strike the match to light the candle, but I was the one who blew it out at the end of the *Havdallah* service, and that was when it *felt* over, with the candly smell in my nostrils. Prayers with Daddy were always in Hebrew, with some bits that were sung; when I prayed by myself it was in English, and I didn't say the words out loud. Sometimes I whispered them, sometimes I said them inside my head like a special kind of thinking with a hard edge that went upwards. I prayed every night and quite a bit during the day when there was something I specially wanted to happen or not to happen. But I never prayed when I was sitting on the lavatory.

I liked Friday best because of the Friday parcel. They couldn't buy presents for me on Shabbos, so when it got near to lunchtime on Friday I'd listen for the lift door shutting, followed by the uneven noise of Mummy's limping footsteps or her voice talking to Gran. They'd come into the nursery in their furs and

hats, laden with brown paper parcels. At least one would be for
me. 'Whatever can it be?' Nanny would say, fetching the
nursery scissors from the cupboard. But if I could untie the knot,
I would. 'I'm called Un-Knottie Hayman,' I used to tell them.
Mummy said I should save the best till last, and this was a way of
saving up the excitement of tearing at the stiff paper which
Nanny would then fold neatly and store behind the vertical pipe
in the cupboard. When we needed brown paper it was always
warm.

I enjoyed playing with the older children, and you never knew
who was going to arrive tomorrow. There were a few boys I
didn't like. The Cohens usually stayed in the room next door to
the night nursery, and you could hear Desley singing in the
lavatory at the end of the corridor because his mummy had told
him it was just as good as locking the door. When I specially
wanted someone to come again soon, I would say their names
very quietly – Gilly, Edgar, Oliver – tasting the sound of the
syllables against my tongue. There was magic in names.
Sometimes I made up pretend names like Rottety Indel
Soundor and Mucky Yollum Pittee. He was the one who liked
touching all the things Mummy wouldn't let me touch. 'Don't
touch, darling. That's mucky. That's horrible.' And she had a
name for the little boy who was suddenly there instead of me,
crying and grizzling. 'Where's Ronnie gone? That isn't Ronnie.
That's Maconochie. Ronnie doesn't grizzle. I wonder when
he'll come back.' She also had a word 'Lippit' which meant I
had to pull my lower lip in to make my face look nice. 'Don't
pout, dear. Lippit.' I hated it when she said it in front of other
people. But if I did something naughty though not really
naughty, she'd say: 'You know what happens to people who do
that. They get spiflicated.' And I'd laugh and run away and get
caught and get tickled under my arms.
    Shit was called 'dooneeze' and doing it was 'having a pain.'
'I've got a pain,' I'd say, and Nanny would fetch the big cold
china pot from the bedside cupboard. When the dooneeze was
more like brown scrambled eggs than sausages, Nanny would
call it 'a worker'.

'Has he had his pain this morning?'

'This morning he had a real worker.'

I had a garden of my own, 'Ronnie's little garden' they called it – a pear-shaped lawn fringed by a flower-bed with a thorny rose-bush climbing up against the tall fence, and thick hedges round the other sides. The entrance was an arch in the hedge low enough to make grown-ups stoop, and other children could come in only if I invited them. Some children were too 'common', and I wasn't allowed to play with Jimmy, the son of the garage man, who lived in the cottage at the other end of the drive. When I had grown-ups or children in there with me, my favourite games were French cricket, which you could play with either a tennis-racket or a cricket bat, and Grandmother's Footsteps. 'Grandmother' stood with his back to the others, who had to steal up and touch him. When he turned round you had to freeze like a crazy statue; and if he saw you moving, you had to go right back to the other end of the garden. But Grannie never played games with me. When I was alone I liked to lie on the grass, looking up at the wispy clouds and listening to the 'Stop me and buy one' shouts of the ice-cream man who rode up and down the cliff-top promenade on his backwards tricycle, the two front wheels supporting the refrigerated box that held six kinds of ice-cream, from water-ices at a penny to family tubs at sixpence. You could hear the sea, and birds, and insects, and cars on the promenade, and a different swish when they were turning into the drive to park, their bonnets nosing into my thick hedge. Then doors slamming and the important voices of grown-ups who didn't know a little boy was listening.

My tortoise, Peter, lived in the garden. Each day I'd find him in a different place. Sometimes I'd look for ages, worrying: if he'd escaped under the hedge into the drive, his shell might have been cracked by one of the heavy cars. But in the end I'd find him hiding against the fence, masked by leaves and almost invisible against the earth. You couldn't stroke him or play with him like a cat, but you could carry him to the middle of the lawn and talk to him. He had sad, tiny, understanding eyes and dry, wrinkled skin like the necks of the old men in the hotel, but still drier, with the same dark sandy dryness as the earth. The skin on the gardener's hands was almost like that, horny and dark with

ingrained earth. I asked him what earth was, and he said it was
made out of sand and leaf mould and vegetable matter from
trees and vegetables from way back before Grannie was born. I
could make earth myself, too. When my skin got all hot and
sweaty, I could rub at it with my fingers, and the dirt that came
away was just like the dirt in the garden. If only I could collect
enough of it in a flower-pot, it would be fun to plant a bulb in it
to see whether it would grow. This idea fascinated me in the
same way as picking my nose or having my nails cut. Suddenly
something that had been part of me was a thing outside me,
hard, touchable.

The earth under the grass was different, hard and flat as a slab
of chocolate, but if you put your face up close against the
hundreds and thousands of tiny, moist, soft, green spears, you
could see tiny holes in the slab and sometimes a slow-moving
worm or quick-moving ants or tiny green flies climbing over the
grass-blades and nibbling at them perhaps, but you couldn't tell,
because their bites were so small. There was life everywhere, but
some of the flies were so tiny that all you could see was a cloud of
busy dots in a sun-ray. Some of them lived only for a day. Did
they know that their lives were going to be so short? Daisies and
dandelions were tougher than ladybirds and midges. They
stayed alive when I picked them, and I'd give them to Nanny to
put in a glass of water. Butterflies didn't live long either, and I
was specially sorry for the Red Admirals. Their wings would get
all crumpled and powdery after they were dead. I helped them if
they got caught in a spider's web I could reach with a stick, and I
helped flies, even if it meant breaking the web. But I never killed
the spider. Once I saw Minnie eating a spider, but she ate flies
too if she could catch them with her paws. She was a very silly
cat who wasted a lot of love by nuzzling against my tricycle and
the bushes and things that couldn't appreciate it.

The grass smelt best of all when the gardener had just cut it. It
would grow again, like hair, and the yellowing green grass-
blades heaped up in the corner were rather like shorn hair the
barber swept into a pile on his floor, only if the gardener let them
stay there long enough they'd turn into compost and then into
soil. Sometimes I pretended to cut the grass myself with my toy
mower, putting cut grass from the pile into the hood so that I

could take it off and empty it back on to the pile. And sometimes
I cut the grass with my toy scissors.

'Why is it so hard to make you lose your cool?' 'Why are you
always polite?' 'Don't you ever lose your temper?' Questions like
these are put to me often by friends, and during five years of
psychoanalysis a lot of time went on trying to discover why I find
it so hard to release aggression. The analyst believed there was so
much aggression in the pressure cooker that I was scared of
fiddling with the valve. These days I do, occasionally, get angry.
I hit my wife once after seven years of marriage and once after
the divorce, but I don't often shout at my daughter, Imogen,
and close friends find it annoyingly difficult to make me angry. I
still find it hard to explain why the boiling-point is so high,
though one reason, probably, is that I was never allowed during
childhood to make a noise in the hotel. The visitors must not be
disturbed.
    Another reason is that quite early in my relationship with my
mother I adopted the habit of masking frustration and anger.
Seeing so little of her, I probably believed I'd see even less if I
displayed unhappiness. Even today, I hear myself – with her
more than with anyone else – preserving an artificially even tone
to conceal impatience. It must also be significant that neither
my brother nor I could ever get into the habit of calling her
'Mother'. Longer, probably, than most sons, we went on saying
'Mummy'. I then started addressing her, in letters, as 'Dear M',
never calling her by name. Today, when he and I talk about her,
we usually say 'she', occasionally 'Mummy', never 'Mother'.
She has difficulty herself with names. For twenty-three years
after retiring she shared a flat with my old nanny, and went on
calling her 'Nanny', as we did, while Nanny went on calling her
'Mrs Hayman'.

I knew that God liked me. The sun shone on the good, they said,
and when I sat on the white wooden chair at the table in the
nursery, painting or doing my jigsaw puzzle of Buckingham
Palace, bright sun-rays slanted through the window from above

the grey roof of the Carlton Hotel to warm my face and throw my shadow on the round white table with a square of gold light all round it. And they lit up the milky clouds of swirling colour in the glass of water I used for cleaning the thin paintbrush. It would have been wrong to paint a picture of God, but I couldn't help knowing what He looked like. He wasn't an old man with a white beard made of clouds. He was more like the sun when it's hidden, a pale, vague, eyeless glow with a comfortable warmth that went to the insides of people's heads. You could hear Him in the soft electric hum of the lift that travelled magically upwards or downwards inside its tall metal cage when Nanny lifted me up to press the button. And His Will was behind everything that happened in the hotel. When Nanny left our shoes outside the night-nursery door, they'd be cleaned overnight. If I pressed the tiny button in the little white pear that was hanging from the electric wire over my cot, the maid would come knocking at the door. The whole world was an enormous hotel that God owned. Under the night nursery was another bedroom shaped exactly like it, with another one under that. And in France and Japan there were other buildings with little boys in them, and there might be two little boys somewhere who were exactly like me and did exactly the same things. Their names wouldn't be Ronnie Hayman but the French and the Japanese for Ronnie Hayman. Everything was organized and everybody had lots of people to look after them even in the middle of the night.

Once when I couldn't sleep I picked up the telephone. The night porter's voice said 'Hello' into my ear and I spoke into the mouthpiece. 'Please may I have a pot of coffee and some toast?' Soon afterwards he was tapping at the door. He'd brought a glass of lemon barley water and some biscuits. In the morning they all knew about it, but nobody was cross.

God wasn't present in the other hotels, where the food wasn't kosher. If any of the visitors came to Bournemouth and stayed at the Carlton or the Norfolk or the Royal Bath, Grannie or Mummy or Daddy would somehow find out and be very cross. But they'd be nice to the people again if they came back to us and said they hadn't really liked it at the other place. I got a lot of presents from the visitors and pats on the head. They all seemed to like touching me, and it was all because of the Jewish religion that they came to this hotel. They were 'our people'.

In the dining-room all the meals were either milk meals or meat meals. For milk meals the table-cloths were checked with brown or blue lines; for meat meals plain white. For milk meals the plates and cups and saucers had black edges and the knives, forks and spoons round handles; for meat meals the edges were blue and the handles were pointed. Breakfast was always a milk meal because you couldn't eat meat if you were going to have milk in your tea or coffee; at meat meals no one could have butter on his bread or cream on his stewed fruit. When it was a fish lunch or dinner, tables were laid with the milk table-cloths, milk crockery and milk cutlery, which meant ice-cream would be one of the puddings. But if a waiter made a mistake when he was laying the tables or used a round-edged spoon to serve vegetables during a meat meal, Mummy would be very angry and call Tonks over to tell him off for being careless.

I didn't know much about other countries, but one of them was called Abyssinia, and there was a little emperor everyone felt sorry for. His name was Haile Selassie. Sometimes his picture was in the newspapers. I also had a pimple called Abyssinia, though I didn't understand why it had that name or what it had to do with the little emperor. The pimple took a long time to get better and eventually Daddy squeezed it and something small but hard came away from me. They wanted to keep it and they put it in a box with cotton wool. 'Ronnie's Abyssinia,' they said, and laughed.

I knew that when I grew up I was going to be King of the World. The grown-ups knew, but they weren't allowed to tell me. It had to be a secret until I came of age, but it was obviously silly to have a different king for each country. It would be better to have one king in charge of everyone. This was the job I was being groomed for. I guessed when a telegram arrived saying HAPPY BIRTHDAY RONNIE FROM ALL THE KINGS. Mummy tried to explain it by saying it was from Mr and Mrs King, Daddy's partners in the antique shop, and their sons, Ashley and Norman. But I understood what was going on when I realized they were a bit short of actors, and sometimes they were using the same ones to play different parts. The straw-hatted manager of MacFisheries in Old Christchurch Road was always to be seen picking up fish by their tails to rearrange them on the white marble slab between the blocks of ice. He had thick glasses and a bristly moustache. Daddy said he wasn't one of our people, but he looked just like a man who came to Shool in a black trilby hat. He had a silk prayer-shawl with blue stripes, just like Daddy's, only not so clean-looking, and with tattered tassels. He kissed it before he put it round his neck and then shook his body backwards and forwards while he prayed, trying to look different from the fishmonger.

One afternoon, paddling, I got to know a little girl with ringlets. Her father was sunbathing and pretending to shield his face with a newspaper, though really he was trying to hide it when he saw that I'd recognized him as the manager of the hotel we stayed at in Lyme Regis. Nanny said it wasn't the same man, but once having guessed at the secret I found more and more evidence. Everything that seemed to be accidental was actually planned by the controller of my training to make me into the perfect person I'd have to be. Things didn't happen unless I was coming along the road towards them. There were spies on my movements hidden in crevices between rocks and under trapdoors. They tapped radio messages in code to warn the groups of actors waiting in various places to get ready for the show they had to put on. I used to wonder what they all did when I wasn't there, and sometimes I caught some of them looking at me in a special way. I knew what they must be thinking: There's the future King of the World. How nice to be so close to him. It was much wiser not to let them know I'd found out the secret. Even when they finally told me, I'd pretend to be surprised. Meanwhile I made up my mind that I'd be nice to most of them. There were just a few who'd have to be punished for being unnecessarily nasty. Naturally they'd all make the excuse that they'd been under orders, playing a part. I had my answer ready: 'Yes, but it's the way you played it.'

2

Another Ronnie

When Mummy was going to have another baby, the midwife moved in to the bedroom next door to the night nursery. She was called Mac, and she wore a starched white head-dress like a nun's, steel-rimmed glasses and a pale blue uniform with a starched white apron and starched white crinkly things like cake-cups to hold her short sleeves to her scrubbed-looking arms. She bustled importantly along the corridor between the flat and her bedroom, getting things ready and talking bossily to Nanny. On the day the baby was going to be born, she wouldn't let me go into the flat to see Mummy, and even Nanny seemed a bit cross. Daddy didn't go to the shop that day and came into the nursery a lot. If it was a girl, she was going to be called Audrey. Finally the door half opened and the upper part of Mac's stiff body tilted into sight. What she said was 'Another Ronnie' or 'A brother for Ronnie', and either way there was something wrong. One of me was quite enough, and if it was all being done for my benefit, why hadn't they asked whether I wanted it?

He was bigger than I expected, and they all said I hadn't been born with so much hair. There was dribble all round his lips and the noises he made weren't very nice. I couldn't understand why Mummy looked so pleased. Mostly he lay on his back just waving his hands about, and later he would wave them about in the same loose way as he sat on the pot doing his dooneeze. But I was jealous of the names they gave him – Anthony Edward.

After I'd tried to kill him with Nanny's scissors, they said that as soon as he grew a bit bigger he'd be my best friend, and meanwhile I must help Nanny to look after him. Daddy said he'd had six brothers, and he showed me a dark old photograph

26

of the butcher's shop in Hammersmith. My burly, bearded grandfather was holding a cleaver and wearing a striped apron. My other Grannie was almost hiding her small, frightened face behind the children. There were only two girls, their dark hair bunchy in front and ringleted behind. But there were seven boys. I could tell which one was Daddy because he looked like me, with the same wavy hair and the same smile. Uncle Joe, the eldest, was in Canada now. He worked in a garage and never wrote to us. Uncle Dan, the youngest, wrote to us from Brooklyn with coloured photographs of a curly-haired American wife and a baby daughter. In Daddy's photograph he was chewing at his rattle. All the other uncles were dead. Some had been killed by childhood diseases, two had been killed in the war. Uncle Harry had been one year younger than Daddy, a brave man, very religious. He died in the trenches. It was lucky that Daddy hadn't been killed by a childhood disease or died in the trenches, but there was something about his face in the photograph that made it look as if he wanted to live, while Uncle Harry's face was much sadder, like Aunt Hetty's now, but kinder and with a far-away look. I asked Daddy what war was exactly, and he tried to say something, but his voice was all cracked, and he turned abruptly away to fumble in his collar-stud box. The photograph was still in my hand, and I saw that one of the dead uncles looked like Anthony Edward. Perhaps he'd die of a childhood disease too.

I could try to find out from Nanny what war was, but it might be one of the questions she'd fob off by saying I wasn't old enough to know yet. There were so many grown-up secrets. Sometimes Nanny even refused to tell me what things were. I found something on the beach that looked like a small, thin, broken balloon of no particular colour, but when I took it to her, she said 'Throw that away at once', and made me wash my hands under the tap people used for washing sand off their feet. We had no towel with us and I had to dry my hands on the back of her coat. I asked her about war while she was pushing Teddy's pram downhill past the Royal Bath Hotel and I was holding on to the side of the handle. She said sometimes there was a quarrel between two countries that couldn't be settled in any other way. I didn't understand how countries could quarrel, but I could picture big, smoky fields called battlefields, full of soldiers in uniform firing guns at each other and riding about on horses in between piles of dead bodies that were buried in trenches. She didn't seem to know what the battlefields were used for when there wasn't a war on.

I was always pleased when Daddy came into the nursery, or when I saw him coming around a corner with his distinctive gait, his hard-brimmed grey trilby hat always at a slight slant. Or when I heard the three-note whistle he used for calling me. He was usually cheerful and always friendly. Even when he was cross, you knew it would soon be all right again. He liked playing games and holding my ankles so that I could 'do a wheelbarrow', walking on my hands, and he saved me the cigarette cards from his Gold Flake and Player's cigarette packets, and let me blow out his matches so that I could enjoy the sulphury smell in my nostrils. I liked the pink-tipped Swan Vestas in wide boxes better than the black-tipped safety matches. I decided that when I grew up I wouldn't smoke, but I'd always carry a packet of Swan Vestas just to light the matches and blow them out.

I wasn't so pleased when Mummy came into the nursery. Nanny would often get told off or be given strict instructions about what to do with 'the boys'. We must have our walks, must have the window open, mustn't go to bed late. With Daddy you nearly always had fun; with her there was always something that needed doing or needed not to be done. She often seemed to be cross with herself, and it was impossible to understand why. You could tell when she was coming: her limp made her footsteps uneven, and the silk stockings rustled.

She didn't like answering questions. I wanted to find out what had happened to her father, whether she had any brothers killed in the war, what the childhood illness was that had left her lame, how many brothers and sisters she'd had. The only uncle I knew about on her side of the family was Uncle Phil, her elder brother, who sometimes arrived at week-ends, always bringing a present for me and a big box of chocolates for her, though Mummy was cross about that. He knew they were bad for her, she said. He had a droopy brown moustache, a big round stomach, a big round face like Grannie's, and he usually wore brown suits. He was much balder than Daddy and the polished dome of his head would have made a fine skating-rink for flies. He'd usually arrive on Friday evenings after Grannie had lit the Shabbos candles, and Tonks would be told to draw the dining-room curtains so that visitors shouldn't see members of the family setting a bad example by arriving in their cars after Shabbos had come in. Uncle Phil wasn't orthodox. He even ate pork, Nanny said, and he was uneasy at mealtimes, mostly sitting in silence, picking at his moustache. Once he absent-mindedly took out his cigarettes after the Friday night supper, but Daddy didn't have to say anything. A glare was enough. The unstruck match went back into the box, the unlit cigarette into the packet.

He didn't possess a velvet Kappul, but the hotel provided crinkly black paper ones for people to put on their head for prayers before and after the meal. Tonks would herd the waiters out of the room, rap with a soup-spoon on the sideboard, and announce: 'Ladies and gentlemen, pray silence for grace.' The paper skull-cap looked insecure on the wide bald dome, but he couldn't take off his Kappul till the blessing had been said over the Shabbos loaf and the bread had been broken into bits so that everyone could start the meal with bread dipped in salt. Even Mummy, who usually ate Ryvita, had to taste it.

Her voice would often sound strained when she talked to Uncle Phil, but Grannie loved it when he came. 'He's my son,' she used to say over and over again in the same affectionate voice she used for 'He's my Ron-boy'. After dinner he'd go up to her bedroom with her, and usually he'd still be in the armchair when I went up to say good-night. One night Mummy and Daddy were there too, and I heard their voices raised quite angrily until I knocked at the door. I kissed them all quickly, knowing they didn't want me to stay. As I closed the door behind me Daddy was saying: 'Now look here, Phil. . . .' I ran to Nanny for my bath.

One afternoon a tall man arrived with an aeroplane for me, and said he was Uncle Isadore. He was thinner than Uncle Phil, and he didn't look like Mummy. He wore a brown felt hat with the brim over his eyes. He came into my garden and I took a photograph of him with my box camera. Had he come back from America? I asked, but he smiled and said no. Afterwards, when I asked Grannie, she said he'd been away, but wouldn't say where. Nanny said she didn't know, and Mummy said she didn't want to talk about him.

'Is he really your brother, though?'

'Yes, now can we please change the subject?'

Teddy was often asleep, but he was always there, and that made everything different. When he was sleeping in the cot, Nanny couldn't come out for a walk, and when he was sleeping in the pram, she often wanted to stay wherever we were, in case he woke up when she started pushing. We didn't go down to the beach so often, or stay there so long, because too much sun was bad for him, and everywhere we walked, we had to take the pram, and instead of holding hands with her I had to hold on to the side. When we went to Horseshoe Common we couldn't go up the winding paths between the gorse-bushes, where the ground was carpeted with fallen pine needles and twisting roots stuck out from underneath the tree-trunks like pipes. The gorse was prickly, with yellow flowers, and there were ferns like thick green lace. It wasn't nearly so much fun on the flat part of the common, and there were too many other blue-uniformed nannies pushing prams. When Nanny talked to them, it was very boring, and she didn't want to talk to me till they'd gone away. But we had to go out for a walk every day unless it was raining.

One day, Daddy came into the nursery with a sad face and said the King was dead. Nanny had been stuffing a lump of sugar into an orange for me, but she put it down and started crying. I wanted to have another look at the telegram the Kings had sent me, but we couldn't find it, so I got a penny out of my money-box and stared at his bearded face. Everybody seemed unhappy all day. Eventually everyone seemed happy again when they were talking about the new King and Queen, whose pictures were in the newspapers. Somebody bought me a Coronation mug with two handles, and somebody else gave me a beautiful golden model of the horse-drawn Coronation coach in a long red cardboard box with troopers of the Household Cavalry on horseback. We kept the tissue paper and packed the soldiers separately each time we put them away, but some of the horses were attached to the coach and it would be hard to stop them from getting broken, especially if I played with them on the floor. Teddy could crawl now, and though he didn't mean to break things, he was always knocking them over. Things were always getting lost too, but usually Nanny could find them. 'Nanny the finder' I called her.

The secret way of keeping things was to use your head like my box camera, and your eyelids like shutters. One afternoon Daddy showed me a place where some of the cliff had crumbled away. It was easy for grown-ups to step across the low wooden hand-rail, but a wire fence had been put up to stop people from going near the grass verge. He wouldn't lift me over the wooden hand-rail. One of his mottoes was 'It's better to be safe than silly'. But the cliff looked so strong. How could it break? He said that sooner or later more and more of it would crumble away. Did he mean that one day there'd be no grass verge? And then would the cliff go on crumbling until there was no pavement? And then until there was no road? And then until the hotel fell into the sea? Eventually, yes, Daddy said, but not for a very long time. Not till way after we were dead.

It was a windy day and the sharp sun kept disappearing behind clouds that were hurrying faster than fluffy things should be able to. All of a sudden I shut my eyes. I was holding Daddy's hand, so I didn't have to look where I was going. I could tell by the brightness on my closed eyelids when the sun came out and when it went in again. Next time I flicked my eyes open I was going to make a brain snapshot of everything I saw. Some of it is still there – the crowdedness of the pavement between the wooden hand-rail and the cars in the road, long overcoats flapping in the wind, a man holding his hat to his head, slanting sun-rays and an Airedale tugging at a lead.

Whether that decision changed the way my memory worked, or whether it would have changed anyway, events afterwards left more of a photographic imprint. Memories of holidays at Newquay, Broadstairs, Swanage and Lyme Regis would all merge together, but individual impressions would remain indelible. Daddy in a boater and white flannel trousers teaching me how to make a volcano by building a big sandcastle, scooping a chimney down the centre, tunelling into the side, pushing screwed-up newspaper in and setting fire to it. ('But don't do it when I'm not with you.') A Shetland pony poking his friendly head over a wire fence and picking up lumps of sugar with loose wet lips. ('Keep the whole of your hand flat.') Mummy in a deck-chair, holding up her knitting to stop me from photographing her. A man in a peaked cap and uniform lifting me up to look through a giant telescope on a stand. A nice teenage girl with long ginger hair letting me play games with a brown beachball which she finally said I could keep. Myself in a floppy sun-hat on a narrow sandy path with waves washing against the rocks below and my plastic pink jelly-mould tossing about in the sea, already out of reach and being carried farther away each second like a toy boat in a real storm. ('We'll buy you another one.') This was the worst thing that had ever happened to me. I loved the pink one more than any of my other jelly-moulds, and however loudly I cried, Daddy couldn't get it back for me.

Many early memories have to do with beaches, but I can no longer differentiate holiday beaches from the beach at Bournemouth. Like many people, I remember childhood weather as being better than it conceivably can have been – as if it were sunny enough for Nanny to take us to the beach almost every day, usually walking down along the zig-zag path. To come up she'd push Teddy's pram into the lift that travelled diagonally up the cliff face on rails, counterweighted by the lift that was making the downward journey. The tickets cost tuppence, or a penny for children. A man tore your ticket in half, and then waited for the bumpy noise which meant the lift had arrived, and for the doors to slide open.

I had a metal spade, and Teddy had a wooden one. We both had buckets. There were inverted rowing-boats on the sand, and fishermen's nets spread to dry. They went out early in the morning. On the promenade people could buy plaice and dabs that weren't quite dead yet. I hated to see them trying to flip out of the pile. On the beach you could buy bananas or oranges from men who walked up and down with wide baskets, but I wasn't allowed to eat between meals.

If you went on to the wet sand near the sea and dug down into it with your spade, you came to water. I could never understand this. The water wasn't part of the sea, so what was it, and would it have been there if you hadn't dug for it?

It was a long walk down the hill to the Pleasure Gardens, but I loved the Bird-lady and the bandstand. The Bird-lady was there every day in the same worn brown hat and old tweed coat, with a crowd of birds at her feet, birds hovering and swooping, birds perching on her hat, on her shoulders and all the way up her arm, birds eating out of her hands. She brought an old leathery shopping bag full of food for them – brown paper bags of crusts, rice, maize and nuts. The nuts were for the grey squirrels, who were very shy. At best one would pick up a nut a few yards away from your feet and sit up on his hind legs, holding it in one paw and cracking the shell with his strong teeth. Sometimes we brought crusts of our own, but the Bird-lady gave me maize and taught me not to be afraid of the pigeons' claws when they gripped my hand. Birds had funny eyes which never seemed to look back at you.

When the food was all used up, we went along to the bandstand. I didn't like violins and cellos, but I loved shiny silver and brass instruments, and soldier musicians in bright red tunics with gold buttons and braided epaulettes, and navy blue trousers with red stripes all down the sides. Nanny sat on the bench by the railings, pushing the pram to and fro until Teddy was asleep, and she always brought a spare knitting-needle so that I could conduct. Some of the bandsmen pretended not to see me, but some smiled, and my special friend was the drummer, who had a grey, downward moustache. Sometimes he let me go up after the concert and have a bang on the kettledrums. He tried to teach me how to do a drum-roll, but my hands weren't big enough to hold the sticks properly. There was nothing I wanted more than to become a drummer-boy as soon as I was old enough. Or a cornet player. The only trouble with military band music was that there were no words. The good thing about the songs on my gramophone records was you could sing them at any time or even just say the words. There was one song that started

> Home, James, and don't spare the horses.
> This night has been ruined for me!

So if we were out for a walk and it started raining, Nanny would say: 'Home James and don't spare the horses.' Then we'd run.

I knew it was an important step towards manhood when I could go to Shool with Daddy on Shabbos. The first face we saw was the caretaker's, with its brownish yellow moustache that looked as if he soaked it every night in urine. Daddy took off his trilby hat and handed it to him. Reaching for a black box shaped like a giant cork, the caretaker would lift out a shiny black silk hat, caressing it with his yellow duster as he handed it over. Daddy adjusted it in the mirror and then we made our entrance – the president of the congregation and his son. With eyes averted upwards as if his chanting were a rope that led straight up to Heaven, the bearded cantor would pretend not to notice as we marched past the platform he was standing on to open the door of the presidential box and sit down on the red velvet seat in front of him next to the treasurer and the secretary. We took our silk prayer shawls out of their velvet bags and kissed them before putting them round our necks. Daddy's lips moved as he muttered a prayer.

Sometimes the cantor gabbled a lot of words together, sometimes he spaced them out, singing joyfully, pleased with God for giving him such a powerful voice. Sitting on the sideways benches, all the other men could see him, and so could the women looking down from the gallery, but the four of us couldn't turn our heads round to look, and the Hebrew chanting went on and on, a strong rope of sound that was wavy and tuneful in some places and almost like moaning in others. The best tunes were the ones we all joined in. I soon got to know them as well as any of the songs on my records, and I joined in as much as I could, gradually learning the phrases without knowing where one word stopped and the next began. *Shellownayvowsh Velownikolaim Leyowlom Voyed.* I loved the gong-like fullness of the vowels and the guttural consonants. *Shollowm. Borrooch. Olaynoo Leshabayach.* Soon I was going to start having Hebrew lessons, and then I'd begin to understand what the words meant. Daddy wished he'd had more lessons when he was a boy. He could read the words in the heavy Hebrew letters that went from right to left with tiny vowels underneath the big consonants, but he didn't know what he was saying unless he looked at the English translation on the facing page.

All the carpet was red and all the windows were stained glass. Hebrew letters were woven into the rich patterns, and when rays of sunlight pointed at them from outside, it looked as though God were reading them. The altar was at the eastern end of the Shool, with a gold star of David on the red velvet curtains in front of the Ark, which had the Scrolls of the Law in it. Hanging from the ceiling was a dim light that was never put out – hundreds of years from now it would still be there. The marble pulpit towered above the white marble steps. Later on the minister would climb up for the sermon, the only part of the service that was in English except the prayer for the Royal Family.

The best song of all was the last, and as soon as it was over, the men would shout *Yishakowach* to the cantor and minister, 'May your strength return.' Then they would all come surging round the side of the presidential box to say Good Shabbos, shaking hands with us. Mr Gallon, the treasurer, sometimes did conjuring tricks with sweets, making a bee-striped humbug appear out of my left ear and giving it to me to eat. The women from the gallery couldn't come into the main part of the Shool, so they couldn't shake hands with us till we were in the hall or the street. I always came back to the hotel feeling I was a very good boy, and one Shabbos I told off an old man called Mr Wigram for getting out of a car.

'You shouldn't ride on Shabbos.'

'You're quite right, Ronnie.'

'So don't do it again, Wiggie.'

For this I was severely told off by Mummy. I must always be respectful to my elders.

When there were festivals, we went to Shool in the evenings, too. As it got darker outside, the colours in the stained glass windows would gradually change, the pale blue ones going darker and darker until suddenly all the lights in the Shool

would come on together, and everything would be cosy. There
were electric candles in brass candelabras on the cantor's desk
and on the altar. Outside, the light would go on fading steadily
till the blue was nearly black.

The nicest festival was *Succos* because everyone had a *lulav*
made of palm branches, which had to be shaken, and an *esrog*, a
fruit like a lemon, that had to be smelt. And each day after the
service we'd go into the *Succah*, where the roof had been slid back
to reveal a trellis that had been decorated with leafy branches
and fruit. The minister would say *Kiddush*, and then we'd all
drink a little glass of red wine and help ourselves to salted
almonds and tiny biscuits spread with chopped liver. 'Don't
spoil your lunch,' Daddy said if I ate too much. The best day of
the festival was the last, *Simchas Torah*, when everyone was in a
jolly mood, and all the Scrolls of the Law were taken out of the
Ark to be carried in procession round the Shool until all the men
had had a turn. I was too small to hold one from the Ark, but
Daddy had bought a very small one with all five Books of Moses
on the scroll in tiny Hebrew characters. The rollers were silver,
and it lived in a little silver ark of its own. I walked behind the
procession carrying my own scroll, and gave all the other little
boys a turn afterwards.

The other nice festival was Passover. You had to go without
bread for eight days, but you could spread matzoh with butter
and jam at tea-time and with butter and marmalade at
breakfast. All the usual plates, cups and saucers were hidden
away somewhere and replaced by special Passover crockery that
was never used except for these eight days each year. The meat
plates had thick blue bands round the edge, but the milk plates,
cups and saucers were my favourites because the edges were
gold. On the first two evenings of Passover there were *Seder*
services in the dining-room. Revd Lazarus, who came down
from London specially to take them, was a big old man with
shrivelled skin under his eyes, blotchy pink cheeks and a white
beard like a goat's. He hugged me and kissed me wetly, saying
he'd married Mummy and Daddy. I said you couldn't marry a
man, and anyway I knew his wife was the short lady with grey
hair. He laughed and said he'd performed the ceremony at the
Shidduch. Did I know what a *Shidduch* was? A wedding. He also

kept talking about a man called Oliver Shollowm, but
something stopped me from asking who he was. Later a frizzy-
haired Jewish lady in slacks talked about him on the beach, and
later still I discovered he wasn't a man at all. 'Olov ha-
shollowm' meant 'Peace be on his soul', and it was a phrase
regularly used by old-fashioned Jewish people after they
mentioned the name of someone who had 'passed away' – they
never used the word 'died'.

Tonks bustled about the room getting everything ready for
the special meal. There was a long table in the middle of the
room with Revd Lazarus at the head of it. The hotel was so full
that some people were sleeping in the annexe, and as the dining-
room filled up, the buzz of expectant conversation grew louder
and louder till Tonks silenced it with a rap of his soup-spoon.
'Ladies and gentlemen, pray silence for Revd Lazarus.' The
service was in two parts, with the meal in the middle. In the first
part there were four questions that had to be asked by the
youngest boy who could speak Hebrew. Next year it was going
to be me. The next section of the service consisted of a long
answer from Revd Lazarus all in Hebrew, but I knew that
Passover was to celebrate the Israelites' escape from Egypt, and
Daddy had given me *The Children's Hagaddah*, which had all the
words of the service in it and a lot of pictures. I was glad I wasn't
an Egyptian because God sent a plague down to kill all the eldest
sons, and I didn't know whether they were all still dying today,
but even if it were only the ones who were alive then, it was
unfair of Him to be on the side of the younger brothers. There
was a picture of the Red Sea parting and the Israelites marching
through, led by two men with long white beards and long sticks,
and there were some pictures you could move by pulling a
cardboard strip. Usually you pulled it sideways, but there was
one you pulled downwards to make the Red Sea close its waves
over the Egyptians. Revd Lazarus's quavery old voice droned
on in Hebrew for a very long time, and I was glad when the
special meal started. There was a funny soup made with slices of
hard-boiled egg in salt water. Uncle Phil screwed up his face,
but I liked it. I liked liking things that other people didn't. When
Nanny rinsed my hair in vinegar after washing it, I poked out
my tongue, enjoying her disbelief at my pleasure in the sour taste.

During the *Seder* service we had to eat some bitter horseradish with a small bit of matzoh, and later on in the meal we ate apple dipped in honey. Then the service started again, but the second half was much more fun, with some very catchy tunes. I tried to join in, and Daddy sang very clearly, putting his face close so that I could join my voice to his. Suddenly everyone was standing and shouting something in Hebrew. 'It means "Next year in Jerusalem",' he whispered. Then they sat down and went on with the praying and singing. The best tune was the last of all, one about a father who bought a kid for two farthings. Each verse repeated the whole of the previous verse with one new line added at the beginning. It was so late by the time it was over I had to kiss them all good-night in the dining-room and go straight up to tell Nanny to put me to bed.

Hannukah wasn't the same sort of festival as *Succos* and Passover, when people had to stop working for two days at the beginning and two days at the end, but it also lasted for eight days and it was one of my favourites, partly because of the *Hannukah* presents and partly because of the lovely, twisty, coloured candles. One of them was called the leader and we used him to light the others. On the first evening there was only one other candle, but one more was added each evening till the eight-branch *Menorah* was full up. The leader had a separate branch of his own that slotted into the centre, so that you could take him out in it to do his lighting work. It reminded me of something that had happened only once when I was very small. As a special treat I'd been taken late at night to the Pleasure Gardens, where there were coloured lamps like glass baskets with oil in them hanging all round the bushes, held by special wooden frames. The lamps looked like gleaming flowers in the darkness, and people were allowed to relight the ones that had gone out, using a funny metal stick with a tufty bit on the end. Daddy got one for me and lifted me up when I couldn't reach a light that had gone out.

The nastiest festival was the Day of Atonement. Daddy said it was the most important day in the year, but they were all in a bad mood because they had to fast for twenty-five hours, and the service in Shool went on non-stop from early morning till dusk. Extra benches had been placed both in front of the box and behind the platform. Full of unfamiliar faces, the Shool was so crowded and so stuffy that all the air you breathed must have been breathed in and out a lot of times by other people. The minister and the cantor were wearing white cassocks and white hats with fluffy white pom-poms on them, and at intervals they blew hoarse fanfares on a special ram's horn called the Shofar. (I drew a mental cartoon in which it wore a peaked hat and drove a car.) We did things we never did in ordinary services like kneeling and beating our breasts. The women's gallery was crammed, and you could see them sniffing at their smelling-salts. Sometimes one of them fainted, but none of the men ever did. In the street outside, people were standing and sitting on the low wall to get a breath of fresh air before going back inside. Even the people who were usually friendly were headachey and tetchy. Once while I was outside, Uncle Phil came out. Not seeing me, he went off quickly down the road, reaching into his trouser pocket. I heard the jingle of coins he shouldn't have been carrying.

Illnesses were the other main cause of interruptions in my routine. Whenever I had a cold or a cough Mummy made me stay in bed, and late in the morning the thick grey hair and thick flushed face of Dr Waistnedge would appear. He had a loud, friendly voice and always called me 'old chap'. He'd swing his case on to Nanny's bed, wash his hands and dry them carefully on the clean face-towel she held out to him. Then he'd launch cheerfully into the routine of making me say 'Aaaaaaahhhh' and 'Ninety-nine', rapping a knuckle against a warm hand that moved across my chest like a smooth crab. Then I had to take deep breaths while he touched me all over my chest and my back with the cold metal of a stethoscope. I wanted them to bring me a toy stethoscope in one of my Friday parcels, but they said there weren't any toy ones. Afterwards he'd disappear with Mummy into the day nursery, and through the half-open door I'd hear their serious voices, but he brightened up when he came back into the night nursery. Taking a little pad out of his case, he'd write a prescription and tear it off. When I asked how long I'd have to stay in bed, he'd say: 'Not long, old chap. I'll pop back tomorrow and see how you're getting on.' Once, after he'd gone, I asked Nanny to read the prescription, but she said doctors always had handwriting you couldn't read and anyway it would be in French. One of the porters would then be dispatched on his bicycle to the chemist at the Lansdowne, and before lunch-time a brightly coloured bottle of medicine would take its place next to the red gargle and the blue milk of magnesia bottle on the shelf over the wash-basin. Meanwhile the wooden bed-table would have been brought from the housekeeper's office and I'd have settled down to the things that could be done in bed – reading *Teddy Tail's Annual*, drawing, jigsaw puzzles, patience and games of snakes-and-ladders or ludo or Chinese chequers with Nanny while Teddy was having one of his sleeps. Mummy would come in several times during the day, but she didn't like playing games. I wasn't allowed to paint in bed except with water in one of the paint-books where colours appeared magically in the picture as soon as you made it wet. After lunch Grannie would look in with some chocolate, and later Daddy would come in on his way back from the shop and stay, playing draughts or dominoes until he had to change for dinner. Nanny would be in and out all day, and before tucking me up for the night she'd rub my chest with camphorated oil. The skin on her hands was quite hard, but I liked the rubbing on my ribs and the smell that was left in my nostrils.

I never enjoyed my toys so much as on the first day of being allowed out of bed. Usually I was kept indoors for the day. In the nursery I had a miniature carpenter's bench with a real vice and real tools, but Nanny said I wasn't old enough to use them yet. Except the wide carpenter's pencil and the sandpaper. The big toys lived in the airing cupboard at the end of the corridor beyond the maids' glass-fronted indicator board, where red discs popped up into holes when visitors rang their bells. There was a toy car with pedals, a Punch and Judy set with painted wooden puppets, a big wooden engine and some big stuffed toys, a giant chimpanzee, a giant teddy bear and a giraffe whose neck had been bandaged to keep it straight and stop the straw stuffing from coming out. The airing cupboard also contained the overflow from the big white toy cupboard in the nursery. So many visitors brought me so many presents. There were clockwork cars, toy aeroplanes, boats, stuffed animals, ping-pong bats – one red one with a rubber ball attached on an elastic, humming tops, shuttlecocks, a xylophone, toy pianos, a magic lantern for projecting slides of Walt Disney films, a Father Christmas mask that smelt of glue, with a cotton-wool beard that was coming loose, a sealing set with little red balls of wax, a tiny saucepan for melting them in and a seal that imprinted a rose on the molten red wax, a box of conjuring tricks including a reversible beer-mug with cotton-wool foam, a fishing game in a box with four fishing-rods that had magnets instead of hooks and lots of painted paper fishes with metal in their mouths ready to be caught, Meccano sets, Bayko construction kits, a lot of jigsaw puzzles and a game called Big Shot, where you fired a silver ball out of a spring cannon and scored points according to where it ended up after it had wound its way through miniature turnstiles and ricocheted off carefully arranged obstacles. Then there were all the things Daddy had brought home from his shop, two musical boxes, a Victorian policeman's truncheon, a locket-like silver box just big enough to hold sixpences you pushed in against a spring, an old kaleidoscope, and a plastic Palestinian cigarette box engraved with a picture of elderly Jews with long beards and broad-brimmed hats at the Wailing Wall in Jerusalem.

One day we'd go to Jerusalem, Daddy said. In the meantime we kept going back to Swanage and Lyme Regis. Daddy would come to the beach every day and bathe with us. Mummy didn't bathe because of her bad leg. She'd sit in a deck-chair with her knitting, wearing a summer dress. I don't think I ever saw her in a bathing costume.

It was in Lyme Regis that I suddenly wanted to hold a bird in my hand. I wasn't going to hurt it. I just wanted to stroke the feathers, very gently, and then let it fly away. Mummy said it was silly, we'd never be able to catch one, but Daddy said we'd try. We put some crumbs on the grass in the garden of the hotel, and he went down on his knees with my butterfly-net at the ready, but no birds showed any interest in the crumbs.

One summer in Lyme Regis Daddy asked me if I wanted to become a businessman straightaway. When I said yes, he showed me a little brass bell with inward-curving sides, moulded to look like claws. I was to take it to the antique shop in the High Street, saying I was the accredited representative of King and Hayman Ltd, Bournemouth, and they could have trade terms if they'd care to place an order for a dozen or more bells. When I came out of the shop saying they wanted a dozen, he gave me the bell to keep.

'That's a feather in your cap,' Nanny said, but it was more like a new pencil mark on the inside of the toy-cupboard door where we notched up my height. It was very important to grow as fast as possible, just as it was important to put on weight. Grannie still called me 'Skinnamalinks', and Daddy gave me four shillings when I was four stone, five shillings when I was five stone, and so on. Once I wanted to wee-wee just before he came into the bathroom to see me being weighed, but Nanny said it would be better to keep it in until afterwards, so as to be that much heavier. It had never occurred to me that if you ate a half-pound of grapes, you'd immediately be a half-pound heavier. So why didn't I weigh as much as all the food I'd ever eaten? All except the weight of the wee-wee and dooneeze.

It was also good to grow out of my clothes. When my Chilprufe underclothes or my socks or cardigans got too small for me, Nanny would put them in the bottom drawer to wait till Teddy was big enough for them, and Mummy and Grannie would take me out shopping. Buying new shoes was frightening. I had to peer through the big X-ray machine in the corner and see the bones in my feet looking as if I were a skeleton. When I wiggled my toes, the bones moved.

The night before my birthday I was specially impatient for time to go by quickly. If only my thoughts would drift over the edge into sleep, the next moment of consciousness would be the beginning of my special day, with a pile of parcels waiting on the floor. Even when they were all opened, and the floor littered with brown paper and string, there were still all the envelopes, and the chance that one or two of them would contain not just a card but a book token or a ten-shilling note. One birthday Daddy bought me a small set of real drums with white wood and silver screws. There were polished wooden drumsticks for playing the side-drum, a fluffy padded drumstick on a pedal for the big drum, a cymbal on a metal stand that screwed on to it, and two more cymbals on leather straps for clashing together.

I knew that on Christmas Day I wasn't going to be the only one who was special. Everybody was. But the excitement of Christmas started a long time before the day arrived. We went out shopping a lot to buy presents, and the shops were all decorated, and in the biggest department stores there were special treats for children. A man dressed up as Father Christmas would give you a kiss and a parcel – the grown-up who was looking after you had to pay for it – and there was a mystery ride, with different scenery every year. You got into the sledge and looked out of the window at all sorts of marvellous things that came whizzing by – angels, flying fish, snow-capped mountains and magic fountains in the background. You knew it wasn't real – it was painted on a scroll and moved by rollers – but it was exciting.

The greatest excitement though was looking forward to Christmas Day, and on Christmas Eve it was almost intolerable that time was passing so slowly after I'd hung up one of Nanny's old stockings – which weren't silk, like Mummy's – from the bedpost.

In the morning, instead of dangling limply, it would be bulging with presents. Some of them would be disappointing, like an orange in blue tissue paper, pushed in to fill up the heel – and there would be lots of things I didn't really want – yet another pencil box, or smudgy new crayons that felt like candles and broke when you tried to write with them, leaving coloured marks all over your hands. But the unwrapping was always fun, not knowing whether or not you'd be pleased with what was inside. Nanny would string the cards up under the criss-crossing paper decorations that were fixed to the picture-hooks all round the nursery walls, frail balls and frills of bright colour, slightly faded from last year and the year before. On Christmas Day I didn't have to go out for a walk if I didn't want to, but we'd push Teddy's pram down the drive to the garage-man's cottage with a present that Mummy had bought and Nanny had wrapped for Jimmy. Nanny didn't really like him. Once we'd seen him sitting all by himself, picking his nose, on the park bench in Grove Road. 'You watch,' Nanny said, 'now he's going to eat it.' And sure enough, his finger went from his nose to his mouth. He

ought to have put the johnnies under the seat. But he might have
been lonely, and on Christmas Day Nanny was nice to him.

It was fun saying Happy Christmas to everybody. On Jewish
festivals I had to say 'Good Yomtov' to the visitors but not the
staff. I liked saying 'Good Yomtov'. It was as if you had
something like a little present in your mouth, and you could give
it to everybody. Once, when I said it by mistake to Tonks, he
said it back just like everybody else. But Christmas was the best
day for all the staff, especially Tonks, because a lot of people
gave Christmas tips. And after lunch there was a special
collection for the kitchen staff, who never got tips because
everybody just ate what they cooked without ever seeing them.
On Christmas Eve the visitors all got a present from Grannie as
they came into the dining-room – a little diary with *East Cliff
Court Bournemouth* in silver print on the leather. After dinner
there would be a dance in the ballroom every evening till New
Year's Eve, sometimes with a cabaret. If it was a conjuror I
could stay up late to watch. One year The Incredible Castellani
produced a fluffy little fluttering dove from a very old lady's
beaded handbag.

At tea-time on Christmas Day there was a special party for all
the children in the Cocktail Lounge, with a red cracker and a
funny paper hat waiting beside every plate. When you pulled
the cracker, you found either a little present or another paper
hat, and a slip of paper with a motto or a riddle. 'What's the
difference between a man who hopes for the best and a steamed-
up pair of glasses?' 'One is optimistic and the other is a misty
optic!' 'What could you eat if you were shipwrecked on a desert
island?' 'You could eat the sand which is there!' We had
sandwiches, bread and jam, scones and cream, cakes, and the
special treat of ice-cream, jelly and trifle all together on one
plate. Afterwards I could go to bed half an hour later than usual.

Usually Nanny would call me at half-past six – 'bath time'.
Sometimes we'd use the green bath in the flat. It depended
whether Mummy or Daddy was using it. If they were, we'd have
to go into one of the public bathrooms, which all had white
baths and weren't so nice. Nanny would soap me all over except
my 'private parts'. I must do those myself, she said. But she
always let me have a nice long lie in the warm water before I got

out to be towelled. With lavatories there was the same irregularity of moving from one to another. I liked it best when I could use the green one in the flat. The others were white, with a cog-wheel lock on the door. It wasn't nearly so nice when Mummy bathed me because she wouldn't let me lie down in the water until I'd been soaped all over, and I mustn't get my face wet until just before I got out of the bath, when I must dry it immediately.

In bed the cold sheets got warm quickly, but it wasn't nice to be left alone. I concentrated on tomorrow and used my magic power to make things happen or not happen. It didn't always work, but if I said 'Oh it's bound to rain tomorrow' it would very likely be sunny, because I was always wrong. So, just by thinking it would happen, I could often stop myself from having to eat bread-and-butter pudding or sago pudding for lunch or having to go for a drive to the New Forest with Mummie and Grannie and a paper bag in case I was car-sick.

I liked the sheet to be so tight under my chin that I could only just get my hand up to pick my nose. If the top sheet got all loose and the bottom one crumpled underneath, there was nothing for it but to toss and turn and kick at it until it was much worse, and then call for Nanny to come and make the bed all over again. If I still couldn't get to sleep, I'd have to lie there listening for sounds in the corridor. Mostly it would be the floor-waiter's footsteps followed by a knock at a door somewhere, or visitors' footsteps followed by the sound of a door opening and shutting, but sometimes my door would open and Mummy and Daddy would look in. With Daddy I'd pretend to be asleep and laugh just before he went out. Then he'd come back and kiss me. He smelt of cigarette smoke, but his voice was always kind. Mummy was sometimes cross.

'Why aren't you asleep?'

So when I heard limping footsteps and the irregular swish of silk stockings, I'd close my eyes tight and try to breathe evenly so that she'd think I was asleep.

When Daddy and I went for walks along the promenade, we'd make plans. We decided to start Hayman's Children's Library. I'd been given so many books that we could lend some to the other children at the hotel. I had a little printing set with rubber letters that fitted into a wooden holder, and an ink pad in a tin like the ones the receptionists had for their date-stamps, so Daddy and Nanny helped me to fit letters into the holder and stamp HAYMANS CHILDRENS LIBRARY into the books. We also put up a sign outside the nursery door: HAYMANS CHILDRENS LIBRARY. But nobody ever knocked at the door to ask what was on the shelves. Daddy said we'd have to do something to make the library famous. I said I'd write a book. He said we could have it printed in the reception office on the stencil machine they used for the menus. I didn't know exactly what it would be about, but there was going to be a boat in it and two boys, and all sorts of incredible things were going to happen to them. There would be a kindly coastguard with white hair and a lantern, and he'd have a dog, a red setter. There was going to be one frightening episode in the night when one of the boys was caught by the smugglers, and they tied him to a park bench. He had his pyjamas on, and the rain was absolutely pelting down on him, but he didn't mind because he knew he was serving his King and Country, and the coastguard rescued him in the morning and rang up his Daddy.

The first time I saw a urinal, I thought it was a tombstone. Someone in the hotel must have died, and the big white slab that was being carried in was a sign that I must get ready to cry. I asked Nanny what it was, and when she wouldn't tell me, I knew I was right. But then another one arrived, and then another. There couldn't have been three deaths. It must be something to do with the hole in the wall. A new wing was being built on to make the hotel bigger, and an enormous hole had been cut in the wall of the landing not far from the nursery door.

What I did not appreciate until much later was how different the new wing was from the old – more modern, more luxurious, with no public bathrooms or lavatories, but a private bathroom for every bedroom, with tiled walls matching the colour of the bath and lavatory. There was a new lift, and a chocolate-coloured carpet in the corridors. In the old wing the bedroom doors were of white-painted panelled wood; in the new wing straight-cut pine with smart handles. Instead of paying two guineas a day all in, the vistitors who wanted one of the better rooms would have to pay three. The new wing was on the south side of the hotel, and the front rooms had an uninterrupted view of the sea. Mummy's and Daddy's bedroom looked out on the tennis-court, and the nursery looked out on my little garden, but Grannie took a room in the new wing.

3

Two Prep Schools

I had secrets of my own but the grown-ups' secrets must be so much more interesting than mine, especially the things Mummy and Daddy wouldn't talk about in front of me. A special look came into their eyes, signalling that they'd go on with the conversation when I wasn't there. And the letters people wrote to them must be full of secrets, because they always tore them up into small pieces before throwing them into the waste-paper basket in case the maids read them. If I'd been a maid, I'd have played at jigsaw puzzles with the pieces on the carpet.

It was a privilege to stay up an hour later than Teddy and to go downstairs for lunch while he still had his meals in my old high-chair in the nursery with Nanny, but I was impatient to be older, especially when people said 'That's not for children,' or 'When you grow up you'll be able to . . .', or 'When I was your age I wasn't even allowed to. . . .' I didn't know that looking forward to adult life was a mistake. It now seems to me almost as if I used up my childhood too fast by wishing it away. Talking to children, I try never to belittle childhood with any of the remarks that were so often made to me about being too young to understand. I was also told that childhood was the best time of anyone's life, but the adults who said this obviously didn't believe it. It was clear that grown-ups were more important than children, and had more freedom. There was so much that children couldn't do, couldn't have, couldn't even know. Anyway, soon I'd be going to school, and that would be the most important step forward yet. The boys I'd seen in school caps and blazers had always looked terribly important, hurrying along with dark blue raincoats and swinging satchels, or playing a game with conkers on a string, or marching like soldiers in a column with one teacher in front and another at the rear. But from the way Nanny talked about school, it sounded as though there might be lots of rough boys, and talking about it made the time come faster when I'd have to go. Or was it because it was coming that we talked about it so much?

The most frightening present I ever had was my school cap. It arrived in a grey cardboard box with tissue paper inside. It had blue and black segments and a shield in front, embroidered with a blue dragon that had a spiky tail and a forked tongue flicking out of its mouth, fierce but friendly. The blazer had wide blue and black stripes. Mummy took me shopping with her and Grannie, who bought me a new pair of short grey flannel trousers to go with it. Mummy let me choose my own satchel, and Grannie bought me a new pencil box – I had two already but one was too good to take to school and the other not good enough. They kept arguing about who should pay for what, but in return for letting Grannie buy the pencil box Mummy was allowed to buy the geometry set, a smart gold tin box with the word Oxford and a dark blue picture of a college on it. I owned a compass already but not such a nice one, and there were dividers, a six-inch ruler, and shapes cut out in transparent plastic, one semicircular, the other two triangular, all marked up with lines and figures.

Mummy took me to school in the car and came up to the classroom with me, but the teacher wasn't there yet. A final kiss on my cheek, and I was alone with nine other boys, who didn't take much notice. Several had loud voices; the tallest had dark, wavy hair and bright pink patches on his cheeks. 'I bet nobody's got such a long ruler as I have,' he boasted, unfolding a two-foot ruler hinged into four sections. I had one exactly like it in my carpenter's bench, but the words never came up through my throat.

The teacher had come in, a small, weather-beaten old lady with leathery skin. 'My name is Mademoiselle Blackbee.' She was holding a pile of flimsy blue copy-books. 'I'm French and we are going to start learning French straight away.' Her accent was different from any I'd heard in the hotel. She gave out copy-books just like the one I had at home. The blackboard was much

bigger than mine, and in flourishy white writing she chalked 'le
20 septembre'. We had to copy it into the top right-hand corner
of our books, and then copy the words in the book into the wide
spaces between the parallel lines.

When a loud bell sounded, she said we could stop. A woman
in a white overall brought in glasses of milk and a plate of white
bread and butter on a tray. Our milk was cold, but there was a
glass of hot milk for Mademoiselle Blackbee, who used a
teaspoon to skim off the wrinkly skin on top. Spreading it on a
piece of bread and butter, she started to eat it.

She taught all our lessons except drawing and painting. The
art teacher was Captain Brough, who had no arms. He gripped
a long wooden brush between his teeth, dipped it in our paint
pots and painted in our drawing books. He also had a thing like
a long wooden cigarette-holder that could grip either chalk or
pencils, and he manipulated it by moving his head. His sleeves
were tucked into the pockets of his jacket and his body looked
very narrow. I wondered how he managed to wipe his bottom,
and what his shoulders looked like. Perhaps there were scabs,
like the ones on my knees. But scabs always disappeared when
the wound healed. Perhaps there was a layer of uneven skin like
Grannie's mole, only red. Or sickly white.

He told us there were only three colours – red, yellow and
blue. Black and white weren't really colours, and all the others
could be made by mixing the three together. He took a big piece
of paper, leaned over to daub it with yellow paint, jerking his
head about to spread it. Then he rinsed his brush by leaning
over the pot of water and shaking his head. When he dipped the
clean brush into the blue paint pot and started painting on top of
the yellow, it went green. When he painted red on top of yellow,
it went orange, and red paint on top of blue made it purple. I
liked him a bit better now. The worst time was when he leaned
over us to correct our drawing. He could talk out of the side of his
mouth while he was sketching, but I didn't like the empty sleeves
to be close to me.

The tall boy was called Herriot, and Herriot was the name
heard more than any other when lessons were over. The other
centre of attention was Mortlock, a scruffy boy with blotchy
cheeks and a hoarse voice like Mrs Levy's. He was scared of

dandelions, and if the boy behind him whispered 'There's a dandelion under your bottom', he'd get up with a loud cry. Mademoiselle Blackbee asked what the matter was, and we all laughed as he tried to explain that dandelions were poisonous. Sometimes we actually brought dandelions into the classroom, but if Mademoiselle Blackbee objected, Herriot always spoke up to explain that we were only doing it to help Mortlock understand that nothing actually happened to you if you sat on a dandelion. Then somebody found out about dandelion coffee, and he was soon convinced that we were going to poison him with it. When Mademoiselle Blackbee assured him it wasn't poisonous, he thought she'd joined the conspiracy against him.

Daddy often asked me how things were going at school, and when I told him about Mortlock, he said I should stick up for him. I knew Daddy was right, but teasing him was a much easier game to join in than some of the others they played. Did Mortlock cry? he asked. He did cry sometimes, but it was all part of the fun, and in his way he seemed to enjoy it. After all, they wouldn't have been able to play the game without him, so it made him more important, and anyway there was no chance that I'd be able to make them do what I said instead of what Herriot said. Nothing was impossible, Daddy said, and he told me the story he'd told before about a poor fisherman who thought he'd never be able to marry because he could never catch more than one fish a day. But he put his trust in the Almighty, Who said that we should be fruitful and multiply. The day after he married, he caught two fish, and two again the day after that, and two every other day, until his wife had a baby, and then he started catching three fish every day. There was nothing that God couldn't do. The only mistake was not to trust Him.

'Mark you,' Daddy said, 'it's a mistake to trust *people*.' He told me another story about a little boy who used to play a game with his daddy, sitting on a wall and jumping off it into his daddy's arms. He always jumped fearlessly, but one day the daddy just stood there without holding his arms out. The little boy hurt himself badly and cried and couldn't understand. 'I did that for your good,' the daddy explained. 'I want you to learn now because it'll hurt even more if you don't learn till later. You must never rely on anyone. Not even me.'

The Day of Atonement is the tenth day of the Jewish New Year. Now that I was six and a half, I could fast till lunch-time, Daddy said. It was right for me to do half as much as a grown-up because I was exactly halfway towards my Barmitzvah, when I'd become fully a man in the eyes of the religion, fully able to accept my religious responsibilities.

I didn't like it when the Shool was crowded, as it was for the two New Year morning services, but Daddy said it was good that so many people came, even if they didn't come for the ordinary Shabbos services, and at New Year we mustn't think harshly of anyone. We must forgive all our enemies. All grievances must be put aside for the beginning of the Jewish Year. Then on the Day of Atonement we fasted to show that we were really sorry for all our sins. It was the day when God made up His mind who would be stricken with illness during the year ahead and which of us would be felled like rotten old trees. That was why sinners were scared – people who'd been shopping on Shabbos and riding in cars and eating pork. They all put on dark suits and came to Shool. And that was why they all looked so grey and headachey.

What I couldn't understand was why the prayer book made us all confess to the same sins, though I liked the singing bit we all joined in at the end of each verse. *Oshumnoo, bogudnoo, dibarnoo – dowfee.* Clutching his prayer shawl against his white cassock, the wailing cantor beat his chest rhythmically on each word, and we beat ours as we repeated each word after him. The idea was to feel bad, but it made me feel good.

Reading the English on the left-hand pages, I found lots of words I didn't understand, but I was pretty sure none of them referred to the secret sin that I never confessed. I knew it was serious because it was the same Devil that taught me how to commit it who had disguised himself as a snake to tempt Adam and Eve. It was in a dream he started talking to me, and I still wasn't properly awake when I started doing what he said, so it wasn't really my fault that time, though of course it was all the other times. Once Mummy caught me in bed not actually doing it, but soon afterwards. My forehead and my whole body were so hot that she said 'I know what you've been doing', and smacked my bottom much harder than usual. I never knew whether she told Daddy.

When my school reports were good, they rewarded me with money. It was important to save as much as I could, they said, so I tried not to spend all my pocket-money on comics, even when we went down by the pier, where the man gave away free surprise packets in crinkly paper. I put the rest of the money into the mouth of a red tin money-box shaped like a bucket with a silver handle and a metal key to unlock the trapdoor in its bottom. As soon as there was enough, they were going to open a bank account for me, and then the money would grow. I imagined sixpences expanding to the size of shillings and two-shilling bits growing as big as half-crowns. Other people would admire my big money: 'I can see that's been in a bank for a long time.'

It was easy to get good reports. I was always given high marks for conduct and praise for trying hard, though I was enjoying what I did in the exercise books. The arithmetic ones had blue covers and squares all over the page. The others had brown covers and blue lines across the page, but you had to rule a line down the side. We started with the date in French, and at the bottom we had to rule a line across the page. It was exciting to have the books collected up by the class monitor, knowing we'd get them back with a judgement in red ink. I was good at sums and spelling and hardly ever got into trouble for making blots or getting smudges on the ruled lines. I liked it when a book was full up and I could ask for a new one, but I kept all the old ones on the bottom shelf of the big toy cupboard. The small white toy cupboard with the blue handle was now Teddy's, but I didn't have to have any of his things in mine.

When I was moved into the next class and the teacher was a man, it was good to know that there were boys in the school younger than I was. Mr Cotter told us that the best way of remembering the two important French ports Toulon and Toulouse was to think of new trousers: they were always too long or too loose. Then he showed us where they were on the map.

One day the headmaster died. Everybody was gloomy and

worried. Teachers came late to class, and rumours went round that the school was going to close. Herriot said that anyway there was going to be a war; and when I asked Daddy, he said it was probably true, but we weren't ready for it. I didn't see why we should have it yet if we weren't ready, but apparently it had something to do with a blotter he'd brought home with three words printed on the shiny side: BOYCOTT EVERY-THING GERMAN. I was told about Nazis, who were obviously nasty, and had a nasty way of saluting, shooting their arm straight out and saying 'Heil', which presumably had something to do with Haile Selassie.

When the war started, Daddy put a map of the world on the nursery wall. The pink British Empire looked quite big, especially Canada and Austrialia, but the unfriendly black countries looked bigger still, especially the USSR, though at least we had France, which was yellow, between us and Germany. All round the edges of the map were diagrams with silhouettes of planes, boats, tanks and soldiers. Each white one represented a hundred or thousand or ten thousand of ours, while the black ones represented theirs. As they had much more of everything, it was obvious we wouldn't have stood much chance if God hadn't been on our side. That was how David had won against Goliath. Whenever I played with my catapult, I thought about Goliath, assuming he looked like the giant in the pantomime *Jack and the Beanstalk*.

The Royal Air Force wanted to requisition our hotel, and Daddy said there wouldn't be much point in appealing. Serious-looking, bald men arrived with bulging briefcases for meetings with him and Grannie, and soon Nanny was packing my toys into huge cardboard boxes. Some were going into store until the war was over; some were coming with us to the furnished house Daddy had rented for us on the West Overcliff Drive. He seemed resigned to the change, Mummy extremely worried about it and Granny very upset. Nothing would ever be the same again, she said, and by the time the war was over she'd be too old to run a hotel. 'Nonsense, mater,' said Daddy, and I tried to cheer her up too, but even when she hugged me she didn't smile. 'The best part of my life is over,' she said. The only one who seemed pleased was Nanny. 'You boys'll have some real home life.'

My new school cap was pillar-box red all over, with the letter H in the middle, and my new blazer was the same red, with an H on the pocket. It stood for the name of the school, Hailey, but the first time I went to Shool in my new clothes, Mr Gallon pretended to think the H stood for Hayman and asked Daddy why he wasn't wearing a red blazer under his silk hat. I started at Hailey before we moved into the new house. Once we were there, it would be only a short walk; meanwhile it was a thirty-minute ride on a yellow trolleybus. I didn't like the old-looking red trams that clanked frantically along the metal grooves cut into the roads, but I liked the smooth electric hum of the trolleybuses, and I loved the long poles that the drivers pulled out from the underside of the bus to fish the conductor-rails from one set of overhead cables to another.

On the first morning there was a distinguished-looking man with thick white hair on the bus. He held himself very erect and smiled at the conductor nicely. I knew I wanted to be like that when I was old, not bald like Daddy. There seemed to be so little point in going to the hairdresser when you had hair only round the side of your head. Why hadn't anybody invented a way of rearranging hair so that the skin didn't have to show in the middle? Daddy's hairdresser had offered to give him a course of treatment to cure his baldness, but he wouldn't agree to Daddy's conditions, which were that he'd pay twice the normal fee if the treatment worked and nothing if it didn't.

Mummy came with me as far as the tall green wooden gate. We could hear boys yelling before we even turned the handle. Then she was limping away across the road to the bus-stop on the other side. I could feel the kiss she'd left on my cheek. The asphalt playground was full of boys in red blazers like mine, running about and kicking tennis-balls and imitating gun noises and aeroplane noises and nose-diving to the ground with outspread arms. A bell clanged, and from going in all directions the movement funnelled into a single surge towards a porch.

With the others I filed past a washroom and a lavatory into a huge room with flaking green paint, skylights, rafters, a dust-coloured wooden floor with grooves like tramlines in it for partitions to separate the three classrooms. There was a desk for each red-blazered boy in grey shorts, but there was a long bench in front of the lockers with boys on it who didn't seem to belong to any of the classrooms. Their blazers made a broad red streak. Mr Bird was standing impatiently at the central table. He looked more like a lion or a walrus, with a bad-tempered, droopy moustache, a flush on his cheeks and a mane of white hair plastered straight back. The last boy still hadn't found his seat when he began barking out names beginning with A and making quick strokes in the register as the boys answered, all using the same word. It sounded like 'Absum', but that ought to mean 'I'm absent'. By the time he got to the G names I still wasn't sure what the word was, so when my turn came I said 'Absum' and it seemed to be all right because he went straight on to Healey and Henderson.

After Young I and Young II, he made a speech telling us to work hard and play hard. Brave men were sacrificing their lives in the air for the sake of our country, so we must all realize the value of discipline. I was hoping the speech wouldn't be too short, because at the end of it he was going to say 'Let us pray' and that would be my cue to get up and walk out. At the other school, St Wulfram's, there had been no prayers; here I was going to be made, uncomfortably, to feel that I was different from all the other boys. I knew where to go, but the door was a long way away, and there was going to be a silence with nothing to fill it except the sound of my footsteps and perhaps Mr Bird's voice shouting 'Hurry up'.

'Let us pray,' said Mr Bird. Every pair of eyes in the schoolroom must be swivelling round to stare at my blushing cheeks. I stood up quickly, catching the brass button of my blazer against the lid of my desk, which clattered loudly shut. One boy sniggered. With my eyes averted from Mr Bird's, I squeezed past the curved back of his heavy wooden chair. If someone stuck out a foot to trip me up as I hurried past the bare knees of the boys on the bench, the whole school would be laughing while I sprawled ignominiously, but it didn't happen, and there I was with the door shut behind me in a small dark room with a stone floor and a strong smell of boot-leather and dubbing. Two of the walls were taken up with open wooden compartments, each containing a pair of brown or black football boots.

Behind the door Mr Bird's loud voice was praying in English. Each time he said 'Jesus Christ' I knew I shouldn't be listening. Then they started on a prayer they all spoke together, breaking it up into phrases. Some of it sounded like bad grammar. How could God forgive them their trespassers? But it ended with the word 'Amen', and then a friendly freckled face appeared in the doorway to tell me prayers were over. I walked quickly back to my seat, accidentally catching the eye of the only woman teacher, Miss Andrews, who smiled.

My new form master, Mr Tilling, was very tall, with iron grey hair in crinkly waves. He used green chalk to write on the blackboard, and green ink to correct our exercise books. In his classes we weren't allowed to touch our faces. 'A hand should never touch any other part of the body except the other hand,' he said. 'The only exception to that is when you're washing or having a bath.' I knew what he meant, and it sounded like a useful rule, but it wouldn't be easy to keep. All the same, I decided to obey. After all, an itch was really quite a pleasant sensation which disappeared if you tickled it. If you didn't, you could go on enjoying the itchy feeling for much longer. The trouble was that when you were concentrating on a comic or what a teacher was saying, you might find your fingers rubbing at your neck or pinching at the cloth on the inside of your sleeve or even that you were rubbing your eyes, which you shouldn't ever do except with your elbow. Anyway, Mr Tilling kept blowing his nose, and I could see him rubbing it through the handkerchief. After a few days I gave up trying to obey except when he was looking.

Sometimes, just as you were closing the lid of your desk, a boy would throw a screwed-up ball of rubbishy paper into it, saying 'Fains'. 'Fains' was the opposite of 'I bags', but 'Fains' was always said about a thing, and you could say 'I bags be first' about doing something. You got rid of the rubbishy paper either by passing it to the boy on the other side of you, unless he said 'Fains' while it was still in your hand, or you could pass it back to the boy who'd given it to you, saying 'Fains infinity', which meant he couldn't ever give it to you again.

Fiske and Muley were the equivalents of Herriot but nastier, and they were boarders, so they had nothing to do when everybody else was in a hurry to go home. Fiske had a friendly face like a crumpled bun with freckles, and he kept tossing his head to get the hair out of his eyes. Muley had smooth, sallow skin and hardly ever smiled. They both had thick bodies but they could move fast. I'd pack my satchel ready to go home, take my navy blue raincoat and red school cap from the hook and stride through the schoolroom, only to find they were hiding behind one of the blackboards, ready to pounce on my cap.

'There's Hayseed, and there's his school cap.'

'Look Hayseed, I'll show you how to make a boomerang.'

And Muley folded the cap around the peak. When I tried to get it back, he threw it to Fiske. When I ran to him, he threw it back to Muley. As the game went on, they both sang:

> Hey little hen
> When when when
> Will you lay me an egg for my tea?

Sometimes they just gave orders.

'Go to Muley.'

'What do you want?'

'Fiske told me to come to you.'

'I don't want you. Go to Fiske.'

'I don't want you. Go to Muley.'

'Why've you come to me?'

'Fiske told me to.'

'Well, I'm telling you to go to Fiske.'

They both had something I envied – freedom from the need to please. They liked each other, but didn't care whether the other boys or the masters liked them. They were always being told off, always losing textbooks and dropping exercise books in the playground mud, always being made to stand in separate corners of the classroom and never allowed the privilege of sitting next to the bell, which gave a boy the right to keep an eye on the clock, waiting for the moment to come when he could put up his hand and say 'Please sir, may I ring the bell?' At the eleven o'clock break and at lunch-time it seemed as if that boy had just given us the right to stream out into the playground or through the other door into the paths around the playing-field.

Once, when Muley was looking out of the window, Mr Bird threw the thick yellow blackboard duster at him, but the sleepy eyes only looked back reproachfully through the rising cloud of chalk-dust. When Mr Bird told Fiske and Muley that he wanted to see them in his study, we used to wait until they'd gone inside and then tiptoe close to the door, keeping count when we heard the cane whistling through the air to thwack their trousered bottoms. They came out like heroes, pretending it hadn't hurt. They must have got very bad reports, and they were always near the bottom of the class, but though Muley wasn't really like Ginger, I often thought of Fiske when I was reading my William books.

4

Some Real Home Life

When we moved into Fremington, I soon saw what Nanny had meant about having a real home life. At the hotel the most important people had been the visitors. I must never make too much noise or run along the corridors or do anything that might disturb them. I had always been conscious of their presence. I had lived a large part of my life in public, almost putting on a performance – the well-behaved little boy – while family life had been scattered all over the hundred-room building, with public corridors separating the nursery from the flat, the bedrooms from the dining-room. Living at Fremington, we all saw much more of each other, and for Teddy and me the smaller audience meant greater freedom.

From the green gate a gravelly drive led up to the garage and the house, which had three storeys and garden all round it. In the corner of the garden, under a pine tree, was the air-raid shelter, with sandbags buttressing the thick brick walls and forming bumps in the tarpaulin roof. The garden was so quiet it made birdsong seem louder than it had on the East Cliff, but inside the shelter silence was total. Teddy and I climbed about on the bunks, shouted against the echoing walls and jumped on the slatted wooden floor. But there was a dank smell like wet sand mixed up with rope and canvas. Outside, the air smelt of sun and pine and rhododendrons and crab-apples. Dangling from the lowest branch of the pine tree, over by the bird-bath, was a rope we could swing on.

There was a place on the roof of the air-raid shelter where your bottom was cushioned by the sandbags under the tarpaulin and you were partly hidden by branches. I'd been given a real army tin helmet and we both had popguns. Teddy was General Woolf, and I was General Hayman. We sat up there with my aircraft recognition book, waiting for German planes to land on the lawn. As I explained to General Woolf, you could tell from the sound of a plane's engine whether it was ours or theirs. Ours had a straight buzz, theirs had an interrupted throb. A fighter sounded lighter than a bomber. Spitfires and Hurricanes were like wasps, Wellesleys like bumble-bees. The Germans had bombers too, but the lawn wasn't big enough for a bomber to land on. Probably it would be a Heinkel or a Messerschmitt. As soon as possible, I would make two wooden machine-guns for us. My carpenter's bench had been installed in the air-raid shelter, but the wood always split when I started sawing it. I needed a grown-up to help, but Daddy wasn't good at carpentry, and it was usually Shabbos or a Jewish festival when Uncle Phil came over from Southampton. He was working in a munitions factory there. Perhaps he could bring two real machine-guns for us, Teddy said.

We weren't allowed to eat the crab-apples. They were so sour you wouldn't want more than a small bite, but Mummy could make them into crab-apple jelly, which didn't taste sour at all. Vegetables were growing in the rear of the garden, and the gardener, who came on Fridays, taught me how to dig with one foot on the spade. 'Digging for victory' we called it. There was something attractive about slogans: 'Walls have ears', 'Careless talk costs lives', 'Is your journey really necessary?', 'Coughs and sneezes spread diseases. Treat all germs like grubs in cheeses' – which was my improvement on the line 'Trap the germs in your handkerchiefs'. Digging for victory was like being careful about the black-out or like observing religious laws. You felt you were doing something good and useful. And it was fun to buy Carter's or Cuthbert's seeds with their promising pictures of what the shaky dry rattle could grow into. I did badly with peas, but some of the carrots and lettuces were quite successful. We also had tomato plants in the conservatory adjoining the dining room.

Every morning Chef arrived on his bicycle, and the other three we'd brought from the hotel staff were Sutherland, the hall porter, Billy, the pantry-man, and Nelly, the maid who'd worked for Grannie ever since she'd had the boarding-house.

There were also three paying guests: Mr Smaller, his wife and their twenty-one-year-old daughter, Ethel, with her long straight hair and her perpetual shy half-smile. In the dining-room they sat at the round table by the window, while we sat at the big oval table in the same formation as in the hotel dining-room, with Grannie at one end and Daddy at the other. Mummy sat between Grannie and Teddy. Nanny sat next to me at lunch and in the kitchen at dinner. Wearing just the waistcoat and trousers of his smart claret uniform, Sutherland would bring the steaming dishes in from the kitchen and place them on mats in front of Grannie, who served generous helpings, which he carried first to the Smallers and then to us. When I asked for half as much bread pudding as she'd given me, she cut the piece in half and put both halves on my plate.

The big sitting-room was reserved for the Smallers; the other one had a desk, a glass-fronted bookcase and the radiogram from the Cocktail Lounge at the hotel. The bookcase was locked but the titles were intriguing: *The Stones of Venice* by John Ruskin, *The Tower of London* by Harrison Ainsworth, *The Story of San Michele* by Axel Munthe, the *Complete Poems* of Henry Wadsworth Longfellow and two companion volumes, Taylor's *Holy Living* and Taylor's *Holy Dying*. At first I thought they were both about Taylor, but I couldn't understand why there was a whole volume about his death, however slow and holy it had been. Even if the books were by him, it was funny to devote as much space to dying as to living unless he thought fifty per cent of your time should be spent on getting ready for Heaven. The old Everyman's Library books had faded green-and-brown spines with dull gold lettering and leaf patterns. I much preferred the new Everyman's I was collecting, with smart red bindings under crisp red dust-jackets and neat black titles in white rectangles. Sometimes Mrs Burke came with her key to take one of the her books away, but she always remembered to lock the bookcase afterwards.

Mr and Mrs Smaller were given the biggest bedroom, facing south, Grannie had the corner one with windows facing south and west, Mummy and Daddy's and the one I shared with Teddy both faced west, and Ethel's, the smallest, was on the opposite side of the corridor from ours. The carved oak staircase came up only to the first floor; the brown lino staircase from the kitchen went up to the second, where Nanny and the staff had their bedrooms. Mummy didn't like me to go up there.

The big bathroom had cupboards all along one wall. When I went to the lavatory after breakfast, I'd move the cork-topped bathroom stool over to use as a table, selecting one object from the cupboard to play with. There was an apparatus with rubber tubing and glass funnels for clearing catarrh by flushing salt water up one nostril and down the other, an old-fashioned manicure set, a variety of syringes, a box of liniment, an old pocket inhaler with a mellower smell than benzedrine, a Friar's Balsam inhaler, an old styptic pencil, dozens of half-used bottles of medicines, gargles and embrocations, and a few small brown bottles of nose-drops and eye-drops, with rubber valves in the caps and glass droppers. Sometimes I used an old eyebrow pencil to do thick drawings on thin pieces of Jeyes toilet paper, which later, for the sake of the war economy, I'd use to wipe my bottom, with the drawing towards my hand, which would have to be washed afterwards anyway.

The smell in Grannie's bedroom was the familiar mixture of eau-de-Cologne, talcum powder and oil of wintergreen. She had rheumatism in her hands, which she treated with a high-frequency apparatus that crackled nastily as it produced mauve electric sparks inside glass tubing. At the end of it was a flat glass bulb which she rubbed against her wrists and the backs of her hands. The first time I saw it I wanted her to do it on my arm, but it felt like bottled electric shocks. I looked up reproachfully and she used some of her chocolate ration on cheering me up.

All over the house the windows were coated with a thin gluey substance. If you just used your nails, it was difficult to peel off very much and anyway it would be dangerous, because it was there to stop bomb-blasts from splintering the glass inwards. Unless the windows were open, everything outside looked blurred, and the straight lines not quite straight. At first I'd thought that bombs were all round – either small, like cannon-balls, and fused, like the ones carried by Wiffskoffski, the bearded Russian spy in the *Pip, Squeak and Wilfred* books, or else big and spiky like the green landmines from the Great War that were on display along the lower promenade, looking as if

enormous conkers were inside the metal shell. I'd also seen
newspaper photographs of bombs that looked like my toy
submarine, only fatter. Later, at the news cinema in Post Office
Road, I saw a film of bombs actually being dropped. The
programmes there lasted just over an hour, and they were
mostly made up of Donald Duck and Mickey Mouse cartoons,
but there was always a British Movietone or Pathé-Gazette news
film showing searchlight beams roving across the sky, tin-
helmeted soldiers manning anti-aircraft guns, barrage balloons
high on thick wires, camouflaged tanks and armoured cars
bumping across muddy fields, soldiers in battledress jumping
over barbed wire, rifles held aloft, pilots lifting up their goggles
and smiling before they climbed wearily out of their cockpits.
And there were Ministry of Information 'flashes' to remind us
that 'Walls have ears' and 'Careless talk costs lives'. Altogether,
films taught me more about the war than photographs in
newspapers or news programmes on the radio, while news
programmes in the cinema had less emotional impact than the
feature films with sad, likeable, poker-faced actors in naval
uniforms using binoculars to scan the horizon for the emergent
conning-tower of a hostile submarine, or the same actors in
R AF blue talking laconically about the Jerries they'd shot
down into the drink.

Aeroplanes were exciting. Some of my friends made models of
them from balsa-wood construction kits. I tried only once to
make a model, but I spent a lot of time studying my aircraft
recognition book, which had pictures of British and German
fighters and bombers, with silhouettes showing dimensions. The
book gave maximum speeds, and a lot of other facts. The Spitfire
could fly at 400 miles per hour; the Hurricane wasn't quite so
fast. Bombers were much slower. The Germans didn't have
anything as fast as our Spitfire. I liked the Spitfire, especially
after seeing a film about the man who invented it, with Leslie
Howard playing the part. There was an awful moment when his
wife heard a rattling noise from his throat, meaning that he was
dying. She nearly dropped the tea-tray she was carrying.

Mummy and I started a National Savings group. Every
Thursday, after school, I'd walk around the West Overcliff Drive
with savings stamps, books for sticking them in, certificates,

a purse full of change, and greetings cards in case anyone wanted to give savings stamps as a birthday present. The units were sixpence, a shilling and half-crown, and you could exchange them for fifteen-shilling savings certificates as soon as you'd bought enough. Mummy said that most of our members could have afforded certificates straight away, but they bought stamps because it was more fun for me. Once a month we took the money into the office and collected our new supply of stamps from the volunteer workers. They seemed to like my idea for a new slogan and they promised to pass it on to the Head Office.

Turn your Notes into National
Silver Savings
Copper Certificates

When the air-raid warning sounded we weren't allowed to play in the garden till the all-clear. I was half hoping that one day I'd identify a German plane, but Daddy said it was very unlikely Bournemouth would be bombed because it was residential, with no strategic targets like ports or munitions factories. After that I added a bit to my night prayers about keeping Uncle Phil safe in Southampton. Sometimes we were woken up at night by air-raid warnings or woken up by Nanny, who said there'd just been one, but instead of using the air-raid shelter, we sat in the kitchen, where Nanny and Sutherland made cocoa, and Mrs Smaller, with her hair in curlers, talked about Birmingham during the Great War. Grannie refused to come down. 'I'm too old,' she said. The rest of us sat around the well-scrubbed wooden table in our dressing-gowns, clutching the brown cardboard boxes that contained our gas-masks. At first I wore my tin helmet but it was too heavy and uncomfortable to keep on for long.

One night I heard a throbbing in the sky. 'That's one of theirs,' I told them, but Mummy looked at me as if I'd said something wrong. Sutherland volunteered: 'It might be one of ours with engine trouble.' But suddenly there was a long-drawn-out whistle quickly followed by another and by two bumps that made the house shake and the windows rattle. Daddy's lips were moving in silent prayer. Then he went to the bottom of the stairs. 'Mater, I think you'd better come down.'

I was scared there might be another bomb while she was on the staircase, but she soon appeared in her hairnet with her pink nightie showing under her dressing-gown. 'It's like I always told you,' she said. 'If it don't have your number on it, you're all right.'

In the morning Sutherland said the milkman had told him that the bombs had fallen on the tennis-court and the bowling-green farther along the West Overcliff Drive. Before lunch Nanny took us along to have a look. Two craters like enormous sand-pits were breaking into the two neat rectangles of green. On Shabbos, Revd Heilbron added an extra prayer in English after the prayer for the Royal Family, thanking God for protecting us.

When Teddy started coming to Shool on Shabbos morning, he had to make do with holding Daddy's left hand, while I held his right. It was my prerogative as elder son. I knew it was mean to insist on it, but I did. When the caretaker swung the door open for us, Daddy would march in first, and I would follow, leading Teddy by the hand. I didn't like it when his warm bare leg touched mine. Once Daddy heard me telling him to sit farther away, and after that he always sat between us, with me on his right in the corner. Sometimes I pretended there was a lever under the bookrest that could make the cantor sing louder, like the knob on a wireless. The best bits were the ones we all sang together. It was good to feel part of a congregation that could sing tunes God liked.

Religion was the main subject at mealtimes. We were the Chosen People, but so many Jews, too stupid to realize how lucky they were, kept breaking the rules. The worst thing you could possibly do was to marry out of the faith, and Daddy was full of contempt for any man who'd let his son make friends with a *shiksa*. There was a lot of talk about people who came to Shool on Shabbos, but did the most awful things during the week, and there were approving sentences that started 'It's a great *Mitzvah* to. . . .' Literally, *Mitzvah* meant 'commandment', but you could say 'It's a great *Mitzvah* to visit the sick', meaning it was a very good thing. Mummy, who wasn't so keen on praying or observing the Shabbos, was more interested in working for charities, Jewish and non-Jewish. She was one of the collection organizers for Poppy Day, and I went round with a cardboard tray of poppies to all members of our Savings Group. I'd been briefed not to sell the silk ones for less than sixpence. Daddy helped the men who worked for Jewish charities; he didn't like it when announcements were made in Shool about how much people were giving, but he knew they wouldn't have given nearly so much if they'd had to do it anonymously.

I was having Hebrew lessons with Mr Younger, who came to the house on Sunday afternoon and charged five shillings an hour. He had rimless glasses and he used wavy underlinings where other teachers would have used straight ones. As I learned what more of the Hebrew words meant, my pleasure in the sounds increased, especially with words like *Bakbuk*, which meant a bottle and sounded like water being poured out of one. But I didn't like the textbook as much as my French and Latin ones. The stories seemed silly. There was one about a mean traveller who gave a boy half a shekel to buy provisions for a journey. The boy came back with a lump of salt saying he hadn't been able to afford anything else. It was also disappointing to realize that nobody spoke the language I was learning except when praying. Talking modern Hebrew, the Jews in Palestine said 'Shabbá' when we said 'Shabbos'.

In the last part of the lesson I could ask Mr Younger questions about the religion. There was a difference between biblical laws and rabbinic laws. The Bible didn't say you had to use different crockery, cutlery and table-linen for meat meals and milk meals. It was all because of one phrase: 'Thou shalt not seethe a kid in it's mother's milk.' The rabbis had built 'fences' around the flower of God's word to stop us from treading on it. It was like leaving margins in exercise books to allow room for mistakes to be corrected. That was why fasts and festivals always began earlier in the evening than they finished, and why we mustn't let even the tiniest trace of milk come anywhere near the tiniest trace of meat.

Mr Smaller wasn't orthodox, so Daddy and I were the ones who did most of the praying. On Friday evening, Grannie would close her eyes behind her spectacles, and, like a

conductor, wave her hands three times in the air before lighting
the Shabbos candles, and then Daddy and I would withdraw
into the small sitting-room with our morocco-bound Singer's
Prayer Books. Part of the service had to be said standing and
facing towards the east. No one would come in to disturb us until
we'd finished. On Saturday afternoon we'd study the Ethics of
the Fathers together, telling the others when we were ready to
say *Havdallah* with them. There was also a long morning service
to be said on weekdays by every male over the age of thirteen,
wearing *Tefillin*. Daddy didn't say it, but I decided to be more
orthodox than he was. I was going to say it regularly, but,
having taken my decision, I could establish my orthodoxy right
now. Because the Bible had commanded that no work should be
done on the Shabbos, the rabbis had added a veto on carrying
anything from one threshold to another. It was therefore a sin to
go out of doors with anything in your pockets – even a
handkerchief – but I discovered that some orthodox Jews solved
the problem by tying their handkerchief around their waist:
instead of carrying it, they were wearing it. This was what I did.
Daddy carried his in his pocket, but he was pleased to be
outdone.

It was exciting to see so many uniforms in the streets, and
Uncle Phil gave me a booklet called *Badges of Rank in the Armed
Services*. It lived on the shelf next to my aircraft recognition book
and I used to peer upwards at the pips and crowns on army
officers' shoulders. We were still going to the bandstand in the
Pleasure Gardens, and my favourite toy was a new trumpet.
When it gave me a sore on my lip, I was terribly impatient for it
to get better so that I'd be allowed to play again. One day Nanny
announced that she was going to make me a uniform of my own.
She cut out the red-and-blue material on her ironing board, and
soon she'd sewn it into a fine red tunic with braided epaulettes,
sergeant's stripes and real brass buttons bought from the
military tailor in the Old Christchurch Road. The blue trousers
were striped with thick red braid just like a real bandsman's.
Teddy of course wanted a uniform too, so she made him a long
blue serge officer's topcoat and blue trousers so that he could conduct with a knitting-needle while I played my drums. The record
of 'Colonel Bogey on Parade' represented the rest of the band.

Daddy had a black policeman's uniform with a shiny peaked cap, a striped armband, a polished wooden truncheon and a silver whistle he would never allow me to blow. He was a special constable now, and he often had to go out on beat in the evening, changing into his uniform as soon as he arrived home from the shop. Sometimes he was on duty in the middle of the night. His main job was to look for chinks of light. One night he found a light on in a window with no curtains. He rang the bell and told a woman that black-out regulations were not being observed. She said oh yes they were – he must be talking about the house next door. As he went back to have another look at the window, the light snapped off, but when he rang the bell again she said she hadn't done anything. 'All right, I'll go and put my foot through the window where I saw the light, shall I? Then we'll know which house it was.'

This became his favourite story. For a while it displaced even the one about the pickpocket who was acquitted and thanked his barrister by presenting him with the watch.

On 4 May 1943, my eleventh birthday, Mr Bird died. Fiske and Muley left the school soon afterwards, and rumours started to go round that he'd had an apoplectic fit while shouting at them, but secretly I knew I must be responsible for his death. Otherwise why had it happened on my birthday and why should two headmasters die so soon after I went to their school? Mr Tilling was appointed head, and luckily he was too pleased with himself to waste time on casting lots to find out who the school Jonah was. He addressed the whole school about the importance of not using the hand to touch any part of the body except the other hand, and I made a serious new resolution to give up my secret vice, but the reign of virtue lasted less than a week. On the eve of the Jewish New Year I made another resolution, thinking that if I could stop sinning for a year it would be easier after that. I promised myself that if I did give in to temptation, I'd write the letter M in red ink on that day's space in my Charles Letts Schoolboy's Diary or 2 M if I did it twice.

It was becoming much harder to decide where to draw the line round my orthodoxy. I'd always felt contempt for the people who said 'I'll go this far and no further', without realizing

I was one of them. When I found out that there was animal fat in bread and ice-cream I gave up eating ice-cream unless it was home-made, but how could I give up eating bread? I discussed it with Daddy, Revd Heilbron and Mr Younger. Each answered differently, but I took some comfort from being told that it didn't matter too much if the quantity of forbidden food to pass through the lips was smaller than half an olive. Some olives were bigger than others, so it presumably meant half a small olive. That took care of the anxiety about eating in restaurants, where obviously you couldn't know whether the cook had been cutting bacon just before he started cutting fruit with the same knife, or had handled meat and then fish, without washing his hands in between. But then it wouldn't be a sin to taste pork, so long as you ate only a tiny quantity, smaller than half a small olive. Mr Tilling said that roast pork was the most delicious meat in the world, so it was awfully bad luck on the Jews who had to die without ever tasting it. But if I asked one of my friends to bring a bit of roast pork to school, smaller than half an olive, I might like it so much that I'd want another bit, and how much time would have to elapse before I asked him again?

Life at school was much pleasanter without Fiske and Muley. My three best friends were Thoulless, Deval and Macleod. Thoulless had bigger freckles than anyone I'd ever known. He came to tea at Fremington and I went to his house. His mother's white terrier barked excitedly when we wrestled on the lawn, fighting until one man was kneeling on the other's shoulders. Thoulless wrote an anti-German limerick into my autograph book, but our friendship was never quite the same after an argument we had when Mr Oldham was out of the room. I wrote on the blackboard 'Thoulless is (1) decent (2) a twerp'. He then wrote 'Hayman is (1) crazy (2) insane'. I said it wasn't fair because one of the things I'd written about him was quite OK.

'Oh, did you mean decent? I thought you meant dekent.'

'What's dekent mean?'

'Gormless. Idiotic. Cretinous. You know. Like you.'

But afterwards I consulted *Nuttall's English Dictionary*.

Deval was French, so he always got the highest marks when we were translating into French, but often I did better with unseens, because his spelling wasn't good, and he was often told off about his handwriting. He had smooth skin and a very round face, with dark hair that fell over his forehead like Hitler's, but he got into a rage if we called him Adolf, and he was touchy about the defeat of France. If England hadn't been an island, he said, we'd have surrendered too. But he was very good at belching, and he was the one who started the fashion of making a double belch into 'Urbs, urbis' and then adding 'feminine, a city'.

Macleod was taller and thinner with lank, light brown hair and bony cheeks that reminded me of Mickey Mouse. We went for bike rides together, and the bike was usually my excuse when Mummy said why didn't we take Teddy swimming with us. We smoked our first cigarettes together in his garden on the day we drank some of his father's whisky. It was good to see the grey smoke curling up towards the trees, like steam from your breathing on a cold day, but much more casually. One day, I decided, I'd learn how to blow smoke-rings. Usually he stole the cigarettes from his father, but occasionally I stole them, two at a time, from the packet of Gold Flake which Daddy kept in his sock drawer. He filled his gold cigarette case from it before he left for the shop and again when he came back. Macleod also had an air-pistol, and we shot at fir-cones with it, but never at birds or squirrels. When the Chief Rabbi came to Bournemouth and preached a sermon in Shool, Macleod was the friend I wanted to tell about it. I led up to it by asking 'Have you ever shaken hands with the man you think is the greatest man in the world?' Of course he hadn't, but he wasn't impressed when I said I had.

My other best friend, a freckled Jewish boy called Abel, didn't go to Hailey. He appointed me second-in-command of his gang, which had thirteen other members, he said. Months later I still hadn't met any of them. He said disguise was very important, especially during a war. He'd sat for a solid hour in front of a mirror, he said, studying his face and considering possible disguises. We went for a fourteen-mile bike ride together into the New Forest and ate our lunch-time sandwiches on a roundabout at the Ringwood funfair. I was very sick and spent most of the next day in bed, wondering whether they'd stop me from going on long-distance bike rides.

He had a real fox-head, cut from an old fur of his mother's, and said he'd thought up a good way of frightening the Germans with it, if they invaded, but first we must test it out. We wired a bicycle lamp to the mask, tying a long piece of string to the handle of the lamp so that we could lower it over one side of the suspension bridge when it was dark enough for the string to be invisible. Anyone who saw the fox-eyes gleaming at him in the dark would have a terrible fright. With no street-lamps in use because of the black-out, the path along the bottom of the chine looked very dark indeed, and Abel said he bet no one ever came there at night except policemen, so we chose an evening when Daddy wasn't on duty. We stood on the bridge for what seemed like a very long time, dangling our patent frightener over the side, but no one came. Then Abel said his arm was getting stiff, and anyway there was no need for both of us to be on duty at the same time. He was the superior officer so I'd better have the first shift of duty. He'd be back in about ten minutes, and then I was to report anything that happened.

I felt sure nothing would, but a few minutes after he'd gone I heard footsteps on the path below. It was too dark to see anything, but someone was coming along the path towards the dangling fox-face. A shrill scream, and then the footsteps were running in the opposite direction. Abel was going to be very cross at having missed all the fun.

'OK,' he said when he came back. 'I'll take over now. Oh, by the way, did anything happen?'

I gave him a detailed report.

'And did you think it was a good imitation of a child's scream?'

5

Longing for Long Trousers

'What are you going to be when you grow up?' Mr Tilling would go round the class, pointing his gnarled finger at each boy in turn. He got irritated when anyone said 'I don't know, sir', and like a searchlight the pointing forefinger moved on to the next boy. I said 'Hotelier, sir', knowing I couldn't really tell whether the word would have anything to do with me in ten years' time. Would I be wearing a black jacket and striped long trousers and standing in the hall to welcome visitors? Or wearing a blazer and long white flannel trousers and standing in the tennis-court, organizing a tournament? It was good to feel that no one would be telling me what to do, but the fact of having to *be* something seemed effectively to reduce my freedom. 'You've got to have security,' Daddy said, and talked about a career in the hotel business, but it seemed silly that I had to choose just one career when there were so many. I'd have liked to be a drummer one day, a detective the next, Prime Minister the day after that and then an ace pilot for the rest of the week. Mummy would have liked me to be a doctor, because doctors did a lot of good, but Daddy said they had to learn by cutting up dogfish. He'd have liked me to be an antique dealer and jeweller, but there was always such a stale and dusty smell in the shop, and they had to stand behind glass counters, spreading out necklaces on black mats and squinting through magnifying glasses at diamond rings, working by electric light all day because the windows were too full of antiques for enough sunlight to get through. Inside the shop Daddy and Mr and Mrs King and Mr Wheatley, the manager, all had to move about carefully, wary of knocking against the pots and swords and plates and dishes

73

dangling from the wall. Mr King liked it because he always had someone to talk to. Nanny, who called him 'the big I am', would imitate the way he'd taught me to imitate Napoleon, putting my right hand inside my jacket, resting it on the middle button. Daddy liked having a shop because Mr and Mrs King were always there, so it didn't matter if he arrived late in the morning and had a sleep before he went back after lunch.

I wouldn't have minded being a pianist. It must be marvellous to be greeted with a crackle of applause as, smiling modestly, you stepped on to the concert platform. Montague Birch, the red-faced conductor of the Bournemouth Municipal Orchestra, always stood back so self-effacingly when the star soloist took his bow. I'd be able to wear evening dress in the middle of the afternoon and pull my sleeves back and fiddle with the knobs on the piano-stool before nodding to signal that I was ready. I could revert to my grandfather's surname, De Koski – Hayman was taken from his first name, Hyman – and if my hair got untidy as I thrashed away at the keyboard, Mummy wouldn't be able to tell me off from her seat in the dress circle. Just before the concerto ended there'd be a terrific flurry of exciting chords and then my face would relax as the applause started, but I'd dab at my forehead with a clean white handkerchief before standing up, just a trifle wearily, to shake hands with the admiring Montague Birch.

The actual business of learning the piano was different. All the windows had to be shut before the lesson could start, because Miss Bellner was terrified of catching a cold. And she was insistent about counting out loud. The first twenty minutes went on scales and another twenty on Czerny's five-finger exercises, not leaving nearly enough time for pieces. Anyway, how could she possibly make me into a concert pianist when she'd never been one herself?. Once she'd broadcast for the BBC, but now she was just a little old lady like so many others I saw in the gallery at Shool. Grannie always called her Miss Berliner, which was her real name, but Bellner sounded less German. One day I'd have to have another teacher, but meanwhile I felt much more in touch with the level I wanted to be on when we met Montague Birch in the street. Daddy knew him from the Rotary Club, and sometimes I had the chance to ask how many mistakes the pianist had made in the concerto last Sunday.

During Revd Dowse's divinity lessons I was supposed to draw maps, but I learnt how to listen without looking up. There was an irresistible glamour in the name I wasn't allowed to utter, Jesus Christ, and I was intrigued by the Trinity, which sounded like 3-in-One oil. But I couldn't make out why it didn't consist of God, Jesus and the Virgin Mary. Who was the Holy Ghost and what did he do? The New Testament seemed to be full of good stories, and there were phrases that had already become familiar from eavesdropping through the door during prayers. Except for some of the Psalms, I'd scarcely heard any liturgical English, and the only sentence with a ring and a rhythm that made it unforgettable was: 'I the Lord thy God am a jealous God, and visit the sins of the fathers upon the children unto the third and fourth generation.' The New Testament was full of exciting language. 'He that is without sin among you, let him first cast a stone. . . .' 'For many are called, but few are chosen.' 'If thine eye offend thee, pluck it out, and cast it from thee.' 'The kingdom of God is within you.' 'For now we see through a glass, darkly; but then face to face: now I know in part, but then I shall know even as also I am known.' 'But by the grace of God, I am what I am.' 'Though I speak with the tongues of men and of angels, and have not charity, I am become as sounding brass, or a tinkling cymbal.' I built up a secret store of fruity phrases, and went over them like a squirrel checking his supplies for the winter. Daddy would have been upset if he'd found out how much of the New Testament I knew by heart.

Revd Dowse devoted a whole divinity lesson to reasons for believing that the soul survives the body's death. It wasn't possible that God, after lavishing so much love and care on creating us, would allow us to be snuffed out like so many candle-flames. Nor would He let the wrongdoers who'd triumphed in this life go unpunished in the next, or the virtuous go unrewarded. Besides, it was inconceivable that human life had no purpose, no meaning; and what would be the point of it if we were merely put into the world to live our lives and beget children who would live theirs? Being perfect himself, God would not create something that was so much less than perfect, except as a means of training us to choose perfection. The boys at the desks on either side of me were taking notes, tabulating the reasons for believing that death wasn't the end.

When Daddy came home from the shop, I asked what was going to happen to us when we died. 'We don't know,' he said. 'There's so much the Almighty doesn't allow us to understand, and there's no doubt it's much better that way. The only thing we know definitely is that our children carry on after us. That's why I don't want you to be sorry when I'm gone. My immortality is you.'

If Hitler was gassing the Jews in Germany, he'd gas us if he invaded England. As Nanny said, the whole thing was silly. If only she could have had half an hour's chat with Hitler, she'd have made him feel ashamed of himself, but the Germans were all afraid of him, so they all did what he told them. The English grown-ups, though, were doing all they could to make it difficult for him. They'd used dynamite to make great gaps in the middle of both piers, because the invading soldiers would have been able to march straight along them once they arrived on this side of the Channel, and all the way down the promenade there were pillboxes for shooting from. There was also a barbed-wire entanglement all along the top of the cliff, as if the German soldiers were likely to climb all the way up, and then climb disappointedly down again when they saw it. You could still play on the beach, but there were no men picking their way between the sunbathers with big clusters of ripe yellow bananas in baskets. You couldn't buy sweets without points or clothes without coupons, and even my visits to the shoe-shop were rarer, though it didn't matter, because my feet weren't growing so fast. Mummy and Grannie still went out shopping together in the car nearly every morning. Petrol was rationed, but Mummy was buying on what she called 'the grey market'. I pictured watery grey petrol, but the car seemed to go all right on it. She also had a battle to keep Nanny from being called up to serve in the ATS. There was a real danger we'd lose her, and Mummy seemed even more worried than usual, but she went along, with her silk scarf round her head, to argue with some women, and soon it was obvious she'd won the argument.

Teddy and I were seeing much more of her now that she didn't have to work so hard. Having done no drawing since art school, she made sketches of us, and it was funny to see our faces coming recognizably to life in her thick pencil strokes, with some lines where there weren't any on our faces and only a few lines to represent all that hair. She played the piano every day, and familiar tunes would make me rush in from the garden to ask 'What's that one called?' 'Schubert's "Marche Militaire"', she'd say without stopping, or 'Tchaikovsky's "Waltz of the Flowers"'. She spent some time each day at the desk in the drawing-room, 'doing the post'. A lot of letters were redirected from the hotel, some from people still trying to reserve rooms, and she replied immediately in her neat handwriting. Daddy would leave letters unanswered for weeks; sometimes she'd reply for him. She wrote the cheques for the school bills, and the notes to Mr Tilling when I was absent because of illness or Jewish festivals. She tore the used stamps off envelopes to collect them for charity, and with a paper-knife she cut off the envelope's gummed back, saving the other half to use as scrap paper.

You never saw her reading a newspaper in an armchair, as Daddy did with his *Daily Telegraph*. At one time she'd taken the *Daily Mirror*, but the pictures weren't suitable for us children, she said. Now she read the *Daily Graphic* at the breakfast table. Not that she liked the sensationalism, she said, but she needed a paper that summed up the news briefly. She borrowed novels from the libraries at Boots and W. H. Smith's, but she read them only in bed at night or on Shabbos afternoon when she couldn't work. Otherwise she always liked to be 'doing something useful' – darning or knitting or crocheting or embroidery. She bought patterns on tracing paper from W. H. Smith's and made covers for cushions and seats for chairs. After Uncle Phil had initiated me into the habit of Sunday afternoon symphony concerts at the Pavilion, she would take me, if no one else could, but she would always bring her knitting, and all through the music I was expecting heads to turn or tongues to tut-tut in protest against the metallic clicking.

She talked a lot about unselfishness and doing good to other people. That was what we were put into the world for. You could tell when people were selfish, she said, because they used the words 'I' and 'me' a lot. In writing letters it was best not to use them at all if you could possibly avoid it. The reason she quarrelled with Grannie so much at mealtimes was that old people made it so difficult for younger people to help them. Mummy had given up the whole of her life to looking after her and assisting her in the hotel, but not only did she fail to appreciate it, she deliberately ignored the doctor's orders. She knew she shouldn't have bread or more than one small potato with each meal, but she had no consideration for the people who had to look after her when she was ill.

Mummy never ate bread or potatoes herself. She never had soup and her favourite main course was cheese and salad. 'You wouldn't like it if I got fat,' she said. Sometimes she and Grannie had a milk table-cloth folded over their end of the table while the rest of us were eating meat. Sutherland had to be very careful about cutlery on those days. She talked a good deal about dieting, but buying food seemed to occupy most of the time on morning shopping expeditions. When I went with them, I'd watch listlessly as Grannie argued with the kosher butcher about the amount of fat to be cut off, and Mummy took advice from the greengrocer about which sort of apples to buy. Grannie didn't mind spending money. ('The best is good enough for me.') But she was appalled when the price of smoked salmon went up to a pound a pound. ('Shockin'.')

Mummy couldn't walk to Shool with us on Shabbos morning because of her bad leg, but she came for short walks with me along West Overcliff Drive or along the suspension bridge that led over the chine or through Cherry Tree Glade. I liked holding hands with her, and there was a new pleasure in kissing when we sat down on benches for her to rest her leg. I put my arms round her shoulder and nuzzled my face up against hers, enjoying the cool hardness of the cheekbone and the warm softness of the cheek which was so different from Daddy's.

But she was liable to fall suddenly into a kneeling position on the pavement. I'd help her up, dreading the sight of torn stockings and bleeding flesh and trying not to meet the eyes of passers-by who didn't know whether to pretend they hadn't noticed anything or to offer help.

It wasn't easy to find things that could give her pleasure to

make up for what she was having to suffer. She didn't want
flowers or books or records, and never wanted to try new kinds of
soap or scent or bath-salts. The most successful present I gave
her wasn't a present at all. One day I carved I LOVE MUM
into the skin of a baby marrow in the vegetable garden, so that
through the kitchen window she'd see the message growing
bigger each day. She thought Teddy had done it, and he said he
would have if he'd thought of it. For years afterwards she would
either write 'Marrow' instead of 'Love' in her letters to me, or
end them with a miniature sketch of a marrow.

At school I was no longer the only Jew. The curly fair-haired
new boy in 3b, Gerald Barker, walked out with me before
prayers. He had a funny north-country accent, and always
wanted to tell me the jokes he'd heard the day before, so instead
of eavesdropping through the green door on the readings from
the New Testament, I had to hear about parrots shitting in
church. At home Daddy had been talking about Barker's
family. Mr Barker kept his shop open on Shabbos, and though
they didn't eat pork, Mrs Barker didn't buy from the kosher
butcher, and Barker ate the school lunch. I hated the idea of
non-kosher meat going into a boy's stomach and helping to
build his muscles, and I didn't like the plump, freckled thighs
visible under Barker's short grey trousers. But Brewer, who
wasn't Jewish and did eat pork, had a more wholesome-looking
body than Barker. They both had fair skin and curly fair hair,
but Brewer was the best athlete in the school, and he looked
particularly good when he was putting on a final spurt to win the
hundred yards, fingers splayed out stiffly on thrashing arms, jaw
jutting with determination, head slightly to one side as he used
all his strength to hurl his body into the waiting white tape. If
only it hadn't been bacon, ham and pork that had gone into
making those muscles what they were. In the playing-field one
morning during break, he offered me half a grape he was eating.
I shook my head, knowing what food his tongue had touched.
'What's the matter? Don't you like my lick?' And he lobbed the
half-eaten grape high into the air with the same graceful body
movement I admired when he was bowling.

I liked football better than cricket, and unorganized games better still. In the playground we used an old tennis-ball as a football, and the goal was chalked on the brick wall. Prisoner's Base was more fun, but rougher, the main cause of scabs on knees. Two boys picked up sides, tossing a coin for first choice. You waited impatiently for your name to be called, knowing they didn't think much of you if it was one of the last. There was a chalk line across the middle of the playground, and if you ran into enemy territory, they could take you prisoner by lifting you off the ground. Then you had to stay inside the chalk marks in one of the far corners of their territory until you were touched by one of your own side, who'd broken through to release you. The alternative was to play war games in the bushes around the playing-field. We imitated aeroplanes and gunfire and argued heatedly about how long you had to stay dead.

Mummy was putting so much pressure on me to be nicer to Teddy that I quarrelled with him more and more. In the end it was decided I couldn't go on sharing a bedroom with him; so when the Smallers left, I was moved temporarily into the big bedroom, knowing I'd have to go into the little one that had been Ethel's when the big one was needed for somebody else. Uncle Phil had it when he came from Southampton for the week-end, and he left his cello in the corner cupboard. One night when I was sleeping there again, I dared myself to get out of bed and play it. Nervously I took it out of its heavy case, sat on the dressing-table stool, watching myself in the long mirror as I held it between my pyjamaed knees, bow in one hand, the other gripping the strings, face concentrated like Piatigorsky's in the photograph in *Life* which had been sent from America. Perhaps I was more cut out to be a cellist than a pianist. But no sooner had I got a few, loud buzzing notes out of it than Grannie appeared at the door in her pink nightdress, hair in metal curlers, angrily telling me I had no right to touch it.

Chef had been ill and didn't want to go on working, so Grannie took over the cooking herself, with help from Mummy and Nanny. Mummy's speciality was apple charlotte, making breadcrumbs out of all the crusts that might have been wasted. Grannie could make cream cheese. She wrapped it in muslin and put it between two plates with a heavy weight on top from the rusting kitchen scales. Yellowish whey oozed out on the lower plate. She was at her most forceful in presiding over the roasting of the joint. At the hotel her closest contact had been with the meat, for even meat bought from a kosher butcher had to be koshered in the home, and it had always been Grannie who marched through the swing doors into the kitchen to take charge of the ritual soaking and salting. The idea, apparently, was to remove all traces of blood. It was very wrong to eat blood. At breakfast, if Daddy found a speck of blood in his boiled egg, he would push it disgustedly away and ask for another.

As Grannie's helpings became more generous than ever, the wartime propaganda about not wasting food was harnessed to the family propaganda about the need to eat. As well as the weekly pocket-money I had from Daddy, I received weekly 'clean plate money' from Grannie if I hadn't been leaving my food. It was OK to leave the fat from the roast beef, the black skin from plaice, and a reasonable amount of cauliflower or cabbage stump, but not spinach or Brussels sprouts. She still called me Skinnamalinks, poking playfully at my ribs, but I collected the money fairly regularly, a half-crown, a threepenny bit and two pennies laid out on the glass-topped dressing-table, the way chocolate used to be before it was rationed. But I refused to eat when she used her own knife and fork to cut a second helping of meat from the dish, or the spoon she'd been eating from to serve the pudding. Mummy couldn't understand why I minded. I told her I was fastidious. She said I wasn't, or I'd always have clean fingernails.

Sutherland was sometimes bad-tempered, and I could never tell when he was joking. Once when he saw me going out into the rain without a coat, he told me that if I was clever enough, I'd be able to dodge between the raindrops. He ate his meals in the kitchen with the other staff, but as they left, one by one, he took over more of the work, and in the end he was eating a solitary lunch, a library book propped up behind his plate. He looked up resentfully if I told him off for eating meat off a black-edged plate, even though I didn't use the annoyed tone the grown-ups would have used, and even though I wasn't going to tell them what I'd seen.

Teddy had started to write poetry, which they all praised, even when it didn't scan. Everybody said how fast he was growing and that he'd soon be taller than his brother. Already he was big enough to wear my clothes quite soon after I'd grown out of them. Mummy seemed to think he was better looking than I was, and never told him to 'Lippit', while Grannie never seemed to worry about his eating habits, though when he was in a bad mood he'd refuse to eat at all. In his worst tantrums he went upstairs to lock himself into the bedroom that was now his. I'd be sent up to plead with him to come back, and when I failed, Mummy would go up and kneel down in the corridor to reason with him through the keyhole. She said I didn't realize how much he hero-worshipped me, but to me it seemed more a matter of his not knowing what he wanted to do except be with me and do what I did. All his hobbies were copied from mine. Sometimes it was quite fun to play games with him, but I had less freedom when he was with me, because she was more concerned to know what was going on. I mustn't forget that he was delicate, she said. He got asthma and hay-fever, and he had mastoids. One day, after the game of General Hayman and General Woolf had developed into a cushion fight, she came storming into the front room to tell us off. We were both out of breath and she seemed very suspicious of what we'd been doing, though all she said was 'Look how flushed his cheeks are'. Did I want him to have another attack of asthma?

Saturday afternoons had a regular pattern. You weren't allowed to play the piano or read or knit, so while Daddy had his sleep, and Nanny played games with Teddy, Mummy and I relaxed in the small sitting-room reading our library books. I liked the Biggles books, John Buchan and Sir Arthur Conan Doyle. Nanny took me regularly to the Westbourne branch of the public library, also borrowing books for Grannie, but Mummy preferred the libraries at Boots and Smith's because the books hadn't been fingered by so many people.

Sunday was my favourite day. We had roast beef for lunch, with Yorkshire pudding and either roast potatoes or baked rice. Grannie cooked the beef, Nanny the Yorkshire pudding. Daddy always listened to the one o'clock news, setting his gold pocket watch by the six pips, and afterwards there were good programmes – *ITMA* with Tommy Handley, and *The Critics*. And there were afternoon concerts at the Pavilion. Uncle Phil was teaching me much more about music than Miss Bellner was. He said that everything in Mozart moved towards reconciliation, and the second movement of Beethoven's Fourth Piano Concerto was a conversation between the instrument and the orchestra. But one Sunday in the middle of lunch he said I was a prig. It was the sort of word Fiske or Muley might have used, but it was incredible that someone in the family should say it. And why was no one sticking up for me? And how could he just go on sitting there, stroking his brown moustache?

It was two weeks before he took me to another concert, and by then I was used to the idea that he didn't like me. But I'd been looking forward to the chance of talking about it when we were alone together in his car. He said they wanted me to have the best education that money could buy, and it was all very well trying to be so religious, but if I wasn't pretty careful I'd get stuck into a little corner of self-righteousness. If I wanted to grow up into a human being, I'd have to find out about real life. I told him about the booklist Mr Tilling had given us. I intended to read *Social Life in the Insect World* by J. H. Fabre: apparently you could learn a lot about human life by studying insects. Uncle Phil said you could learn about life only by living it. He seemed to disapprove of the way I was being brought up. It had never occurred to me that there was any other way. Daddy always seemed to know what was right, and so did Mummy. When she punished me, she always said: 'You've got to learn what's right.' Surely I *was* learning. But all the time Uncle Phil had been sitting there, munching silently and listening to what they were telling me, he'd been thinking what he'd have said if he were in charge. I knew Christians thought we were wrong to believe we were the Chosen People, but it was strange that an uncle could think my parents were wrong about what they believed to be right.

Suddenly, without intending to, I was asking 'Why didn't you ever get married?' He didn't answer at first, and my words seemed to stay hanging in the air.

'They don't want you to know, but I don't see why you shouldn't. I have been married. She wasn't Jewish.'

'You mean you married a *shicksa*?'

It was shocking but exciting. He had been there all the time, right in the heart of the family, eating meals with us and talking to us like anyone else – a man who had done the most outrageous thing you could possibly do. 'In my eyes you'll be dead if you marry her.' That was what a Jewish parent was supposed to say if his son was thinking of marrying out of the faith, and Daddy had pretended not to recognize people in the street because they'd let their son bring his non-Jewish wife into their home.

'What happened to her? Did she die?'

No, she was still alive but it hadn't worked out, and now they were divorced.

'Are you still friends with her?'

They'd gone on seeing each other for some time after the divorce, but didn't any more.

'But why did you never tell me about it?'

I was their son, and it was against their wishes he was telling me now. If I was *his* son, everything would be different. I tried to imagine what it would be like to be his son. I'd never seen any photograph of him when he was my age.

'I won't tell them you told me.'

And I didn't even tell Nanny, but when I kissed Mummy good-night – the cold cream was already smeared all over her face, so I had to plant the kiss carefully on her forehead just under the hairnet – I had the feeling of knowing a secret that belonged to the grown-up world.

Periodically food parcels would arrive with American stamps on them. Uncle Dan and Aunt Valerie sent us powdered milk, tinned kosher sausages, tins of salted cashew nuts, whipped cream, corn off the cob, bars of Hershey chocolate, packets of spearmint chewing-gum and an ice-cream mixture called Frizz. It had a fine, rich, creamy taste, better than the ice-creams of the Stop-me-and-buy-one man. Their letters said they still intended to come over for my Barmitzvah. Please God the war would be

over by then. In the colour photographs Aunt Valerie looked
very pretty and smily, but Cousin Marian looked rather bulgy
in her bikini.

When Daddy invited Aunt Hetty and Uncle Ben to come
with their children for Passover, I knew I'd have to give up my
bedroom again, but I was looking forward to sleeping with
Cousin David in the sitting-room. We had one Put-U-Up
already, and Mummy bought another at Harvey Nichols.
Cousin Barry, the eldest, could sleep in Teddy's room, because
Teddy would be asleep by the time he went to bed, and Cousin
Rosalie would have Ethel's room.

Two years older than I, David was the nicest looking and the
nicest of them. Barry was sallow-skinned, self-important and
scowling. Nanny, who had names for everybody, called him the
Indian prince. If we went out for a walk, he boasted about his
sense of direction; if we played croquet on the lawn, he knocked
other people's balls into the flower-beds. Aunt Hetty was short,
dumpy and over-affectionate. She kept saying we liked our
Auntie, didn't we, and pulling our faces against the hard shiny
fabric over the big, floppy breasts. Uncle Ben was tall and bony,
with metal-rimmed glasses and a polished-looking forehead.
They both talked the sort of English that would have earned me
a lot of red underlinings at school – 'That isn't no good', 'Don't
talk silly, Dave', 'Wasn't you?' And Nanny was soon mimicking
Aunt Hetty for saying 'Definitely' so much.

We'd brought a lot of Passover crockery from the hotel, and it
was nearly a full day's work for Nanny and Sutherland to
unpack it from the crates in the cellar and wash it, packing the
other crockery away, rinsing all the cutlery in boiling water and
emptying the larder of all food that wasn't kosher for Passover.
Instead of flour we used matzo meal. Fruit and vegetables were
all right, but everything that came in jars, like pickles, or in
bottles, like tomato ketchup, was exiled for eight days to the
garage and replaced by special jars of honey, jam and
marmalade, bottles of cordial and packets of butter that had
been approved by the *Beth Din* and stocked by local grocers for
their Jewish customers. There were even boxes of chocolates and
bags of sweets stamped with the *Beth Din*'s seal of approval.

At the Seder service it was now Teddy who asked the

questions. 'Why is this night different from all the other nights?'
he said in Hebrew, though we all knew the second night was
going to be exactly the same, and when the second night came,
the question made even less sense. Daddy read the service on the
first night and Uncle Ben on the second. Some of his tunes were
different from Daddy's, and not so good. Barry sang very loudly,
forcing his voice from the back of a tightened throat and often
glancing up to make sure God was listening. We all said 'Next
Year in Jerusalem' both nights with great fervour. If only Hitler
would let the German Jews go to Jerusalem instead of gassing
them, perhaps the war could be over sooner. Teddy had written
a poem about an argument between Hitler and God:

> Send down the Israelites,
> Send them to me.
> I can look after them
> Better than Thee.

I said it ought to be Thou, but Barry said I was a spoilsport and
got his own back on Teddy's behalf when I corrected his
pronunciation of 'Quand Madeleine', the march on the other
side of the 'Colonel Bogey' record. Barry corrected mine.

Dave kissed me a lot, which was a bit soppy, and once, when
he was holding me, he asked, 'Why are you so nice?' I didn't
know what to say, and he let go. We went for a lot of walks
together, taking it in turns to be a royal personage. 'Yes, your
Highness'. 'But isn't your Highness forgetting that. . . ?' The
idea was to make passers-by curious, but most of them were too
discreet to stare. With Dave there was always plenty to talk
about, and in bed we'd go on chatting for ages after we'd put the
light out. No one else was sleeping on the ground floor, so we
were unlikely to be told off, but the possibility added to the
excitement. We criticized all the grown-ups, and nearly always
agreed on what was likeable about them and what was silly. I
could send us both into long fits of giggles just by saying
'Krennie'. It wasn't even a good imitation of her accent, but her
presence had been invoked.

The big sitting-room had a deep bay window and a straight
curtain on rings, forming a D-shaped space Dave, Teddy and I

could use as a stage to put on concerts for the grown-ups with songs and recitations and piano pieces. The pianist had to go out into the room to sit down at the rosewood baby-grand but he got applauded when he appeared between the curtains, and at the end of the piece he could disappear again behind them after he'd taken his final bow. We made programmes with a lettering pen in red and black ink, and sold them for threepence when the grown-ups came in. Then, after seating them in a row of chairs, we disappeared into our magical space behind the curtains. They could talk out loud, but we could only whisper while making our final preparations: it had to be as much like a real theatre as possible. Once Mummy shattered the magic by shouting out 'Ronnie, you can't keep grown-ups waiting like this'. If she were willing to play the game of being an audience she should have played it properly. But a short while ago I was surprised and touched to find that she'd kept two of the programmes.

Aunt Hetty said that by the end of the war I'd be big enough to go up to London on my own, and, if Mummy and Daddy would let me, I could stay in her house if I went to St Paul's School. He wanted me to go to a public school because he'd never had the chance himself, and the only public school that provided kosher food for boarders was Clifton College. St Paul's took day-boys and it was in Hammersmith, only ten minutes' walk from the house. I could look forward to red London buses, concerts in the Royal Albert Hall and sharing a room with Dave.

The Common Entrance and scholarship exams couldn't be all that much worse than those at the end of every term, and it was better than looking forward to a birthday, because it wasn't just a matter of unwrapping presents and being one year older. I'd be able to wear long trousers, and I'd have had my Barmitzvah. I'd pray every morning with my *Tefillin* on, and I'd count as a man when ten men were needed to make up a *minyan* if somebody wanted to say *Kaddish* on the anniversary of his father's or mother's death. *Kaddish* was good for the soul of the departed, so it was a great *Mitzvah* to make up a *minyan* for it.

The exams were going to come just after my thirteenth birthday, so they arranged coaching for me in French and Latin, as well as extra Hebrew lessons to prepare for my

Barmitzvah. The French teacher, Mademoiselle Malevigne, had
a small flat in a house that belonged to Daddy in Post Office
Road near the news cinema. She was paying him rent and he
was paying her fees. She was a tiny, wrinkled old lady with
pince-nez, which she kept readjusting whenever her hands
weren't too busy grabbing at her blouse to rub at her breasts,
which seemed to need tickling all the time. I did an imitation of
her at school, and the boys said it was incredible.

My extra Latin lessons were with Mr Oldham at school every
Thursday after the last lesson. When it was sunny we sat with
our books in the grass behind the cricket nets. His fingertips were
stained yellower than Daddy's with nicotine. 'Never smoke
when you grow up,' he advised, brushing spilt ash off his
trousers. 'It's a filthy habit.'

Every Sunday morning I went to Hebrew classes at Shool.
The classroom was in the room with the sliding roof that became
the *Succah* during *Succos*. Both the desks and the benches were
very narrow, and Revd Heilbron was fond of giving us extra jobs
like sorting the old books in the big cupboard on the platform of
the hall under the wooden board that was inscribed in big gold
letters, first in Hebrew and then in English: 'Out of the mouths
of babes and sucklings hast Thou ordained strength.' Daddy
wanted to get the Shool's library going again, with me as
honorary librarian and David Symons as my assistant. David
was a very smily boy who put the word 'Sir' at least twice in
every sentence he addressed to Revd Heilbron, but Revd
Heilbron liked it. Respect for one's seniors was a very good
thing, he said. David and I made out file cards for all the books
in English, books like *A Guide for the Perplexed* by Moses
Maimonodes and *A Short History of the Jewish People* by Dr Cecil
Roth. Some of the books had nice shiny dust-jackets with
pictures of archaeological excavations or men in beards and dark
hats, but most of the books were old and dusty. We still hadn't
started on books in Hebrew, which would have taken much
longer to catalogue, when time became different. There had
always been endless quantities of it. I used to say 'Nanny, what
shall I do next?' Even when I started school, life hadn't seemed to
change very much, but now it was difficult to cram in everything
that had to be done before I went to bed, and I realized that I

didn't have time to be an honorary librarian. The lessons with Mr Oldham and Mademoiselle Malevigne made the evening shorter on Tuesday and Thursday. There was an hour's piano practice every day except Shabbos. There was homework and there was all the extra work I had to do for my Barmitzvah.

Ambitiously, I'd volunteered to sing not just the *Haftorah*, an excerpt from one of the Books of the Prophets, but also two *Sedras* that were scheduled for the Shabbos nearest to my thirteenth birthday according to the Jewish calendar. The five books of Moses had been divided into *Sedras*, and by singing one or two each Shabbos, the minister and the cantor took us through them each year. I was going to sing two rather difficult *Sedras* from Leviticus, mostly about leprosy and ritual washings. Each word had to be sung to one of about eight simple three- or four-note melodies, and the Scroll of the Law, which was all I could have in front of me, contained neither the vowels nor the musical notation, which were both in the books everybody else would have, so they'd all know if I made any mistakes. But after years of joining in the choruses, I was at last going to have a solo, and be sure that God and everybody else was listening. There wouldn't be any applause at the end, but at least there'd be shouts of YISHAKOWACH, May your strength return.

I was walking back from Hebrew classes one Sunday when the air-raid warning sounded, and within seconds a German plane was flying so low over the treetops that I could see the pilot's goggled face. An enemy as close as that! Throwing myself flat on the pavement, I realized all I'd done was to present him with a bigger target, but I was too scared to move or look up or do anything except hope he wouldn't think it worth circling back to machine-gun a boy in short trousers. The loud engine noise was receding already, and when I looked up the sky was empty. I ran all the way home, so eager to tell the others about it that I forgot to take shelter till the all-clear sounded. Usually there was no resemblance between the safe things that happened to me and the dangerous things that happened to Biggles and the heroes in *Hotspur*, *Boy's Own* and stories by John Buchan. I'd have done anything to avoid the adventure, but as soon as it was over, I knew it was the most important thing that had ever happened to me, and I understood why there were men who wanted to work

as spies and secret agents. You felt more alive when you'd
narrowly escaped being killed. Time wasn't an endless space
you could take for granted.

In the afternoon, when Teddy and I were sitting on the sun-
warmed tarpaulin roof of the air-raid shelter, it seemed
impossible that there had been an enemy plane in the blue sky,
now reassuringly full of clouds and birds and quietly buzzing
bees. Suppose I *was* dead? Suppose that what happened after
death was that God made you think you were still alive?
Everything went on inside your head exactly as it would have
done, so it was only other people who ever found out that you
weren't there. Perhaps it was just a figment of my dead
imagination that Teddy was sitting there with my tin helmet on
his head pretending to be General Woolf. I seemed to be seeing
the popgun in his hand and the scabs on his knees and, all down
the side of one leg, the imprint of the pine-needles he'd been
kneeling on, but perhaps the real me was on a slab in a hospital
mortuary. Except that my soul was more real than my body, so
these unreal fancies about being alive were more real than the
corpse on the slab.

Later on in the afternoon I had a Hebrew lesson with Mr
Younger. He wore a crocheted Kappul on top of his wavy grey
hair, and when he took off his rimless glasses there were deep
dents above the bridge of his nose. He always had three
fountain-pens in his waistcoat pocket, one for red ink and one for
green. His handwriting was very neat, both in English and in
Hebrew, but he had no sense of humour, and though I didn't
have to call him Sir, I did have to be very careful not to upset
him.

Once I made the mistake of asking 'How do you spell it?'
when he was telling me what vowel to put under a Hebrew
consonant in my spiral-topped vocabulary book. He stood up
abruptly, marched out of the room, collected his coat from the
hall-stand and slammed the front door. After supper he rang up,
and when I answered the telephone he sounded very cross. He
called me Ronald and told me to fetch my father. Afterwards
Daddy looked very serious, but said he wanted to hear my
explanation before he made any comment. When I said I had
intended to make Mr Younger laugh, he told me to write a

letter, assuring him I hadn't wanted to be impertinent and that I
felt as much respect for him as a good pupil should for a good
teacher. If I could find a suitable quotation from the Ethics of
the Fathers and a way of working it in, so much the better. As I
was writing my letter, Mummy started playing something
familiar on the piano, but when I went in to ask what it was, she
refused to tell me until I'd finished the letter. I went back as soon
as I'd stuck the stamp on. She said it was 'Anitra's Dance' from
the 'Peer Gynt Suite' by Grieg. I'd heard it on the radio but
always thought the announcer had been calling it 'The Beetroot
Dance'. My mental picture had been of plump beetroots
prancing.

Mr Younger was coming twice a week now. Besides coaching
me how to sing the two *Sedras*, he wanted to explain everything I
needed to know about the religion. I hadn't chosen to be a Jew.
It was just lucky that I'd been born into the true religion. But
now I had to accept full responsibility for my beliefs. So if I had
any questions about Jewish laws or about anything else, I was to
put them to him. These lessons should be regarded not just as a
preparation for one day, however special, but for my whole life
as a Jew. He knew I'd have one question in particular, and he
was going to answer that straight away without my even
needing to put it. Every boy was puzzled how babies came into
the world, and some parents liked to explain it themselves, but
Daddy and Mummy had shown their confidence in him by
expressing the wish that he, as my religious instructor, should
tell me. I knew already, no doubt, that a baby grew from a seed
inside the mother's womb, but did I know what made it start
growing or how God had made sure that it didn't start inside the
womb of a woman who wasn't married, like Nanny for instance?
Well, what happened in fact was that it never started to grow
until the husband slept with his wife.

It seemed odd that sleeping in the same bed could start the
growth, and anyway Mummy and Daddy had single beds, but
he didn't stop talking long enough for me to say anything.

'The husband's penis', he explained, 'is inserted into the
wife's vulva, but it can only be inserted when erect, and
when erect it can emit only urine, not semen. No, the other
way round, only semen, not urine. God has devised the human

organism with such loving ingenuity that there's not the slightest danger of urine being passed into the vagina or semen being wasted in the lavatory. Just as a flower is pollinated or a chicken's egg fertilized – I expect you've seen boiled eggs with a speck of blood in them but I hope you haven't eaten any – the female eggs or ova, which are produced regularly, irrespective of whether sexual intercourse has taken place, can be inseminated by the male sperms, which are fired from the penis like bullets from a machine-gun during the orgasm or climax, which is the most pleasurable part of sexual intercourse. This is what sparks off a pregnancy.'

A picture was forming in my mind of Mr Younger, with his rimless glasses either in his hand or on the bedside table, inseminating the long-nosed, sharp-chinned Mrs Younger to spark off the pregnancies that had led to the births of Rebecca, Sarah and Shulamith, but it disintegrated into a welter of guilty alarm as I realized that the name of my secret sin was onanism. The thick fluid that left marks on the sheets which no one had ever mentioned was semen, and the sin of wasting it was second in seriousness to murder. In biblical times I could have been stoned to death.

'Now is there anything you don't understand? Anything you want to ask me?'

I didn't want to talk about it. But in biblical times you were married when you were very young, which removed the temptation I'd tried so hard and so unsuccessfully to resist.

It was only a few weeks after this that Macleod grabbed my arm just after the bell rang for break and said: 'Let's walk round the field.' This was where we always went when we didn't want to be overheard. 'Have they told you how babies are made? I think it's absolutely disgusting. Really horrible. I've decided quite definitely I'm never going to do it if that's what it's like. Are you?'

It was exciting to meet Uncle Dan. Neither Uncle Phil nor Uncle Isadore looked at all like Mummy; here was a man very much like Daddy, but sixteen years younger, and talking with a soft American accent, while Aunt Valerie looked even better than she did in the photographs. It was like suddenly having a film star in the family. I told her she looked like Vivien Leigh, and when I took her up to show her the *Picture Post* photograph from the film of *Anna Karenina* which I'd stuck up on the inside of the big white toy cupboard door, she couldn't deny the resemblance. They both had the same delicately scooped-out nostrils and the same slender neck with dark ringlets creeping round the side of it. Aunt Valerie had very white teeth and her smile was like a flash. One of her eyes was made of glass, but you didn't notice it wasn't moving like the other eye unless you looked at it hard. Cousin Marian was a lumpy eleven-year-old girl who hugged me a lot and said she wanted to marry me as soon as we were both old enough. I said we could decide later.

Aunt Valerie seemed pleased when I started to call her Aunt Vivien. All her clothes were glamorous, and so were Uncle Dan's suits. He wore lighter colours than Daddy in lighter-weight materials – pale grey and powdery blue, stylishly cut. He always smelt nice too. He used an electric shaver and he promised to send me one from the States as soon as I needed to start shaving, and to keep me supplied with the same after-shave lotion he used himself. But his tone of voice changed when he talked about loyalty. The history of the Jewish people was a history of persecution. Just as the war against the Nazis had tightened the bond between the British and their American cousins, persecution through the ages had produced a solidarity in the Jewish people. That was why family feeling mattered more to us Jews than to Gentiles. Each family group was part of one big family, and I must always remember that loyalty to my family was part of loyalty to my people. Even if he and Aunt Valerie and Cousin Marian didn't live as close to us as they'd like to, there was nothing to stop us from writing to each other more often. If ever I wanted his help or advice, all I had to do was send a letter.

They'd brought six packets of Frizz, and a lot of chewing-gum in long strips you unwrapped out of silver paper. It was nicer than the fat white sugar-coated pills of gum you got in the English shops. They also had a reflector for sunbathing. It looked like a silver-coated kite, with three hinged sections. If you rested it against your knees while you were lying in the sun, with its sides at the correct angles, it could triple the strength of the heat, making your skin three times as brown. That was how Aunt Valerie got herself so tanned.

Weeks before the Barmitzvah, presents started to arrive. I kept a list in an old pocket diary for 1942, devoting a day's space to each present and putting a tick in the corner when I'd written the thank-you letter. The list soon spread into April. I was given six fountain-pens, four propelling pencils, five wallets, three copies of Dr Cecil Roth's *A Short History of the Jewish People*, five book tokens for half a guinea, three for a guinea, two for two guineas and one for five guineas. Mr Younger gave me *The Giant Book of Jewish Humour*, but it had no dust-jacket round the artificial leather binding, and a pencil inscription had been rubbed out under his ink inscription on the fly-leaf. Daddy bought me a new bicycle, and Nanny a new Dunlop tennis-racket, but the most exciting present, from Mummy and Grannie jointly, was hanging in the wardrobe – two suits with long trousers. A dark blue suit with a waistcoat, and a black jacket and striped trousers for me to wear in Shool on the actual morning. I kept opening the wardrobe to finger the long trousers. One afternoon, when I was having a smoke to celebrate the freedom they'd bring, there was a knock at the locked door.

'It's Aunt Vivien.'

I stubbed the cigarette on the sole of my shoe and threw it into an empty drawer before letting her in.

'We want to take some snaps of that Cherry Tree Glade, and we thought maybe you'd like to come. We could get some of you and Marian together. Dear, did you know there was smoke coming out of that drawer?' There was neither reproof nor complicity in her tone, and we were both smiling as I put the cigarette under a tap. Nothing was damaged except the white lining paper in the drawer. 'So what do you know? Who's just about to be a man?' And she put her arm round my waist. 'Come on. Let's go find the others.' I shall never lose my brain-snapshot of the grey curl of cigarette smoke drifting out of the closed drawer.

After the Common Entrance results, which were better than I'd

dared to hope, the masters all said they expected me to win a
junior scholarship to St Paul's. Mummy and Daddy were both
counting on it, though I knew they'd be nice about it if I failed.
The exam had to be taken at the school, and it lasted three days.
I was going to stay with Aunt Hetty, but Mummy and Daddy
would come up to London with me on the Sunday morning to
stay for the rest of the day. They said I could have a quiet
bedroom to myself in Aunt Hetty's house if I wanted to spend
the final afternoon revising, or I could go to my first concert at
the Royal Albert Hall. Marjorie Lawrence was going to sing
Brünnhilde's closing scene from *Götterdämmerung*, with Basil
Cameron conducting. I'd seen pictures of her performing from
her wheelchair, and I'd heard her on the radio.

I wasn't prepared for everything to be so huge. Compared
with Bournemouth West, Bournemouth Central was quite big,
but it hadn't occurred to me that a railway station could have as
many platforms as Waterloo. In the bustling crowd, against the
trundling of luggage trolleys, the shouting of porters, the
loudspeaker voice trying to sound calm and the babble of voices
from the crowd, Mummy and Daddy suddenly seemed small. I
was nearly as tall as she was and her lame walk made her look
shorter as she clung to Daddy's arm, following the porter
through the crowd, past the W.H. Smith kiosks and the tea and
sausage stalls, under a grimy arch to a thick queue. London taxis
(like the ones I'd seen in films) were arriving in rapid succession,
loud engines rasping while porters bundled luggage up into the
space beside the driver. I'd never realized what the spaces were
for, or seen so many taxis. When we drove out into the sunlight, I
saw red buses like the ones in my London jigsaw puzzle.

Then Westminster Bridge and the Thames. It wasn't a stream
like the one in the Pleasure Gardens but a massive river right in
the middle of the town. Then the Houses of Parliament. The
wide pavements were full of people who weren't taking any
notice, but there they were, the most important buildings in the
world, with Big Ben spiking up into the sky and the House of
Lords still intact, and the enormous space where a German
bomb had done what Guy Fawkes had failed to do. And here I
was at the centre of things. This was where Queen Elizabeth had
made speeches and Disraeli had said 'Justice is truth in action'. I

hadn't expected the streets to be so wide and noisy, with so many buses and taxis and cars and dirty lorries going so fast in so many different directions, but without even seeing the school, I wanted desperately to belong in this great city. Suddenly, above us, Big Ben started to gong out the chimes I'd heard so often on the radio before the news. Now there was only a taxi window between me and the invisible bells, and when I tugged it open there was nothing. 'Ronnie, *please*,' said Mummy, and I closed it. But nothing could have quashed my excitement. It was exactly as if I'd never been in London before. I had been, when I was about five. I remember two photographs of me taken at the zoo. In one I am riding a donkey; in the other a chimpanzee has its arm around my shoulder. But it's only the photographs that I remember, the experience of the zoo, like the first experience of London, had vanished. But I still have a clear image of the blonde Australian soprano being pushed on to the platform of the Royal Albert Hall in her shiny metal wheelchair.

The summer was full of good news. Hitler's suicide in the bunker. My success in the scholarship exam. Churchill's demands for unconditional surrender, the arrival of the Russian army in Berlin, the birth of four kittens, the surrender of Berlin, the surrender of Hamburg, the unconditional surrender of Germany. Pulling the newspaper through the letter-box was almost as exciting as unwrapping a parcel, and even the poker-voiced radio newsreaders sounded pleased, though if I'd been Stuart Hibberd or Frank Gillard I'd have wanted to shout YIPPEE and dance round the microphone. Watching Daddy's happy face as he sat in the armchair by the wireless, I remembered how grim he'd looked a few years ago, listening to news about the Germans advancing. Even now it was a bit frightening to think about what would have happened to us if that advance hadn't been stopped. German army trucks screaming to a halt outside the Shool and Erich von Stroheim barking orders as SS troops rounded the congregation up for gassing. It must be true that God was on our side.

Japan couldn't possibly hold out for long. It would all be over in time for me to start school in London, and soon we'd be back in the hotel. Grannie was worried about the state we'd find it in. I wasn't worried about anything. I was wearing long trousers and I had my own wireless set. After years of borrowing Nanny's portable when I wanted to listen in bed to *Monday Night at Eight*, I had one that was hardly bigger than a book. The sound came on as you pressed two silver buttons to flick the lid open, and the news that pushed its way through the tight mesh of silvery wires was always good news. I also had a new cricket bat with pale orange rubber on the handle. Lovingly I massaged linseed oil into it, wanting it to look as old as possible, but it would have been cheating to put a bandage on when it didn't need one. Not having to swot for exams, I practised in the nets after school, and played a lot with Teddy and Nanny in the front garden, though they could only bowl underarm. We used the old cork cricket ball in case it got lost in the tangle of undergrowth between the rhododendron bushes and the outside privet hedge. My new red leather ball was for use in the nets.

The day no longer started with a cup of tea in bed brought by Nanny. Now that I was a man, no food or drink must pass my lips until I'd said my prayers. I had to take my new *Tefillin* out of their little velvet bag and put one on the centre of my forehead, like a miner's lamp, the leather straps holding it in position. The other went between the biceps of my left arm, facing towards my heart. I then had to bind the long leather strap all the way down my arm and three times round my hand to form the letter *Shin*, standing for *Shaddai*, one of the names for God by which we avoided pronouncing his real name, which was too holy for the lips. At first the morning service took me twenty minutes, but within a few months I'd got the time down to eight. The actual praying took only six, but it was at least a minute's work to put the *Tefillin* on, and it took just as long to put them away, winding the long leather thongs neatly round the projecting edges on one side of the little black boxes.

I'd never enjoyed school so much as I did that term as a member of the long-trousered élite. At break Macleod and I would saunter around the playing-field, planning a new gang we were going to start, not for any reason, just to have something in existence with us at the head of it and some boys who were members and some who weren't. The members would have to take an oath of allegiance, swearing to keep the gang going after we both left at the end of term.

There was a new English master, Mr Mousehold, who'd had one leg amputated just above the knee, but he was younger than any of the other teachers. He had long, straight, blond hair and he'd been in the RAF. He made us write an essay every week, but it was fun because he thought up interesting topics such as 'What would you most like to see invented that hasn't been already?' I wrote that I'd like something that bore the same ratio to television as the gramophone to radio. 'Jolly sound idea' was the comment in his fluent, flourishy red handwriting. 'No doubt this will become a reality within the next few years.' His voice took on a serious tone when he talked about the atomic bomb. 'For the first time in the whole history of the human race,' he said, making emphatic pauses like Mr Churchill's, 'it is within the power of Man to produce an explosion of such devastating amplitude that the whole of humanity could be wiped off the face of the earth. If you don't know what amplitude means, look it up. This is a fact of such profound significance that it is almost impossible for the imagination to grasp it, but one fact is clear. After two world wars there can never possibly be a third. Nations will have to find some new way of settling their disputes if they want to avoid a holocaust. Holocaust means global catastrophe.'

Mr Mousehold was appointed Assistant Headmaster, and he had several weeks as Acting Headmaster because Mr Tilling had his appendix taken out in a nursing home, where they forgot to remove one of the swabs when they sewed him up after the operation. Making the announcement about it before prayers, Mr Mousehold was angry when we laughed. How would we like it to happen to us? The next day he made a speech about swearing, which was not only bad for us and for the school, but for the English language and the civilization of which language was the custodian. He glared round, defying us to laugh, but nobody wanted to. If any of us heard another boy using foul or ungentlemanly language, he said, we were to report it to him immediately, and this would not be regarded as sneaking because moral standards were involved, and so many gallant airmen, soldiers, and sailors, many of them ex-public-school boys, had given their lives in the fight against barbarism. We were members of a doubly privileged generation. They had died so that we could have a better world to grow up in, and we could never be asked to make the same sacrifice because a new weapon was in existence that guaranteed there could never be a Third World War.

Soon after this speech Macleod and I heard Cartwright saying 'ballsitch'. Neither of us knew what it meant but we were pretty sure it was a swearword because he'd said it so vehemently. But how serious was it? We wouldn't be expected to report people for saying 'damn' or 'blast' or 'bloody', though actually 'bloody' was quite serious because it meant 'by our Lady' and I tried never to say it because she wasn't mine. Anyway 'Gosh' and 'Golly' both mean 'God', and you couldn't count them as swearwords. Though if you didn't, how could you ever find enough words to keep swearing for a whole minute without repeating yourself? If you couldn't do that, according to Thoulless, you'd be debagged and dunked in the swimming-pool on your first day at a public school.

Two weeks before the term ended I won a race. Though I'd always had to make a conscious effort not to imitate the splayed-fingered way Brewer held his hands when he was sprinting, I loved the feeling of going all out in a final spurt and then letting myself collapse on to the grass with heart thudding and chest heaving, knowing there was no more effort to be made and waiting for my breathing to get back to normal. It was so incredible that for once I'd beaten Brewer, I couldn't be sure it had actually happened. In the French lesson afterwards, while Mr Oldham was writing on the blackboard, I whispered to Deval: 'Who won the hundred yards?' Deval didn't know, but the next time Mr Oldham turned his back, he whispered to Brewer: 'Who won the hundred yards?' And I heard Brewer whisper back: 'Hayman.'

I was spending over an hour at the piano every day now, working simultaneously at the 'Moonlight' and 'Pathétique' Sonatas. I could hardly believe my fingers were ever going to move fast enough for the third movement of the 'Moonlight'. 'They won't,' said Miss Bellner, 'unless you do twenty minutes of scales and twenty minutes of Czerny every single day. You always want to run before you can walk.' It had been a mistake to tell her I wanted to learn the Polonaise in A flat Major. I had

Paderewski's recording of it, though Miss Bellner maintained
that Pachmann was the better pianist. Her uncle had once had a
lesson from him.

I also wanted to be a composer and bought a ruled
manuscript book from the music shop. After a lot of experiment-
ing and an argument with Mummy, who came in and told me
not to strum, I composed my Prelude in C Major (Opus 1 No. 1),
but Miss Bellner was unimpressed. I had no grasp of harmony,
she said. I went back to the music shop and paid six shillings and
sixpence for *Harmony – a Simple Systematic Treatise on the
Harmonisation of Melodies and Basses* by T. Keighley, Mus. D
FRCO, etc. I could understand about tonic triads but got
confused over modulation, and she said she didn't have time to
explain.

My pocket-money had been increased by threepence a week
when I won the scholarship, and I made frequent sorties on my
new bicycle (which was now equipped with a speedometer and
a mileage gauge) to the stamp shop in the Post Office Arcade. I
paid fifteen shillings for a Penny Black, but mostly I bought
stamps in packets, tempted by something rare or triangular
displayed in the little windows of transparent paper. The
promising bulge behind would always turn out disappointingly,
but Teddy was glad to be given my duplicates. He'd also taken
up autograph hunting soon after I did, though he hadn't yet
started on my latest craze, which was to collect photographs of
musicians cut out from the *Radio Times* and the monthly
supplements HMV and Columbia issued to bring their record
catalogues up to date. I used stamp hinges to stick the pictures
into a loose-leaf drawing book, trying to arrange the musicians
in order of merit within each section, but separating the British
from foreigners. Heddle Nash was my number one British tenor,
but I wouldn't have known how far after Gigli and Jussi Björling
to put him if all the tenors had been grouped together, or how far
after Heifetz and Yehudi Menuhin to put Ida Haendel. It was
difficult enough deciding whether to put Moiseiwitsch before
Solomon, Gladys Ripley before Kathleen Ferrier, and Eva
Turner before Isobel Baillie. I tried to be objective but I liked
Gladys Ripley's smile, and perhaps Marjorie Lawrence wouldn't
have ranked so high among world sopranos if I hadn't seen her.

This mattered enormously – to see a great musician or actor, not on a film but in real life.

Part of the excitement in buying gramophone records was in deciding which was the best recording to have. Sometimes Uncle Phil advised me; sometimes I consulted the book in the reference library. The man in the record shop claimed to stock what he recommended, but he may have been recommending what he had in stock. One afternoon, when a record I'd ordered hadn't come in, I gave in to a long-standing temptation and spent the money on a baton, so that I could conduct records and watch myself in the mirror. But during Tchaikovsky's fantasy overture, 'Romeo and Juliet', I got too close to the mantelpiece and broke the baton. Obviously it was a punishment for my giving in to temptation.

6

In a Dark House

My life seemed to change colour when I unpacked my suitcases
in Aunt Hetty's house. Either there was less sunlight in London
or it was because of the darkened wallpaper in my new home.
There was so much I'd been looking forward to – red buses,
Underground trains, being with Dave, the Royal Albert Hall,
Aunt Hetty's curly chips and having red bottles of a fizzy drink
called Tizer the Appetizer on the table at every mealtime – but
it was all greyer, grimier, grimmer, greasier than I had
expected. We ate in the kitchen, where the smell of fried onions
clung to the faded brown wallpaper. The holes in the table-
cloth, the patches of floorboard showing through the old lino,
the peeling paintwork, the frayed curtains, the worn stair-
carpet, the dusty broken lampshades, all reflected the same
weary sadness that was in Aunt Hetty's small, dark, resentful
eyes. She wore her dressing-gown and slippers to cook breakfast,
first for Uncle Ben, who had to leave the house by ten to eight,
then for Cousin Barry, then for Dave, Rosalie and me. After
she'd been to the bathroom she changed into a housecoat that
looked very much like the dressing-gown, but she padded
constantly about the house in her slippers, except when she went
out. She said she worked too hard, but I never saw her attack a
cleaning job energetically, the way Nanny did.

There was only one bathroom, and the small, smelly lavatory
was next to it; in the morning, with six of us to use each room, I
couldn't dawdle in either. I had to keep my toothbrush,
toothpaste, soap, flannel and nailbrush in my blue flannel bag
which I was allowed to hang from the dented brass knob on the
door of the overcrowded cupboard. It smelt of toothpaste and

wet flannels. The bathroom door had frosted glass on it, so you could see dim shapes from outside – Uncle Ben's tall, lean body or Aunt Hetty's short, squat one, or Cousin Barry jutting his chin towards his own reflection or Cousin Rosalie standing back to admire hers. If it was Dave's plumper-waisted figure beyond the glass, I could rap on it with my knuckles, and go in to start cleaning my teeth while he was washing his face. There was just enough room for two of us between the chipped bath, the towel-rail and the door. The bath usually had a washboard in it.

We ate in the front room when we had guests – mostly Minnie and Flossie Levine or Aunt Golda and Uncle Hymie, Uncle Ben's sister and brother-in-law. Then Aunt Hetty would put a lace cloth on the long table and make one of her high teas, with rollmops, two other kinds of pickled herring, anchovies in a tin with the jagged lid curling upwards, bread and butter, matzoh and a round cake with thick yellow icing, bought from J. Lyons. Otherwise the table was topped with a legless billiard-table supported by six wooden blocks. Chalking their cues between each stroke, and keeping score by sliding markers along the dark wooden scoreboard that hung like a picture on the faded brown wallpaper, Uncle Ben and Cousin Barry played billiards and snooker with a ritual running commentary of half-jocular threats and insults, disparaging each other's shots, boasting about what they were going to do next, making excuses when they failed to do it. I knew I'd never be any good at this sort of banter, but I was pleased when Uncle Ben started to teach me the game, interrupted, if Cousin Barry was in the room, by a barrage of contradictions.

Cousin Barry wanted to be a chemist. 'He's quite brilliant,' said Aunt Hetty. 'He's got the most brilliant career ahead of him. You mark my words, Ronnie. Your cousin's going to be a great man.' Known as his laboratory, the room next to the bathroom was equipped with a bench supporting an elaborate mesh of glass tubing and retorts, a Bunsen burner, test tubes in a rack, and shelves with jars of coloured crystals and bottles of colourless liquids, all neatly labelled. There were two big brown glass jars marked POISON. I wasn't allowed into the room unless Cousin Barry invited me. Now that I was sleeping in his old bed, he was sleeping in the laboratory, immediately underneath Dave and

me, so he could hear if we talked in bed. One night he appeared
in his pyjamas, grumbling that we were keeping him awake, and
raising his fist so high I thought he could only be threatening,
but a hard punch landed on my undefended ribs.

Aunt Hetty spent most of the day padding about in the
kitchen. Her skin was greasy, particularly on the nose; her
chicken soup had yellow circles of grease floating on the top; her
chopped liver was fatty, and there was always a sauceboat of
greasy gravy on the table. She served both roast and boiled
potatoes at every meal, and Cousin Barry would mash his up
with a fork, pouring gravy over them. He, Dave and Uncle Ben
were orthodox enough to wear Kappuls all through supper on
Friday and lunch on Shabbos, but they ate in their shirt-sleeves
and read the evening papers all over the dinner-table. Uncle
Ben did the football pools, and went to dog racing at the White
City. He offered to take me, but Aunt Hetty said he mustn't. He
drank several glasses of Forest Brown Ale at each meal and
feigned incredulity when I admitted that I didn't like the taste.
'Go on, Ron. Have a glass. It'll do you good. I'll tell you
something, Ron, and if you take my advice now, you'll never
regret it, not till your dying day. Do you know why I look so
young? Well, how old do you think I am? Go on. Don't be afraid.
You tell me what you think. All right. I'll tell you. I'm nearly
forty-eight, and I don't look a day over forty, do I?'

Over-loud guffaws from Cousin Barry. 'You don't look a day
over eighty, Dad.'

'Don't take any notice of him. He gets stroppy when he can't
win at snooker. But seriously, Ron, the reason I look so young is
beer. It's all thanks to Forest Brown Ale. The secret of life is
beer.'

'The secret of life is ears,' said Cousin Barry, licking at Cousin
Rosalie's left ear. From touching it gently with the top of his
tongue, he started to suck at it with loud slurping noises, while
Rosalie smiled uncertainly. Sometimes Cousin Barry took just
the lobe inside his mouth, sometimes the whole ear.

'Barry, I do wish you wouldn't do that at mealtimes. You're
supposed to be setting your Cousin Ronnie a good example.'

But he just grinned at her, displaying his big yellow teeth. He
knew she couldn't be angry with him for long.

When they were actively unpleasant to me, or outspokenly
derisive about my parents, she at first tried to restrain them, but
soon accepted defeat. I told myself that they were jealous of us,
but this didn't help me to weather the abuse from Barry and
Uncle Ben about Jack and Sadie. They implied that when my
grandfather's butcher's shop had been sold, my father had
somehow made off with an unfair share of the money; they
ridiculed the hotel; they accused me of thinking a lot of myself;
they made unfunny jokes about the weekly chickens that Daddy
contributed during term-time. At first I tried to argue and
contradict, but I was shouted down. Later I preserved a hurt
silence, not knowing where to look.

  Home life was uncomfortable in every way, and more
cramped than I'd bargained for, but the school was more
spacious. Inside the thick stone walls of the red, Gothic,
cathedral-like carapace were wide stone corridors, wide stone
staircases and big wooden-floored classrooms. Eric Cookman,
son of the Hammersmith Synagogue's president, had promised
to keep an eye on me during my first few days. When the bell
rang at twelve minutes past nine, he took me up the stairs to a
huge, tiered lecture-hall. All the boys who came in looked
Jewish. A short, spectacled boy with a loud voice started talking
up at us from a lectern. 'That's Neville Banner,' whispered Eric.
'He's a prefect and his father's a Socialist MP.' He was making a
speech of welcome to the new boys, and telling us where to sit in
hall if we were having the vegetarian lunch. Then he began a
story about a stuttering Jew who applied for a job as a radio
announcer. The boy was enjoying himself when he imitated the
stammer, but he failed to get much of a laugh with the punch-
line, in which the man attributed his rejection to the anti-
Semitism of the selection board. Neville Banner's confidence
was undeflated. 'Never mind. You think about it. You'll see the
point later on in the day, and suddenly you'll burst out
laughing.'

  At lunch-time Neville Banner and Eric, who were both ahead
of me in the queue, accepted meat meals from the serving hatch
and sat down among the non-Jewish boys. According to Eric,

there were about 110 Jews in the school, but one table was enough to accommodate all the vegetarians. Our table was the nearest one to the platform where the masters were eating, some still wearing their gowns. When I got to the serving hatch I said 'Vegetarian, please', and the white-overalled woman, who already had a plate of meat in her hand, put it down to pick up a plate with a crumbly piece of Cheddar cheese on it, and some lettuce. The noise of boyish talk and clinking cutlery seemed much louder than the mealtime noise in the hotel, and I was incredulous that so many Jews, including a president's son, were eating meat. The next day I took sandwiches, and ate them walking up and down the long, white-painted, brick-walled corridor in the basement. I kept passing two boys, one tall, one short, who were walking up and down together, whistling 'Sheep may safely graze' in harmony. A moustached master dressed in the khaki uniform of an officer stepped through a doorway and looked at me oddly. The door he shut behind him had a notice on it saying Junior Training Corps.

For the physics and chemistry lessons we had to sit at high double desks in big laboratories. The teacher's desk was a long demonstration bench with a Bunsen burner on it and a sink cut into one end underneath a high tap. At the far end of the room were similar benches for us, with two high stools against each, Bunsen burners all along them and sinks at either end. The chemistry lab made Cousin Barry's look very small. We would be dealing, said Mr Whicker, the chemistry master, with substances that could be dangerous if we were careless with them. Sulphuric acid on the skin would not only be painful, the skin would never look the same afterwards. But the safety rules were elementary, and we should not expect sympathy if we ignored them. He had very fair hair and eyebrows that disappeared into his blond skin, the same way that his quiet voice seemed to fade into the sunlight filtering in through the tall Gothic windows. I craned forward against the hard edge of the desk, nervous of missing one of the safety rules. Next time we came, he said, he would divide us into pairs, so that each boy had a partner for the practical experiments. I knew I'd be absent next time because of the Jewish New Year.

The physics master, Mr Hampton, was like an elderly boy,

with round cheeks, a friendly grin and a loud voice. Terrier-like white hair circled his globular pate. If only he'd been the geography teacher, I whispered to Hughes, he could have had the northern hemisphere tattooed on it. He was in charge of boxing, he told us, and he hoped to see a lot of us in the gym. He smiled as he explained his system of Avoidable Errors. In our study of physics, we'd find that certain mistakes were unnecessary. We'd often be called upon, for instance, to draw a stick half immersed in water, showing the approximate angle of refraction. Boys often drew the bend in the wrong direction. All he wanted to do was help us, but in his experience the best way to help boys was to beat them when they failed to avoid avoidable errors. He was grinning so amiably, I wondered whether beating could be the same as caning. Since we were all new boys, he said, trying to find our feet in the school, he wouldn't want to punish our bottoms just yet, so for the first two weeks of the term he'd be quite prepared to assume that even avoidable errors were unavoidable.

Revd Peros, the cantor in Hammersmith Shool, was a bass, and the New Year service sounded about two octaves lower than it did in Bournemouth. Instead of being in the middle of the Shool, the altar was at the front, only a few yards away from the ark, and all the benches faced towards it. The presidential box was in the corner, but there was room for only three men in it, so Eric wasn't sitting next to his father. I wondered whether he'd make a New Year's resolution to eat only kosher meat.

After a two-day halt in my new routine, I didn't want to resume it. I knew I'd have to miss school again next week for the Day of Atonement, and again the week after that for the first two days of *Succos* and again for the last two days. There was only one day of school now before Shabbos and it hardly seemed worth going. My sandwiches were waiting on the table in a neat parcel of greaseproof paper, held together by a rubber band, my satchel was full of new textbooks, and new exercise books containing homework that would already be out of date by the time I arrived. My new school cap and new scarf were waiting on the hall-stand, and there was no excuse for giving in to the fear in

my stomach, no possibility of saying I wasn't well enough to go. I
had chilblains on most of my toes, which had provoked a sneer
from Cousin Barry. 'He's used to central heating.' But I could
still walk.

The school bell was just finishing its warning chimes as I
rushed up the stone steps through the heavy doors into the dark
entrance-hall, where the prefects were detaching themselves
from the radiator, ready to start awarding detentions to
everyone who arrived late without a good enough excuse. I
ran up the stairs to my locker, hung my cap, coat and scarf
on the peg inside it, and took my satchel to the lecture-hall
where Neville Banner made a speech about the excellent
Jewish principle of starting the New Year by forgiving one's
enemies.

The morning began with a double chemistry period. Not
having a partner, I was told to join Hughes and Langton, who
seemed to have cemented the friendship that had started on the
first day of the term. Langton had delicate, girl-like features,
Hughes had a husky, open-air look. It was like joining in a game
of mothers and fathers with two children who couldn't refuse to
let me play with them. They tried to keep me abreast of what
they were doing, and it was fun to see liquids changing colour,
like paints in the first lesson with Captain Brough, but they kept
using words I didn't understand.

With the other subjects it was much easier to catch up. French
was the easiest of all, in spite of Mr Gordon's air of ferocity.
'Santa Barbarossa,' he'd shout, clapping his hand to his
forehead in melodramatic despair at our stupidity. He wanted
to be thought a character, but he was more likeable than the
masters, who obviously wanted to be liked. Some stayed sitting
at their desks all through the lesson, others paced incessantly,
stepping on and off the platform. Mr Coombs, the economic
history master, was a great pacer. Tall, pale and serious, he
wandered ruminatively up and down, hitching up the baggy
grey flannel trousers that were too loose around the waist. I
thought I'd arrived at a useful conclusion when I suggested in
my first essay for him that, in conflicts of opinion, the truth lay
somewhere between the two extremes, but he wrote 'Obviously'
in the margin.

With all my previous periods in bed, I'd been impatient to be allowed up again. I didn't feel ill this time, but then I'd hardly ever felt ill before. The difference was that my usual hunger for the future had been displaced by fear. I was so homesick for the past that I wanted to make the house into a hotel and Aunt Hetty into an approximation of Nanny. It was reassuring and slightly surprising when she shuffled into the room with trays of food. She accepted the idea that I had to stay in bed, agreeing it was better not to tell Mummy and Daddy. It would only worry them. It wasn't as if they could do anything to help.

It felt odd to be making out cheques in favour of Mrs H. Hatter, but Daddy wanted me to do it, and he was paying the money into my bank account every month. She'd thank me, tuck the cheque into the torn pocket of her worn, flower-patterned housecoat, and carry on talking as if nothing had happened. 'Now that you're old enough to understand,' she kept saying, as the secrets came tumbling out from Mummy's and Daddy's past. I listened with a mixture of guilt that I was learning what they didn't want me to know, and greedy relief that at last, without looking for it, I'd discovered a source of information. Grannie's husband had been a tailor, like Uncle Ben, but he was a shy, unsociable man, while she always enjoyed being at the centre of things, a good talker, and a good cook. From taking first one lodger and then two, she'd made the boarding-house into a flourishing business. All he wanted was a quiet life, so one morning, when she woke up, he wasn't there. She never saw him again. Altogether she'd had an unhappy family life, what with Sadie getting infantile paralysis and both sons marrying *shicksas*. Didn't I know about Uncle Isadore? Oh yes, that was why we didn't have anything to do with him any more. Uncle Phil had divorced his, but Uncle Isadore refused. Grannie told him she never wanted to speak to him again. It wasn't until years later that she saw him in a park in Bournemouth with his wife, and then he was the one who wouldn't speak to her. Walked straight past without so much as a look. 'Who is that woman?' asked his wife. 'I don't know. I've never seen her before in my life.' 'But she's calling you.' 'She must be a lunatic.' 'Then how does she know your name?'

In her clear insistent voice, Aunt Hetty quoted with unchallengeable authority the exact words of conversations she couldn't possibly have overheard. But there were undertones of resentment in most of her stories. 'All my life I've had to work like a slave. You know that, Ron.' As if less deserving people enjoyed easier lives. Uncle Phil for instance. 'He's cost your Grannie his weight in gold. She says that herself. Because he's never learnt to stand on his own two feet. He was her favourite son, and she spoilt him for life. Do you know how many businesses she's bought him? She can't believe he's no good. But that's the way she's made him. Each time he wants money, she gives it to him, so why should he work for it? I don't suppose you remember the garage she bought him just before the war? You do? Well, he doesn't know any more about cars than I do, but there he was in a white overall with a spanner in his hand, tinkering about with engines, and calling the manager every time he got into trouble. No wonder it lost money. It's a good thing she's got plenty.'

There was also a lot of talk about money at mealtimes. The Hatters considered themselves to be poor and us to be rich. They didn't seem to know any really rich people, like Lady Salmon and the Kahns, who owned big cars, wore diamonds and mink, and handed out huge tips to Tonks and the other waiters and porters, making them all specially obliging, even if other people had to be kept waiting. When Daddy came to Dunsany Road, he usually gave money to Dave and Rosalie, but when he wasn't there, they weren't at all respectful to him, taking their cues from Uncle Ben and Cousin Barry, who both seemed to think it was wrong that we should have more money than they did. Aunt Hetty said it was true that when my grandfather died, Daddy took more than his fair share of the money from the sale of the butcher's shop. He had a big quarrel with Uncle Joe. That was why he never wrote to us from Canada. Certainly Daddy had been very good to her, she must give him his due. Without him Barry couldn't have gone to London University, but as soon as he was a famous chemist, he'd return every penny to his Uncle Jack. That was what he was like, Barry. Didn't want to be in

anyone's debt. Actually he took after Jack in a lot of ways.
Uncompromising and very religious. Did I know how my dad
had come to move into Grannie's boarding-house? Hadn't he
told me that story? Well, when he was trying to set himself up in
Bournemouth as a young auctioneer, he'd been staying with a
Mrs Feldman, who claimed to keep a strictly kosher house. One
Sunday he wanted to have lunch in bed, and she brought him a
glass of milk on the same tray as a plate of cold chicken. He took
one look at it, grabbed the tray out of her hands, threw it all in
her face and started packing his suitcase while the milk was still
dripping down her dress. He moved into Grannie's boarding-
house the same day, and never moved out. He'd helped her with
all the business arrangements for buying the hotel. He'd always
been a good businessman. But in those days he used to be very
moody. Wouldn't speak for days on end. Locked himself in his
bedroom, and wouldn't go to work. Wouldn't get up, even.

As soon as Dave got back from school, he'd come up to see me.
He told me about his humming programmes. He could
remember music just as accurately as if there were a score printed
inside his head, he explained, and he had a special way of
humming, imitating all the instruments of the orchestra. At
present his humming repertoire consisted of seventeen sym-
phonies, twelve piano concertos, five violin concertos and one
cello concerto, but he was adding to it all the time. It took him
thirteen minutes to walk to school, and he usually started with
an overture on Monday morning, spreading the three movements of a concerto or the four of a symphony over the next three
or four journeys, but it all had to be worked out very carefully, so
that he didn't get stuck in the middle of a concerto or a
symphony over the week-end. He always prepared his programmes so as to know what he'd be humming on each journey
over the next few weeks, and he showed me his programme
sheet, neatly written out with red underlinings and all the
composers' names in capitals. Brahms figured a lot.

Cousin Rosalie would bring me cups of tea, and most evenings
Uncle Ben would come up with beer on his breath and a glass in
his hand. 'Come on now, seriously, Ron. That would get you
back on your feet in no time if only you'd drink it. You won't?
Oh well, better drink it myself, I suppose.'

The only one to show his disapproval was Cousin Barry, who called me a 'bloody little malingerer'. Then Daddy arrived, saying he was in London for the day on business. It was possible that one of them had telephoned him, but he seemed surprised to find me in bed. I said I was very nearly better, and probably I'd start school again at the beginning of next week. He persuaded me to start in the morning.

It was going to be very hard to catch up in physics and chemistry, and it was surprisingly hard to find myself a partner. It seemed that I was the only one who hadn't been let into the secret of partnership. There were twenty-four of us in the class, so I couldn't be an odd man out. Yet I was. There ought to be a boy looking for me just as anxiously as I was looking for him, but where was he? Absent? Why hadn't Mr Whicker made a list showing who was meant to be whose partner? Several boys were absent each time, and for weeks I was tacked on either to Hughes and Langton or to one of the other pairs. Finally it emerged that I was meant to be partnered with Finlay, a tall, broad, pudding-faced Scot with thick hair brushed straight back.

On Shabbos afternoons Dave and I would go for long walks. We invented a game which continued from one walk to the next, looking for a car or lorry with the registration number one, then for a two, then a three, and so on. Whoever saw it first scored a point, and though we couldn't write our scores down, we could check them by adding them together. The total should always be one less than the number we were looking for. Our other Saturday afternoon hobby was reading Shakespeare's plays out loud with Cousin Rosalie, dividing the parts up between us, letting her play all the women and some of the unimportant men. In *Hamlet* she was Guildenstern, Cornelius and Marcellus, but when Dave played Rosencrantz with a Yiddish accent, she gave one to Guildenstern, although she'd played her first speech without.

Dave was a good mimic, and at mealtimes he'd have the others in fits of laughter at his impressions of men we met in Shool. 'Vot a goot leetle poy. Not vun mornink since ees Parmitzvah izzy forgettink is *Tefillin!*' Not to be outdone, Cousin Barry would do his imitation of Revd Peros, though this consisted mainly of his hawking in his throat and pretending to spit into a dirty handkerchief before singing loudly in his forced tenor. But Aunt Hetty would laugh delightedly: 'What a good voice he's got, my Barry!'

Upstairs in the bedroom Dave and I sang a duet version of Handel's *Messiah* with hummed imitations of the orchestral accompaniment. In oratorio it was all right to pronounce the name Jesus Christ, and from regular Christmas visits with Nanny to performances at the Pavilion and the new Winter Gardens, I was familiar enough with the airs and most of the recitatives not to have much difficulty in singing from the score. Dave was having singing lessons with Olive Duveen in Shepherd's Bush. On Sunday afternoons, if we weren't going to the Albert Hall, I'd accompany him at the piano in 'Oh Star Divine' and 'Where E'er You Walk'. He talked a lot about Miss Duveen and what she'd taught him about the real meaning of *espressivo*. He was impressed by her reaction when he complained that Gigli had sung 'Return to Sorrento' as an encore at a recital he'd been to. She took the signed photograph of him out of its frame on top of her piano and tore it up. I was less impressed. If she hadn't wanted it, she could have given it to him in case any of his friends or relatives collected autographs.

I was having piano lessons at school with Mrs Tilson, a plump, businesslike lady with her light brown hair in a bun, a mole on her cheek and her spectacles on a cord round her neck. She was much more encouraging than Miss Bellner, and less fussy, but I'd rather have been with Mr Tilson, the school's official music teacher. He had distinguished-looking grey hair and a deep, likeable voice, but when I asked him whether he could take me on next term, he sucked at his pipe and said his wife was a better teacher. I practised every day before I started my homework, and sometimes I pretended I was giving a recital in the Albert Hall. One evening when I took a bow in the direction of the window, I heard jeers and ironical applause from the street. There were boys outside and only the lace curtains were drawn.

The tickling game that Dave and I played in the darkness was spiced with all kinds of dangers. The biggest was that Cousin Barry would hear us giggling, storm upstairs and switch the light on. He'd have been furious at the sight of our naked bodies.

The rules of the game were that you had to stand absolutely still while the other man tickled you, and he scored a point if he made you laugh. Genitals weren't out of bounds, but I never touched his, and didn't like it when he touched mine. We evolved techniques of tickling to catch each other off guard. There was the long, slow, gentle scrape with the back of the fingernail along the back of the spine. The way to resist was to tense the surface of the skin against the insidious funniness of being touched, and the way to penetrate Dave's resistance was to pause just long enough for him to relax, resuming in a different place. If I still got no giggle from him, I'd stop again, pausing either more briefly or for much longer, trying to build up a pattern of expectations and then dodge through it. Standing on his bed, in the very dim light from the windows of the house next door, we lightly explored each other's bare bodies, the back of the knee, the hollow between the shoulder-blades, the line under the buttocks, the slightly damp armpits. I didn't like the hairs that were growing in his, and I didn't like it when I could feel goose-pimples on his skin. But we both got so absorbed in the game that we forgot how cold we were.

7

Corridors of Continuity

During the war we'd all avoided the East Cliff, not wanting to see the hotel from the outside when we couldn't go in. Even after Japan surrendered, we couldn't expect to have the building back for some months, and I first saw it again on an afternoon in the Christmas holidays, with the concave green rooftiles glinting in the cold sunlight. In the drive there were slopes and curves I'd forgotten, but something seemed to be missing. On the south side, the white balconies still jutted boldly outwards towards the sea, and on three of them words in big gold letters, EAST CLIFF COURT, proclaimed the hotel's existence. Suddenly I knew what was missing. My garden. The hedges around it had been cut down and the lawn dug up. Brown earth, stones, weeds and some broken sandbags.

'Now you must prepare yourself for a shock,' Mummy said before we went in. 'Grannie cried when she saw it last week, but Daddy says it'll look quite different once it's been redecorated.' The revolving door was folded flat and the glass in it was cracked. Inside, where the potted palm used to stand, was a sack of rubbish. The carpetless floor was covered with torn paper, empty tins, sand and bits of old newspaper. The polished wooden counter of the reception office was scratched all over with names and drawings of hearts with arrows through them. Loose electric wires were sticking through holes in the walls and ceilings. In the lounges the wallpaper was dirty, torn, and scribbled on, with big holes eating into the plaster. The sign still said LISLE LOUNGE, but inside was a dartboard-sized circle of darker colour on the wallpaper with dart-holes all round it. The lift wasn't working, and we walked up the

115

carpetless stairs. When Mummy asked whether I wanted to see
the nursery, I said no.

Going back for my second term was quite different from going
up for my first. Excitement was replaced by resignation and
anxiety. I couldn't tell Mummy and Daddy what it was like at
Dunsany Road – it would have been too much like sneaking,
and anyway there was nowhere else they could have sent me. At
school the worst ordeals were on the rugger field, in the gym and
in the physics lab. It wasn't the pain of being beaten that I
feared. I'd watched him beating other bottoms, and he didn't
hit hard, but I didn't enjoy watching and didn't relish the idea of
being watched. There were still three of us who had managed to
avoid all the Avoidable Errors, but we couldn't expect our luck
to last, especially when he kept on adding to the list.

My favourite subject was maths. In quadratic and simultan-
eous equations, there was always a neat way of finding an
answer which was incontestably right. I enjoyed ruling lines
under solutions – $x = 7$, $y = 13$. And in geometry I enjoyed
writing QED for *Quod erat demonstrandum* at the end of a proof. I
also enjoyed translating in and out of French and Latin, but it
wasn't quite as satisfying because there was no single, perfect
solution to each problem, only an infinity of possible approx-
imations. You could go on crossing phrases out, scribbling
improvements above them, varying the syntax, and the closer
you got to perfection, the messier the page looked. It was good to
have loose-leaf files instead of exercise books, but even when I
decided to scrap a page and substitute a fair copy, I knew I
wouldn't be able to resist the temptation of defacing it with
alterations.

If I spent longer than necessary on my homework, it was partly
because I felt safe while I was sitting with my books at the card-
table in Dave's bedroom; going downstairs was like going into
enemy territory. Apparently Uncle Ben had been making a
special effort to behave well last term. Now he often came home
drunk, shouting, thumping the table and swearing in Yiddish. If
the little black cat was curled up asleep on his armchair, he'd
throw it off and try to kick it. He was paid on Fridays, so Friday
nights were the worst. He'd come in threatening Aunt Hetty:
'I'll show you who's master in this house.' When Dave ignored

him, humming as if nothing were happening, he got furious.
One night he knocked the Shabbos candles over, slapped Aunt
Hetty, and before Dave could come to her aid, stormed out of
the house, with a furious Yiddish oath, which must have been
quite terrible. Aunt Hetty seemed to be groaning mainly
because of the damage he'd done to his chances of going to
Heaven.

There was a new ordeal at school, too. It had been decided
that I needed 'remedial exercises'. I had to go to Corporal
Williams, who was in charge of physical training, a muscular
man with a face like a boxer's and dull blond hair brushed
straight back. He always wore a thick white pullover. 'Let's
have a look at your chest,' he said. I'd been aware that the ribs
on the right side did not come out quite so far as the ribs on my
left. This, according to Nanny, was because I'd had acidosis as a
baby. Corporal Williams told me that whenever I was carrying
anything heavy like a suitcase, I must carry it in my left hand,
and he devised a series of exercises which I had to do with him in
the gymnasium, spending an extra forty minutes there every
Monday, when it was already quite bad enough having two
periods of PT each week.

Dave's friendship had made everything else bearable; and I
was unprepared for the loss of it. 'Breach of relationship'
sounded as abstract as a phrase in a history book, but there it
was, in his neat capital letters, underlined twice in red ink and
once in blue, on the top line of a page torn from a foolscap pad.
Underneath, the details were tabulated as neatly as the items in
his humming programmes. For the first offence he would break
off his relationship with me for twenty-four hours, for the second
forty-eight, and so on. Notice would be served on me by means
of a Hebrew letter, Aleph for the first breach, Beth for the
second, and so on. Once I had received notice of a breach, I must
make no attempt to communicate with him verbally or by
writing notes or by sending messages through third parties. In
the event of any such attempt, the next period of breach would
ensue automatically on the termination of the current one, and a
warning would be issued in the form Aleph + Beth, Beth +
Gimmel or whatever. Examples of characteristic behaviour that
was liable to punishment under the new system were:

1 leaving an undue amount of food uneaten on my plate;
2 giving disrespectful answers to my elders;
3 leaving articles of clothing or wrapping paper from parcels on my bed, socks on the floor, or shoes or slippers in positions where other people were liable to trip over them;
4 leaving electric lights or fires burning in empty rooms;
5 occupying the lavatory for more than five minutes or the bathroom for more than fifteen;
6 failing to clean the bath after using it;
7 reading in bed for more than five minutes after he wanted to go to sleep.

These examples were listed for my benefit, and it was clearly to be understood that they were only examples – that is, a breach could ensue from any other misdemeanour which he judged to be of equal gravity, and it was to be understood not only that he was the sole judge, but that no appeal could be made against his judgement.

When he handed the sheet of foolscap to me, turning away from my tentative smile, it had been folded in six, just like the letters I used to receive from him at Fremington. I knew that even if he never actually initiated a breach of relationship, he'd deliberately broken something that could at best be repaired – never again made as strong as it had been. With schoolfriends there had always been a religious barrier; with him there had seemed to be almost no limit to the closeness that was possible.

I didn't know what to do with the piece of paper. It would be sneaky to leave it somewhere Aunt Hetty might see it when she was cleaning the room, and it wasn't something I wanted to carry around in my wallet. If I packed it in my suitcase, Nanny might find it when she was unpacking and show it to Daddy. Finally I tucked it inside the special prayer book that I used only on the Day of Atonement.

Dave usually came to bed at about 10.30. Rosalie, who had a room to herself, was usually in bed by ten, while Cousin Barry often went out in the evening. He was secretary of the local Jewish Youth Club and treasurer of a local organization for Jewish Defence against anti-Semitism. When Daddy came to

London, he used to argue with Barry, saying that defence was a form of attack and therefore more likely to provoke anti-Semitism than reduce it.

Aunt Hetty and Uncle Ben occasionally went to the cinema together, but spent most evenings in their slippers, sitting in the long, low, worn armchairs on either side of the kitchen grate, listening to the wireless, and reading the three evening newspapers, the *Standard*, the *News* and the *Star*. 'You know Ron,' Uncle Ben would say, 'the country's in a terrible mess.'

Aunt Hetty, Uncle Ben, Dave and, when he was in, Barry, all used the bathroom and lavatory at about the same time, and from waiting until after they'd all finished, I gradually got into the habit of going to bed much later than they did. When Dave was coming upstairs, I'd hear his soft humming before I heard his slippered footsteps. I started packing my books together, ready to leave the bedroom to him. Sometimes we'd chat for a few minutes, sometimes he'd greet me only sulkily or not at all. Downstairs in the empty kitchen, I'd spread my books over the table, and, unless Barry was still out, I'd feel enormous pleasure at not having to confront any of them again until tomorrow. Soon the creaks and footsteps above me would stop. By the time I went upstairs to undress in the dark, Dave would be asleep or at least pretending to be. Meanwhile I was free. I used to get up and wander about the kitchen, looking through the creased newspapers for pictures of girls in bathing costumes. I'd help myself to a glass of lime-juice cordial or orange squash or Tizer, and look in the larder cupboard to see whether there were any new jars of pickles or pots of fish-paste, in which case I'd read the labels. If there were any letters lying about, I'd read them, and I'd open the cupboards and drawers to look through the contents. Finally I'd settle down to work, feeling much better able to concentrate than I had upstairs. To be at school by 9.12 I had to leave the house by nine and get up not later than 7.45, but there was no need to be in bed before twelve, and sometimes I stayed up till 1.30.

The later I was, the more I dreaded the moment of going to bed. Aunt Hetty and Uncle Ben slept with their bedroom door ajar. I counted the stairs, knowing which ones creaked, and with my books in one hand, I held on to the wall with the other, because the banister creaked too. Uncle Ben would be snoring and Aunt Hetty breathing loudly through her mouth, each breath almost a sigh of complaint. It was safe to put the light on in the bathroom or the lavatory, but not to close the door, and I was nervous of waking them by dropping something. Did I know what time it was, I'd be asked. Had I any idea how much it cost to pay for the electricity I'd been wasting? I couldn't feel completely safe till I was between the cold sheets, reaching under my pillow to find the Kappul I would put on in the dark to say my night prayers.

By the time I'd finished my morning prayers, Dave and Rosalie were almost ready to leave for school, so I was alone with Aunt Hetty while I ate my breakfast – fried egg on toast or egg fried with broken-up matzoh. When I came home from school, she gave me a cup of tea and a piece of cake at the kitchen table. She was now the only one to spend much time talking to me. Even when she was trying to be cheerful, her doleful voice sounded as though she wanted me to notice how brave she was being, rising above everything she had to put up with. She told me about food prices in the shops, illnesses in Uncle Ben's sisters' families, neighbours, what people had said to her in the street and what she had said to them. Once when she was waiting in a crowd to see the King and Queen pass by, she told the woman next to her that her brother Jack was the spit image of Winston Churchill. Most of all she talked about Barry and Dave and how wonderful it was to have two such wonderful sons. Daddy thought very highly of them, she said, and favourable comments from acquaintances were passed on to me as if she were quoting verbatim. 'You don't know how lucky you are, Hetty, believe me. I'd give anything for my Hymie to be more like your Dave. He's a hard worker, he's good looking, he's religious and he always has such a nice smile when you meet him in the street. A real nice boy, God bless him.' Later on, when she told Uncle Ben the words would become even more complimentary.

If her short-range memories were inaccurate, the stories about her childhood must be unreliable, but at least she was willing to talk in detail about the butcher's shop. The older boys had been allowed to help in the sausage-making, while the older girls had to help with the housework and with looking after the younger children. My grandmother kept the house spotless, and the table-linen was always perfect, especially on Friday evening.

But there was something in the quality of Aunt Hetty's story-telling that had changed since the beginning. Like Mr King in the antique shop, she enjoyed talking for talking's sake, and it didn't much matter to her whom she was talking to. While the others were reacting against my presence in their home, her resentment had accumulated over the years against Mummy and Daddy. Towards Daddy she felt a mixture of admiration, affection, jealousy and malice, but the negative elements were less concealed now that the weekly cheques, together with the weekly chickens, were taken more for granted, while her dislike of Mummy came out into the open. Why had she and Daddy never come to stay in Dunsany Road when they were in London? They knew how welcome she'd make them, but no, her house wasn't good enough. Mummy wanted to be in a hotel and have a bath every morning and go shopping in Selfridges. Some people didn't know how much they were missing in life if they couldn't muck in, the way ordinary people did. Of course, one had to make allowances for her bad leg, and maybe she hadn't had as much happiness in life as she'd have liked. Well, some-thing must have gone wrong, or she'd never have tried to run away from home, would she? Before she got married, of course, that was, but then a fifteen-year gap between husband and wife was an awfully big one, wasn't it? Of course it was. Anyone could see that. In some ways it might have been better if Uncle Dan had married her when Daddy asked him to. Well, I wasn't a child any more. I was old enough to understand these things, wasn't I? Daddy had been closer to Grannie than he had to Mummy. In age, of course, she meant. Well he still was, wasn't he? She wasn't telling me anything new. And I knew that Mummy had this terrible polio as a child. Perhaps that was why she'd found it wasn't so easy to live away from home. She'd been at the Bournemouth art school when she tried to run away, so perhaps some of the other art students had put her up to it. Just one week in London, and back she came. After that she'd never left Grannie's side, and Daddy was living permanently in the boarding-house because he trusted Grannie to keep a real kosher home. By the time he said to Uncle Dan that one of them

would have to marry Sadie, Dan was already in love with this
very pretty American girl who had only one eye. And my dad
was a fine, upstanding man who always did what was right.
That was why she couldn't refuse to look after his son when the
boy needed a good kosher home near the school. It's a funny
thing, she said, life. You never know what you're being
rewarded for, and what you're being punished for. Anyway
Teddy and I were two fine boys that any Jewish father could be
proud of, and she for one was glad things had turned out the way
they had. Uncle Dan had only a daughter and he'd always
wanted a son. Well, any Jewish father does, because otherwise
who'll say the prayers for his soul to go to Heaven? And who'll
keep the family name alive?

Letters from Daddy were frequent but irregular, while letters
from Mummy arrived every Monday morning, answering mine
which had been posted to arrive by the first post on Shabbos
morning. (Nanny would tear the envelope open.) In Mummy's
last letter of the term the postscript was 'Don't forget to get off
the train at Bournemouth Central, not West.' This time it was
the hotel I was going home to. Mummy wasn't waiting on the
platform but outside, sitting with a green silk scarf around her
head in her new green Rover. She put out her cheek through the
car window to be kissed.

As we drove past the Lansdowne clock, it chimed the three-
quarters. The Metropole Hotel had been bombed to rubble, but
the clock tower on the municipal building was still erect, still
sending out the same reassuring chimes that had punctuated my
childhood. She parked in the drive just by the porch. A new hall
porter in the familiar claret uniform with brass buttons hurried
down the stone steps to take my case. Sutherland appeared
behind him, the head porter's uniform making him look wider.
The revolving door was working again, the cracked glass had
been replaced, the steps inside recarpeted and there was a new
palm-tree in the old wooden stand. Miss Black, who had twice
been to Fremington to have tea with Mummy, was installed at
the main desk in the reception, wearing spectacles now, and
there was a new blonde telephonist operating the switchboard.

The wooden counter gleamed with new varnish, and I remembered the fountain-pen on the stand, its pointed handle chained to its holder. The hall was full of people. The old brown carpet was back in place, There was new wallpaper on the walls, and the wooden-backed armchairs that used to stand opposite the lift were in their old position, their seats newly covered with tapestries Mummy had done during the war.

'My big schoolboy,' said Grannie, stepping proudly forward out of a knot of chatting people to give me a big hug. 'My Ron-boy. There's some cold chicken for you in the dining-room and there's some lockshen soup. Tell Tonks to have it hottened up.'

When I went down the stairs, there he was. A front tooth was missing but the grin was the same. We shook hands, and he said how tall I'd grown. When he led the way to our old table in the corner, I remembered his flat-footed stride.

If Bournemouth, which had seemed huge, now seemed quite small, the hotel was still big, with big rooms and a big garden, without any washing hanging out in it. All the streets near Brook Green seemed to consist of grimy brick terraces, identical houses backing on to small gardens with little in them except vegetables and washing; whereas Bournemouth was full of clean hotel buildings with balconies and tennis courts and big lawns with big flower-beds aflame with bright colours, especially the yellow of marigolds. Instead of sulky Rosalie, a black-coated waiter would hand me my plate of food, and Nanny would look after me again, and I'd leave my shoes outside my bedroom door every night. Then, all through the twelve weeks of summer term, I'd have the eight weeks of summer holiday to look forward to.

Rituals provided a corridor of continuity through the first-class and third-class compartments of my life. Every morning except Sunday I strapped my *Tefillin* on my forehead and on my left arm. Every Saturday morning I went to Shool. Every night, after rubbing Valderma into my acne spots, I'd make sure before I got into bed that the Kappul was under my pillow, ready for my night prayers.

The religion may have contributed to my self-consciousness: the God I believed in never stopped watching me, so I often thought about what it must be like to see me from outside,

especially when I came from my bedroom in the hotel to one of
the public rooms. Going into the dining-room for lunch or
dinner felt like making an entrance on a stage, and even when I
was alone, I found myself doing things as if an invisible camera
were whirring away, recording my movements in close-up.

Nanny helped me to be aware of other people's attitudes to
me, passing on remarks she'd heard. 'I'd do anything for Master
Ronnie,' said one of the still-room maids. Which must mean I
was all right. So why didn't Mummy see me like this? She
compared me unfavourably with Mr Feather, a dandyish
bachelor who danced obsequious attendance on his mother, a
handsome but over-made-up old lady with white hair. 'He's a
model son,' I was pointedly told.

Every night, before going to bed, I had to kiss Grannie,
Daddy and Mummy good-night. Usually there was no problem
in finding Grannie, who most often went to bed before I did, so
all I had to do was take the lift to the top floor, knock at her door,
give her the ritual kiss and break off two pieces of milk chocolate
from the bar that was waiting for me on the dressing-table.
Daddy would sometimes be in the card-room, less often playing
than watching one of the games in progress on the green-topped
card-tables, or he might be in the hall or one of the lounges
chatting with the visitors. Sometimes one of the porters would be
able to tell me where he was. Mummy would often work late in
the reception, but you couldn't see whether she was there – you
had to ask one of the receptionists, pretty, blonde Miss Bright or
tight-lipped Miss Black, who was never actually unpleasant but
always looked as though she was going to be. When Mummy
wasn't in the reception, she was often in the stores. To get there
involved a long walk through the swing doors by the still-room,
past the kitchens and the two huge refrigerators, one for milk
things, one for meat. Before I went back to London each time,
Mummy would take me with her to the stores and I could choose
any food and drink I wanted.

In Bournemouth I was free to go as often as I liked to plays at
the Pavilion and Palace Court Theatre, to cinemas and concerts
and once we went to the Hippodrome at Boscombe to see Laurel
and Hardy, live, on the stage. In London I couldn't go to the
pictures without Aunt Hetty's permission, which was granted

only on Sunday afternoons and on Saturday evenings during the winter when it got dark early. In the summer, Shabbos went out too late. I missed seeing Gielgud in *Crime and Punishment* through not being allowed out on evenings when I had school the next day. 'Not when you've got all that homework to do,' she said.

On Sunday mornings Uncle Ben would collect everybody's trousers, and, standing at the ironing-board in his dressing-gown, press them all under a steaming cloth. He could get a neat, knife-edge crease, but he liked a lot of praise for it. I cleaned my own shoes, and every Monday I packed all my dirty shirts, underclothes, pyjamas and handkerchiefs into a lumpy brown paper parcel, which I posted to Nanny. It arrived back on Friday in a neat parcel with a green-and-white East Cliff Court label, filled out with my name and address in Nanny's capital letters – MASTER RONNIE HAYMAN. Aunt Hetty already had a big enough pile of washing to keep her bent over the bath most of Monday, scrubbing at the corrugated washboard. On Monday evenings there was condensation all over the bathroom walls, ceiling and cupboard doors.

Mealtimes at the hotel were quite unlike mealtimes in Dunsany Road. Instead of shirt-sleeves and quarrelsomeness around the kitchen table, with Uncle Ben shouting, Barry sucking at Rosalie's ears and Dave humming while he turned pages in the *Evening News*, there was ceremonial and brightness. It was like the moment in the theatre when the curtain went up to reveal a brilliantly lit drawing-room. Like actors who had to spend hours in their dressing-rooms preparing for their entrance, visitors at the hotel retired to their bedrooms to get ready for the meals, tidy their hair, arrange their make-up and put their jewellery on in front of dressing-table mirrors. A black-clad waiter, flunkey-like, would swing the glass doors open for them to stride past, conscious of other people's eyes on them. The wall behind the sideboard and the wall behind our table were both covered with rectangles of mirror. Some people came to be seen or have their nubile daughters seen, others came to look – unconfirmed bachelors and hopeful widows of all shapes and ages. Our business seemed to consist partly of selling people to each other.

The hotel was at its fullest over the week-end. Before the cold fried fish Friday supper, the entrance of the visitors was like a parade past the mirror walls that multiplied the bright ceiling lights and picked up the sparkle from dangling diamond earrings, necklaces and bracelets. Permed hair glistened. Bosoms bulged under décolleté dresses. Diamond tie-pins and gold signet-rings twinkled. I thought of the advertisement I saw in London on the Underground showing six soldiers on parade: *Six minds with a single thought – a Bravington ring and the girl is caught.* Not these girls. I also liked watching rich men. Some looked immensely distinguished, with thick, wavy, iron-grey hair, aquiline noses and delicate, fine-textured skin, as if they washed their faces in milk. Others looked tougher, more commanding, with coarse-edged voices, wide pores in their noses and confident eyes that made the waiters slightly frightened, transparently eager to please. Power endowed even ugly men with a glamour that clung like powder to their faces.

Tonks still had the same technique of mixing vinegar, oil, salt, pepper, mustard and sugar in a metal gravy boat, stirring them busily with a fork as he hurried down the blue runways, and he hadn't lost his bent-backed prowess at herding waiters out of the room, already clutching the soup-spoon he'd use for his rap on the sideboard. 'Ladies and gentlemen, pray silence for grace.' I was often the one who performed, glad at having an opportunity to impress, especially when there were girls listening. The fuller the room was, the harder it was for him to choose his moment. If some people still hadn't had their pudding and their black coffee, they'd be annoyed at having to wait till grace was over, but if people began to drift out of the room, Mummy would grow restive.

'Aren't you ready yet, Tonks?'

'Just four more sweets over by the window, madam.'

When Shabbos went out before seven o'clock, there was a Saturday evening dinner-dance. The men wore dinner-jackets, the ladies long dresses with stoles around bare shoulders. On Sundays there was a tea-dance in the ballroom and another dance after dinner. The band was a trio of saxophone, drums and piano, led by the pianist who'd worked for us before the war. Charlie Richards his name was, but I'd always called him Captain Richardson. Dancing became a means of pleasing

Mummy and of getting to know girls. Like many of the husbands, Daddy didn't enjoy it, preferring just to sit at the shiny, black, round-topped table in the corner of the ballroom, smoking and chatting with Grannie. Chairs were dragged up for visitors to join us, and I listened to inconsequential chats about business, politics and family relationships. Almost all the parents made the same complaints about their children – no gratitude, no respect, no appreciation for the way everything was made easy for them. 'It wasn't like that when I was a child.' At the same time, they told us how lucky they were to have children who were so fond of them, so dutiful and so clever.

I didn't like watching the unbalanced, limping steps Mummy took on the dance floor, but she loved dancing. There were two dance-hosts, Mr Kynaston and Mr Hargreaves. At dinner-dances they sat at the table just inside the door; in the ballroom they sat at the table next to the drums. When the music started they'd stand up promptly, stubbing out their cigarettes, and walk over to smile at a lady with an inclination that could have been either a bow or a movement forward to make their voices audible above the music. 'May I have the pleasure of this dance?' It was all right if just occasionally they went up to one of the pretty girls, but they were there for the sake of the women who weren't in demand. Mr Hargreaves had permed-looking waves in his greying blond hair and the face of a second-rate actor. His body was quite thick but in the tango, the quick-step and the slow foxtrot, his patent-leather shoes would weave elaborate patterns as his strong arms kneaded his willing partners into following him. Mr Kynaston, who was taller and leaner, depended less on his footwork, more on charming conversation. His bottom stuck out slightly as he hunched deferentially forwards, fascinated by everything his partners said. His pale blue eyes were almost invisible behind glinting gold-rimmed glasses.

Mr Hargreaves never asked Mummy for a dance because he knew she didn't like him. According to Nanny, who retailed a lot of gossip picked up mainly from the housekeeper and the telephonist, Mummy kept him on because of Miss Levin, a short, large-breasted lady of about thirty-two, with thick, dyed-looking blonde hair draped over one shoulder. Her rich parents brought her to the hotel at least twice a year for three or four weeks at a time, determined that she should find a husband. Instead of looking, she made dates with Mr Hargreaves, met him in pubs and gave him expensive presents. Mummy liked dancing with Mr Kynaston, who could be relied on to offer her at least two dances, and more if there weren't too many other ladies who needed him. She also enjoyed dancing with me, and making embarrassing jokes about 'duty-dances'.

Like the bedroom at Fremington which I'd at first shared with Teddy, the night nursery had become his room, while I was shifted around according to what was available. When the hotel was fairly empty I was put into one of the grand double rooms facing the sea. There I'd have a private bathroom with a coloured suite, pink, green, or blue. But in August and at Christmas, when the hotel was always full, I'd have to sleep either in the vestibule of Mummy's and Daddy's flat or in a tiny room – normally the housekeeper's office. When a bed was put into it for me, there was just enough space to move round it. Most of the time when the hotel was neither full nor nearly empty, I was given a small single room looking out over the tennis-court and next door to the Oak Room, which was kept as a family sitting-room. I used it more than anyone else did. It was decorated and furnished in Tudor style with half-exposed beams on the ceilings and walls. In the corner by the latticed windows there was a shallow cupboard with a latticed glass front. Somebody had once told me that behind it was a blocked-off passage that nuns had used as an escape route during the Reformation. I knew the hotel dated from 1926, but couldn't exorcize the picture of nuns climbing on each other's shoulders to squeeze into the narrow space, tucking their habits around their bottoms.

I accompanied Mummy and Grannie on some of their shopping expeditions. When Mummy parked the Rover outside the grocer's, the greengrocer's, the kosher butcher's and the three department stores, Beale's, Bright's, and Plummer Roddis, I helped Grannie to get her weighty body out of the car, and then offered my other arm to Mummy. We always had our mid-morning coffee at the Cadena Café, where an invisible string trio played old favourites. Sometimes we took Teddy with us, and

Grannie with the two of us. Teddy (*right*) is the younger by nearly four years.

The promenade at Bournemouth when I was about six.
Courtesy Dorset County Libraries

(*top left*) Aged two and a half; (*top right and below left*) Mummy seldom took me out for walks, but I often went with Daddy; (*below right*) with Nanny.

sometimes, as a special treat, we stayed in town to have lunch at one of the restaurants. Mummy would call the waitress 'Miss' and, saying we were vegetarian, inquire whether there was any meat in this soup or that sauce. The puzzled girl would retreat into the kitchen, reappearing with information that would be either incomplete or belied by the appearance of the dish, which was then rejected. 'If there's any doubt at all,' Mummy would explain, 'we're not allowed to eat it.'

Telling me that I had good taste, she'd take me with her to the dress shops in Westover Road, saying she wanted my advice. Habitually she opted for navy blues, dark greys and blacks, never explicitly referring to her lameness, but rejecting other dresses as 'too young' or 'not my style'. My role was to persuade her to be less conservative. When I succeeded, I'd be told how glad she was that I'd made her buy the green dress. I was then expected to take more interest in her diet, but I didn't like the presence of the Ryvita packet on our table and the dark pot of yeast extract next to the pepper and salt. I wanted the hotel dining-room to be totally unlike the kitchen in Dunsany Road, which meant sticking as elegantly as possible to the norms of correct behaviour. I was uncomfortable when Grannie gestured with her knife or Daddy talked with food in his mouth. I corrected Nanny's grammar and Teddy's table manners. His relationship with Mummy was closer than ever. They cuddled a lot, held hands and called each other 'darling'. She was proud of us both, but in a de-individualizing way, presenting us as a tandem. 'Meet my sons.' Worse still she made no attempt to conceal her preference for his looks. When visitors, in his absence, praised mine, they'd be told to 'wait till you see the other one'. It was impossible to forgive him for her insensitivity.

Mealtime conversations still centred on Judaism as if it were a club. 'He's one of our people,' was said proprietorially, and often they'd be glad to infer from a news item in the *Jewish Chronicle* that they could say it of a politician, film star or artist they hadn't known to be Jewish. Court cases and scandals that put Jewish-sounding names into the headlines provoked head-shaking and tut-tutting, while it was like blackballing would-be members when they said 'Of course, he's only half Jewish' or 'Her brother married out of the faith'. At first I joined in these

games with relish, passing on any news I picked up about Jewish
musicians. When Montague Birch died and a Jewish conductor
was appointed, we discussed whether he should be invited to a
meal at the hotel.

In Bournemouth before the war there had been only one other
Jewish hotel, which hadn't been considered as a serious rival,
but now several others were competing for the same clientele.
The most luxurious of them had opened before the war was over,
and Daddy thought this was taking unfair advantage of our being
out of action. Visitors who came back to us after trying the
others complained about the vulgarity. They'd been given too
much to eat, and hadn't met such a nice class of people.
But Daddy would come home from the shop with stories
of people who'd been embarrassed to meet him in the Old
Christchurch Road because they were staying somewhere else,
while the four old ladies who were permanent residents with us
would take malicious pleasure in watching Grannie's face drop
when they came back from having tea at one of the other hotels
and told her how full it was. It was all very well for Mummy and
Grannie to speak scornfully of grilled grapefruits, free cocktails
and cabarets with star Jewish comedians: the luxuries our rivals
offered were obviously a threat. Some of our staff defected to the
other hotels, and if former customers now staying at one of them
were bold enough to drop in on friends staying with us, Mummy
would pretend not to see them, while Grannie would overwhelm
them with a friendliness that could hardly fail to make them feel
guilty.

The first time I fell in love with one of the girls at the hotel was
while some boys from St Paul's were staying there. Louis
Solomon was a big-boned, pimply boy in the biology form a
year ahead of me; his brother Michael, who was also doing
biology and a year behind me, was neatly built and confident in
his way of moving, with sleek black hair that he was always
combing. Annette was the same age as Michael, but her figure
and her upswept hair made her look older. It was almost
unbearable to be close to her without touching the full breasts
that pressed ripely against her pullover as if to get as close as they
could to your hand. She had a plump tongue and plump lips
that needed no lipstick. She was always nice to us, but not to

Katie, her younger sister. When Annette, Louis, Michael and I played doubles at ping-pong, Katie had to run after the ball in the long end of the room. But when one of us was dancing with Annette, there were always two of us left with Katie, being as nice as we could be to her in the hope she'd put in a good word to Annette.

It was Mummy's idea we should go to the funfair at Christchurch. She wanted us to take Teddy and Katie, but we took only Annette: I sat next to her on the bus, and Louis shared a dodgem car with her, while I shared one with Michael, but he sat next to her in the ghost train, saying how frightened Katie would have been if we'd brought her. Annette, who was more frightened than she'd admit, wanted to hold Michael's hand, but Michael said no, not unless she promised to hold hands with him all the way back on the bus. She gave in, charmingly, and after that it was hopeless. They were always going for walks together, and I lived in dread of seeing them kissing. If I'd been sitting next to her in the ghost train, I'd have been only too glad to hold hands unconditionally. So Louis and I played singles and sat on the edge of the ping-pong table, talking sadly about the ways of women. He said her body would soon lose its shape, and anyway I'd soon be in love with someone else. Meanwhile there was a sort of third best pleasure to be had out of talking about her, but it didn't make up for the awfulness of watching her eyes gleam when she looked up at Michael.

The next time I fell in love, it was with a waitress, who had even less idea than Annette of how much she mattered to me. In the summer Tonks always took on some commis waiters from a training school in Birmingham. Meek, pale boys in thin white jackets and thick black trousers bustled uncomplainingly about the crowded dining-room, obeying the tail-coated waiters, who ordered them brusquely about, using a different tone from the deferential one they put on for the visitors. I got used to seeing overworked boys stooping to pick up teaspoons that fell off waiters' overcrowded trays or running back into the kitchen for an extra portion of cauliflower when Mrs Silverberg decided she'd like some after all, or going to find a clean napkin because Mr Lotinga had spilt coffee on his. But Yvonne was the first commis girl I saw submitting to this sort of treatment, and even

inside the shapeless black cotton dress and flimsy white apron
her figure was as disconcerting as Annette's. Her black-
stockinged legs were like a ballerina's, with delicate ankles and a
thrilling curve to the muscle on her calf. When she was serving
hors-d'oeuvre over my left shoulder, I knew her body was
touching the hard back of my chair, and I leaned as hard as I
could against it, as if my back could pass a secret message to her
through the leather and the wood.

At first I asked her questions about the menu. 'What is Potage
Garbure?' 'How is the veal cooked today?' But she talked so
softly I could hardly hear her, and she blushed when she had to
describe soups by their colour. Sometimes she even went back to
the kitchen for information, and there was no way of showing
that all I wanted was to be her friend. Soon I began coming
down to lunch and dinner before the gong sounded. One
evening I started down the staircase just as Tonks was raising the
padded drumstick in the air. He grinned at me as if he'd guessed
why I was early; I said 'Good evening, Tonks' as if he hadn't.
She was still laying our table. There was a checked table-cloth
folded across it diagonally so that Mummy and Grannie could
have a milk meal while Daddy, Teddy and I ate meat. In the
Oak Room, thinking about her instead of concentrating on
H.A.L. Fisher's *History of Europe*, I'd imagined myself being as
suave and worldly-wise as Dennis Price or George Sanders.

'Good evening,' I said, not quite daring to pat her shoulder as
I squeezed round into my seat. 'So how do you like being in
Bournemouth?'

'Very much,' she said.

I then asked how long she'd be here and did she go swimming
much. But how could I suggest a secret meeting on the beach
when she kept glancing down at the table-cloth to fidget with
knives and forks that were already in place? Looming up blackly
behind her, Tonks told her to lay two extra places for guests at
Mr and Mrs Greenbaum's table. Anyway Teddy was coming
down the stairs, so we wouldn't have had time to make any
arrangements.

'Where's Mummy?' he said. When she came in through the
waiters' entrance, we both stood up and he held her chair back for
her, opened her napkin for her, sat down next to her, his hand on

her arm. If only I could write a note to Yvonne, suggesting a midnight swim. But I couldn't have married her, because she wasn't Jewish, and I knew that somewhere in the world, probably in an English-speaking country, was the one girl destined to be my wife. There was just one girl, I'd been made to believe, who was 'right' for me. But if I took Daddy's advice and married someone fifteen years younger, she'd still be a baby, and I couldn't even start looking. But his advice was based on his own experience, which would have been quite different if Mummy had married Uncle Dan, or Grannie's boarding-house hadn't been strictly kosher or the other Jewish landlady's had.

Yvonne's presence made food unimportant except as a pretext for brief, unequal conversations. There was always a chance we might exchange a smile. At lunch on Sunday we did, but only a brief one because Daddy was saying he didn't want his Yorkshire pudding soaked in gravy. Either I'd have to write her a note or telephone from upstairs and ask to speak to her. But Tonks would recognize my voice and tell Mummy, while the telephonist might listen to our conversation and tell Nanny. With Annette the pleasure and pain in thinking about her after it became hopeless had been spiced with uncertainty about whether I'd have stood a chance if I'd been more self-confident. With Yvonne it still wasn't hopeless, but what could I do?

One warm evening I walked to the Lansdowne with Nanny. She had to change Grannie's library book, and I had to return a biography of Voltaire and collect C. V. Wedgwood's *William the Silent*, which I'd reserved. As we walked past the Carlton Hotel on the way back, we saw two lovers holding on to each other so tightly that the man seemed to be pushing the girl into the hedge as he pulled her towards him. Their voices were murmuring very softly, like pigeons. Preparing for School Certificate, I decided, was much less important than building a private little nest of murmurs in a hedge.

'They ought to be ashamed of themselves,' said Nanny.

'I don't know why you say that.' Getting ready to tell her how important love was.

'Chef's a married man with a nice wife and two children, and that Yvonne can't be much older than you are.'

8

Losing Faith

After School Certificate I found myself in the 'Modern Special'. Our new form master, Mr Fletcher, called us 'gentlemen', while the history master, Mr Harding, who was going to be our form master next year, promised to get several of us into university by treating all of us as if we were already undergraduates. He'd take it for granted that we were all going to pass the Higher Certificate exam in two years' time. Only a fool could fail it. What interested him was who would do well enough in it to win a state scholarship; to be sure of a place at Oxford or Cambridge, even a state scholarship wouldn't be enough. We'd need to sit for an open scholarship.

Together, Mr Fletcher and Mr Harding were going to control our lives for two years. They were friends, but quite dissimilar. Mr Harding took discipline for granted; Mr Fletcher made sure he was entitled to it. 'Efficiency, gentlemen. I insist on efficiency.' Sometimes he called it *Tüchtigkeit*. He admired the Prussian virtues. He had iron-grey hair brushed neatly backwards, and he laid out his breakfast tray every morning in exactly the same way, he said, so as to notice at once if anything was missing. He held his square-shouldered body erect on the swivel chair that must have been his own property, because all the other masters had round-backed wooden armchairs. He issued us with a roneoed sheet of the abbreviations he would use when correcting our essays and translations and with a white panoptic chart showing all the common suffixes and affixes in the English language derived from Greek and Latin roots. He advised us to keep a commonplace book for copying down quotations that specially appealed to us. When we used one aptly in an essay, we were rewarded with a neat green c.q. in the margin – his abbreviation for 'classy quote'.

Mr Fletcher's recipe for winning a scholarship to Oxford or Cambridge was efficient organization of time, which meant not wasting any. We could improve our French and German vocabulary, as he did his, by equipping ourselves with two packs of mnemonic cards, made of white cardboard, and uniform in size. His were three inches by two inches. The French or German words should be written in a neat column on one side of the card, with the translation on the other. By carrying cards about with us, we could work even when we were waiting in a bus queue or sitting in a lavatory, testing ourselves constantly by covering up one side of the card. Skate drew a cartoon of Mr Fletcher absent-mindedly wiping his bottom on a German vocabulary card, and we all liked to mimic his clipped diction. 'Efficiency, gentlemen.'

In my two previous forms, 5x and 6x, I'd been aware of belonging to the junior half of the school and hadn't had much contact with boys in higher classes, except Eric Cookman and Neville Banner. In Modern Special I somehow made friends with two boys who were in the history eighth, Mr Harding's form. Nigel Firth was slim, dark, girlish, and he cultivated all the virtues of the English gentleman. I could imagine him going to the city in a bowler hat, black jacket and striped trousers, carrying an immaculate umbrella. Raymond Da Costa was sandy-haired, plump, Jewish and spoke with a drawl. I usually sat next to him during prayers, admiring his gold ring and gold-capped fountain-pen. He was editor of the school magazine, *The Debater*, and he asked me whether I could get the hotel to advertise in it. I said I'd ask my mother. I'd have been quite willing to ask her without any incentive, but he then said he was looking for a successor, and if I could persuade her to advertise, I could be the next editor of *The Debater*. I liked the idea of being editor, but didn't like the position he'd put me in. Either he thought I'd make a good editor or he didn't. Why should bribery come into it? I thought about not approaching Mummy, which would have made me feel virtuous, but there was no particular point in that, so I did ask her, and of course she said yes. The succession was assured.

If my conscience was guilty, I could salve it by working hard. I should have devoted more time to games, and if they'd played soccer instead of rugger, I probably would have done, but it was no fun being pushed in the mud, and I concentrated all my energy on getting to either Oxford or Cambridge. The idea of escaping from the Hatters and the hotel was like the idea of Heaven, and I was not programmed to believe in salvation by grace. Providentially, Mr Fletcher was supplying a new orthodoxy.

The more stringent its rules, the greater my chances of distinguishing myself by exerting my will-power. Skate and Lea never made any mnemonic cards until he said he wanted to inspect everybody's; I had been cutting up menu cards Mummy sent me from the hotel and, at the risk of annoying Aunt Hetty, kept some on the table during breakfast and tea. To use them at dinner would have provoked too much derisive hostility from the three males. My relationship with Dave was even worse since a quarrel we had had when he was listening to Brahms's Third Symphony on the radio and wanted the kitchen light off. I wanted it on because I was reading. He banged my head against the wall, and I fought back until Aunt Hetty separated us.

Like Fiske and Muley, Skate and Lea were a pair who enjoyed getting into trouble together. They were always being given detentions for lateness, always making far-fetched excuses for not having finished their homework, always having to stay back after class to see Mr Fletcher privately, and when they had to see the High Master there was a rumour they were both going to be expelled. Their reports must have been awful, but they could get fun out of anything when they were together, and it was fun for the rest of us to be with them. They made up rhymes about the masters, and talked loudly about lingams and yonis. They had girl-friends who came to watch when they played for the second fifteen in the match against Westminster. I'd have liked to be friendly with them but found it easier to get on with Imison, a serious Catholic who commuted from Tunbridge Wells, and with Blake, who wanted to be a solicitor. My friendship with Blake, though, was never quite the same after he'd invited me to Sunday lunch in Richmond with his widowed mother and his sister Amelia. Knowing I wouldn't be

able to eat meat, he'd persuaded them to buy two lobsters.
Embarrassed, I explained we were allowed to eat only fish that
had fins and scales.

'Why is that?' Amelia asked.

I knew I had to be careful. I quoted a German proverb Mr
Fletcher had taught us: *Der Mensch ist was er isst.* Well, if people
consisted of what they ate, so, presumably, did fish, and lobsters,
like seagulls, ate certain things that, well, in the eyes of the
Jewish religion, weren't altogether clean. Of course I didn't
mean that eating lobsters was the same as eating whatever it was
that seagulls ate when they flew in the wake of steamers, and
anyway the Jewish dietary laws were formulated for a society in
which standards of sanitation weren't nearly as high as ours.
Pig-meat went bad in the desert, and if only a *Sanhedrin* could be
convened today to repeal some of the outdated laws, lobsters
would no doubt be OK. The harder I tried to camouflage what
I'd said, the worse I made it. I tried to turn it into a joke by
telling them about one of the permanent residents at the hotel, a
widow, who'd rejected a gâteau by telling the waiter 'No thank
you. I like to keep my tummy tidy if I can.' But nobody laughed,
and Blake started talking firmly about cricket.

Along one wall of Mr Harding's classroom was a stand-up
reading desk like the ones in public libraries for newspapers and
magazines. It was big enough to read *The Times* on, and it felt
very grown-up to have it at our disposal every day, though I
couldn't understand why the front page was devoted to births,
marriages, deaths and the personal column, making you open
up the massive paper before you saw a single headline of news.
Mr Harding also displayed copies of the *New Statesman*, the
Spectator, *Time and Tide*, *The Listener*, *The Economist*, and the
Political Quarterly. 'If I can teach you one thing,' he said, 'it'll be
that yesterday's news is today's history.' Like Daddy he had a
round bald head and a persistent cheeriness; but unlike Daddy
he had a toughly challenging capacity for irony. 'If I had to
define history in one word, I'd say "continuity".' There was no
tradition of centralized government in Germany as there was in
England. Hitler belonged to the same story as the sixteenth-

century principalities, while Tsarist despotism in Russia should be seen in the same perspective as the dictatorship of Stalin, which was no more benevolent and a good deal more ruthless. More efficient, certainly, but more destructive for that reason. Matthews, the class Communist, argued with him about that. Matthews was pale and pimply with spectacles, dark, tousled hair and an unabating, indignant appetite for history. Even during the break he sat at his desk reading and scribbling notes into a spiral-topped notebook. He had more facts in his head than any of us, but according to Mr Harding he twisted them all sideways.

We still had lessons in economic history from the long-legged Mr Coombes, who still wore grey flannel trousers and still paced about the classroom hitching them farther up his waist. Karl Marx's mistake, he told us, looking Matthews firmly in the eye, was to forget that his own theories, like everything else, were conditioned by their period. If only, I thought, Karl Marx could have had the benefit of Mr Coombes's advice, that mistake could have been avoided.

History was to be my main subject in the university scholarship exam, and, thanks to Mr Harding, it had come to consist less of facts and dates than of trends and relationships. But he was an atheist. 'We're all historians in this room,' he'd say encouragingly, 'and we have to recognize that Western civilization is a Christian civilization. In other words, a legendary explanation of evolution and a sadistic story about a crucifixion have inspired all the pivotal works of art and architecture in our culture. But the fallacies that have stimulated our most creative impulses have also provided excuses for the most vicious wars and persecutions. The Jews are not, strictly speaking, a race. Add *We Europeans* by Huxley and Haddon to your general reading list. The so-called racial intolerance of the Nazis must be seen as belonging to the same strain of religious intolerance which was characteristic of the Catholic Church in the Middle Ages, and which erupted again very nastily in the Spanish Inquisition and the Thirty Years War. It's all right, Matthews, I know what you're going to say. Of course I concede there were also economic motivations, but Catholics and Protestants were also killing each other because of

their creeds. The theory was that true believers had a moral
duty to kill the heretics who might lead other true believers
astray. Besides, there's always the chance of a death-bed
conversion to the true faith, in which case you're saving their
soul at the expense of their body. Of course you're sending them
straight to Hell if they don't repent at the stake, but you're
increasing your own chances of going to Heaven by fighting on
God's side.'

When I talked about Mr Harding to Revd Kleinmann, the
gentle Hammersmith minister who was giving me Hebrew
lessons, he told me that Judaism was the most tolerant religion in
human history. Unlike the Catholics, who were always trying to
drum up converts, we made it very hard for Gentiles to be
accepted in the Jewish faith, and by the same token we had
never butchered the people who disagreed with us. Revd
Kleinmann was very tolerant himself, a soft-spoken man, with
fair hair, a quiet wife and three young children. He was much
hated by Uncle Ben, Barry and Dave, who mimicked him
tirelessly. Barry said he was too tolerant towards anti-Semitism,
and Uncle Ben said he couldn't even keep Revd Peros in his
place. 'Kleinmann's just putty in his hands. Lets him get away
with murder.' I tried to defend Revd Kleinmann and I liked
him, but he couldn't settle the doubts Mr Harding had raised.
Hadn't there been a certain amount of religious intolerance in
Jewish history? What about all those tribal wars? And if we
believed that Judaism provided the only path to salvation, why
had we made it so hard for potentially virtuous pagans to
convert?

I was also troubled by a doubt that had been raised by Nanny
and later encouraged by the New Testament line about the
sounding brass and the tinkling cymbal. If a man observed all
the Jewish laws, he was a good Jew, but was he a good man?
What about the orthodox who prayed with *Tefillin* every
morning, as Barry and Dave did, but were uncharitable towards
other people? Was it more important to be pious or to love one's
neighbour? 'All God's commandments are important,' said
Revd Kleinmann. 'We have no means of grading their
importance.' But in that case it might be just as bad to eat bread
baked in a tin lined with lard as to masturbate or fail to honour

my father and mother. Anyway, weren't the dietary laws sometimes an obstacle to loving one's neighbour? If I meant Gentile neighbours, said Revd Kleinmann, then deliberately so. The dietary laws had been formulated by the rabbis to discourage fraternization with the heathen. Even today there would be less assimilation if Jewish parents realized that letting their children eat pork was the first step towards letting them marry out of the faith.

The incessant quarrelling in the gloomy kitchen at Dunsany Road made me long for the white linen table-cloths and napkins at the hotel, though Mummy had become more aggressive towards Grannie, who was relapsing further and further into a long-suffering silence, while Daddy seemed to be getting less pleasure out of mealtime conversations. Provocatively calling the dance-hosts gigolos, he said we'd be better off without them. Always touchy when her rights were being threatened, Mummy said she wasn't the only woman who'd hardly ever be able to dance without Mr Kynaston and Mr Hargreaves. She won the argument but lost the advantage a few weeks later when she was seen with Mr Kynaston at a tea-dance in one of the non-Jewish hotels. For several days Daddy didn't speak to her, trying to carry on friendly mealtime conversations with just Teddy and me. I was still having ballroom dancing lessons on Tuesday and Thursday afternoons with Mr Kynaston, so I had to be very vague about what I was going to do after lunch or I'd have been forbidden to go.

Dancing was a help in overcoming my shyness. With only a mild flutter of nervousness I could walk over to any girl in the ballroom. 'Excuse me, but would you like to dance?' So long as you reached them before anyone else, even the prettiest girls invariably said yes, and with any luck we'd soon be dancing cheek-to-cheek. But these girls didn't seem to mean anything by snuggling up close on the dance floor. Skate and Lea seemed to experience no difficulty in making their girl-friends into mistresses. None of the girls at the hotel wanted to be my mistress, and most of them didn't even want to be kissed. One night in London, when Dave was asleep, I dared myself to sleep with a prostitute. As soon as I decided that I would, my body started to tremble. Quickly I ran through all the objections, rejecting them one by one until I came to the danger of venereal disease. When I retracted my decision, the trembling stopped, and it didn't take long after that to fall asleep.

Mr Fletcher mentioned Aldous Huxley more than any other writer, and when I bought a Penguin edition of *Crome Yellow*, I was reminded of the master by the hard, sharp eyes, the cleanly chiselled features and the determined chin in the photograph on the back. They must be the same age too, about ten years younger than Daddy. I enjoyed the novel so much that I started buying Huxley in hardback, and soon the rich brown of the dust-jacket round the collected edition was almost as dominant on my bookshelves in the old nursery as Penguin orange, Pelican blue or Everyman red. Huxley liked using words like 'rachitic' and 'stertorous', which I had to look up, writing them down on mnemonic cards, but the novels seemed to open up a world that was full of free love. None of the girls who danced cheek-to-cheek had the sexy sophistication of Myra Viveash or Lucy Tantamount. I made a note in my commonplace book of Mr Mercaptan's recipe for a tolerable existence: 'Readable books, amusing conversation, civilised women, graceful art, dry vintage, music, with a quiet life and reasonable comfort – that's *all* I ask for.' But in *Point Counter Point* it was very worrying when Rampion said the soul was like a cancer, eating up the real, human, natural reality, spreading and spreading at its expense. I'd always thought of the soul as tucking neatly and comfortably into the body like an invisible leather tongue in a shoe. I felt the same recoil as when Uncle Phil had told me that if I wanted to grow up into a human being, I'd have to start learning about life by living it.

If I thought of a vast, swarming mass of animal and insect life, counting myself in with the midges in the air and the tadpoles in ponds and the cows lying lumpishly about in fields, I had to recognize that I was just an infinitesimal blob. To see me, God would need a miscroscope as well as a telescope. But the assumption behind all my praying had been that He might consider altering His plans, making it rainy instead of sunny, just because I asked Him to. And after so many years of tying my handkerchief devoutly round my waist, after emptying my pockets of coins and pencils before it got dark on Friday evening,

I still hadn't been rewarded with a willing girl-friend, when, at this very moment I was miserably thinking about it, hundreds, thousands, millions of couples were happily making love. Wouldn't God prefer to watch them?

The same religious routine was still running through my life. Every day still began with morning prayers and ended with night prayers. Supper on Friday and lunch on Saturday began with the taste of bread dipped in salt, ending with the grace, which, like the Shabbos service in Shool, contained tunes that had threaded their way through my life. But when I read the translations, I realized it was insulting God's intelligence to think He'd be taken in by such banal flattery and sugary praise. If I were God, I'd be very annoyed with creatures who didn't understand that I could create for myself all the gratification I needed. Monks and nuns were particularly tiresome, thanking me by wasting the whole of the great gift I'd given them, but Jews were bad enough. I'd put them into the world to live. Why didn't they get on with it?

'You know, Dad,' I said one morning when we were walking down the Old Christchurch Road towards the Shool, 'if I were God I'd prefer humanity to carry on as if I didn't exist.'

He looked sideways at me disapprovingly.

The Thirteen Articles of the Jewish faith each started with the words 'I believe with perfect faith. . . .' Four years ago, that had seemed quite reasonable, but the most I could have managed now was 'I believe with imperfect faith'. As Professor Joad might have said on *The Brains Trust*, it all depended on what you meant by God. But how could I be sure that the definition implicit in the Thirteen Articles was absolutely right and the definitions implicit in all other religions absolutely wrong? If God was omnipotent, why had He condemned so many babies to be brought up by families who'd convince them that He had a son? In Shool, though, when I saw all those old bodies swaying devoutly under prayer-shawls, it seemed impossible that so many men had lived so many years without going through a period of doubt. Since they were all still there, they must have come out on the right side of it, so perhaps I would too.

I told Revd Kleinmann I needed his help to refute the

arguments of a Catholic friend who was trying to convert me. His light brown moustache twitched like a rabbit's whiskers, and there were long pauses, while he turned away to lift huge volumes of the Talmud off his shelves, licking a pudgy finger before leafing through closely printed Hebrew pages to find quotations from rabbis whose names were familiar from Shabbos afternoons spent with the Ethics of the Fathers, though I hadn't realized then how often the Fathers disagreed with each other. I soon began to wonder whether the constant recourse to books wasn't a stratagem to afford him time for hesitation, and since studying the Reformation with Mr Harding, I'd been alerted to the difference between aprioristic authoritarianism and empiricism. Rabbinic philosophy couldn't but be more medieval than modern. After seeing Ann Casson as St Joan at the King's Theatre, the line I wrote down in my commonplace book was 'What other judgement can I judge by but my own?'

If I couldn't overcome my doubts, sooner or later I'd have to tell Daddy. Religion had always mattered more to him than anything else, and for at least five years my orthodoxy had mattered more than his own. I'd voluntarily gone further than he had, and he valued my piety as if he owned it. Now I was going to deprive him of it, and he was a more vulnerable man than I'd ever realized when I was younger. One day towards the end of breakfast in the dining-room, Teddy, who'd been having an argument with him, smacked his face. I was tingling with impatience for Teddy to be smacked back. But nothing happened. Eventually Teddy got up and walked away, unpunished. I said nothing, but when Daddy and I were going upstairs in the lift, he said : 'I hope you noticed my self-control.' I'd always loved him more than anyone; I now had to start feeling sorry for him, not so much because of the dance-host or the slap as because of what I was going to do. I knew that if I won a university scholarship, he'd be proud of me, but when I told him I'd lost my faith, the news would be as hard for him to take as would news that he had an incurable disease or that one of his arms was to be amputated. 'You're my immortality,' he'd told me.

Certainly I couldn't ruin his happiness during the preparations for Teddy's Barmitzvah. Nor could I undermine his excitement about the State of Israel. In his after-dinner speeches at functions held in the hotel, he was saying that the year from May 1948, when Israel was given its independence, till May 1949, when it was admitted to the United Nations, was the most important year in the history of the Jewish people, and we must all realize how privileged we were to be alive now when so many generations of our ancestors had looked forward to this moment each time they said 'Next year in Jerusalem', but had not lived to experience it. We were doing Wordsworth at school, so I read some of 'The French Revolution' to him. He copied out the lines

> Bliss was it on that dawn to be alive,
> But to be young was very Heaven!

During the next speech he made in the synagogue hall I saw him fumble in his waistcoat pocket for a piece of paper, but he quoted the lines without looking at it, meeting my eye on the final syllable.

The longest letter he ever wrote to me described how he'd arranged for a course in modern Hebrew to be included in the curriculum at the Municipal College, and for Israel to be toasted at a Rotary Club lunch. Revd Heilbron had said he was too busy to teach adult classes in modern Hebrew, so Daddy approached Dr Shorter, a fellow Rotarian, who promised to start a course at the Municipal College if Daddy could find a tutor and at least twenty-five students who'd commit themselves to paying six shillings and sixpence per term. Daddy's pleasure at succeeding was intensified on the Shabbos after the course had been launched, when the devious Revd Heilbron announced from the pulpit that members of the congregation were invited to enrol for the modern Hebrew course he was starting at the synagogue.

It would have been nice if God had resolved my uncertainty by giving me a sign, but I didn't pray for one because if He was there and at all interested, He'd know what was going on in my mind. Even if I prayed for a sign, the absence of one wouldn't prove that He didn't exist. He might just be testing me. I'd never become an atheist like Mr Harding, but his description of agnosticism made it sound like the only tenable position.

It was safe not to put my *Tefillin* on in the holidays because
nobody ever came into the Oak Room before breakfast; during
term time I put them on and, without praying, stood for five
minutes with the prayer book open in front of me in case Aunt
Hetty came in. I still went to Shool on Shabbos both in
Hammersmith and in Bournemouth, joining in the singing so
that neither Uncle Ben nor Daddy should suspect anything.

When everyone was praying quietly, all I did was move my
lips, but I still had to sit down, stand up and bow at the right
moments. It was all very uncomfortable. The Jewish religion
had effectively begun out of the moment Abraham refused to
please his father by bowing in front of an idol he didn't believe
in, and here was I still pleasing mine by bowing in front of
nothing. Abraham's father was more obviously in the wrong
because he couldn't have been made by an idol that he'd made
himself, but it would have been Jesuitical to argue that nothing
had created us and that was what I was bowing to. Theoretically
it was still possible that God had made us in His image, but we
really ought to be invisible if so, and wasn't it much likelier that
since we'd made Him in ours, His invisibility had made it
necessary for Him to have a visible son? There was a note in my
commonplace book of Pascal's observation that if triangles had
a god, he'd have three sides.

Guilt was beginning to spread over everything I did. It
shouldn't have been necessary to feel guilty about working, but
it was partly an excuse for withdrawal. In Bournemouth I didn't
want to play with Teddy or spend my evenings in the lounges
with Daddy and the visitors; in Hammersmith I needed to keep
away from the family. After three years of creeping up the stairs
in the small hours of the morning, clutching at the wall and
avoiding creaks, there was now a real need, with the vital exams
approaching, to work the long hours I'd been working from the
start.

Both Mr Harding and Mr Fletcher thought I was going to win
a scholarship to Oxford or Cambridge, while Mummy and
Daddy both wanted me to have the university education that
would provide me with opportunities they hadn't had, though
obviously they had misgivings about the education I'd had
already. They'd made sacrifices for me to have it, Mummy said,

and they were willing to go on making sacrifices, but they didn't want it to take me away from them. Perhaps I didn't realize how much I was hurting them by some of the things I said, especially when the way of life I was criticizing was the one that had made it possible for them to send me to St Paul's. Besides, I didn't realize how much effect I was having on Teddy. My influence on him ought to be a good one.

Mr Harding insisted that the object of university education was to prepare boys for life in general, not for one career in particular, but the idea of becoming a barrister was edging ahead of other career possibilities, and he couldn't advise me about which university or which college to apply for until I'd decided whether or not I wanted to read Law. I couldn't understand how people decided what to do, when it was impossible to know in advance what doing it would be like. I'd never have come to St Paul's if I'd known what it would be like to live with the Hatters. How could I know what a barrister's life would be like?

The barrister who sometimes came to Shool was dignified, with a very pleasant smile; George Sanders had given a suave performance as a generous attorney defending a beautiful girl who couldn't pay his normal fee, winning her love even before he got her acquitted against impossible-seeming odds. I was also very impressed by the barrister father of my new friend John Ludkin. The whole family was impressive. John's sister was a novelist, her husband a publisher, John's uncle a politician whose books on economic history were recommended by Mr Harding, and John himself was going to sit for a scholarship to Trinity College, Cambridge. He was a mathematician, but his conversation was full of quotations from Auden and Isherwood, Evelyn Waugh, Louis MacNeice and Stephen Spender, 'Are you washed in the blood of the Lamb?' he'd inquire. His drawl was affected but his self-assurance was genuine. 'Never explain, never apologize,' he kept telling me, and I tried hard not to. He found it no effort. I discussed almost everything with him except what to read at university. I went to stay for week-ends at his parents' flat in Bayswater; he came to stay at the hotel. He maintained that mathematics and religion were mutually exclusive. I asked him about Lord Edward's mathematical proof of God's existence in *Point Counter Point*: that if m over naught was infinity, m being any positive number, both sides of the equation could be multiplied by naught, which would mean that any positive number was the product of zero and infinity. The universe must therefore have been created by an infinite power out of nothing. John's answer was that both naught and infinity were concepts unrelated to experience, and that in any case to multiply both sides by naught would be to reduce the equation to $0 = 0$.

When I told Mr Harding I'd decided to read Law, he said I should put down Trinity Hall, Cambridge, as my first choice. If I won my scholarship, as John would undoubtedly win his, our colleges would be next door to each other. Meanwhile Teddy wanted to go to St Paul's, and Aunt Hetty said he could stay at Dunsany Road. It was up to me to stop it from happening. But would I be able to? Uncle Ben, Aunt Hetty, Barry, Dave and Rosalie all behaved quite differently in the presence of Mummy and Daddy, and, intent on 'not telling tales out of school', I'd been so secretive about my suffering that they were both suspicious when I reacted so violently against the idea of sending Teddy to the Hatters. If it hadn't been all right there, why hadn't I said so before? Had I offended the Hatters in some way? Criticized them?

I had to do everything I could to save Teddy, and I started by giving him a description of the treatment he'd be letting himself in for. He said he wasn't surprised to hear they were two-faced, but he was quite prepared to make sacrifices for the religion. I couldn't tell him I'd stopped believing in it, or he might have told them, and I couldn't tell him how suspicious I was of the word 'sacrifices'. But I had to do something. I went on arguing with Daddy, who promised to look into the possibility of sending him to a flat in Earls Court, where the widow of an old friend from the Board of Deputies of British Jews might be glad to have a lodger. But when it turned out that she didn't keep a kosher home, Daddy seemed to think he'd done all he could to find an alternative, and the more vehemently I talked, the less they wanted to listen.

I waited till I was alone with Mummy.

'Do you realize how malicious Aunt Hetty is?'

'What do you mean?'

'It's the things she says. The way she talks about you and Daddy behind your backs.'

'I think she's had quite a hard life. You have to make allowances.'

'I do. But they're all extremely jealous, and I *know* Teddy would be extremely unhappy there with them.'

'But where else could we send him?'

This was the argument they both used as if it were unanswerable.

'All I know is you mustn't send him there. Really. It's one thing to send somebody there when you don't know what it's going to be like, but honestly, now that I do, it would be idiotic to make the same mistake twice.' I shouldn't have said 'idiotic'. The shutters were coming down. In an unconsidered bid to keep them open I went on talking. 'She told me that Daddy asked Uncle Dan to marry you. That you weren't really in love with him. That Grannie made it all happen. I didn't believe her. I'm not asking you. I don't want to know. I'm just telling you the sort of thing she says. Do you want Teddy to hear that?'

Her eyes were closed. 'I don't know. It's probably true. I don't really remember.'

When the telegram arrived from the senior tutor at Trinity Hall, congratulating me on winning a scholarship, Daddy immediately asked what I wanted for my reward. He'd asked me the same question when we got the news about my state scholarship, so this time I had my answer ready: 'A holiday in Paris.'

He booked me into the Oxford and Cambridge Hotel, which sounded appropriate, he said. It was in the Rue de Rivoli, almost next door to a souvenir shop owned by Mr Goodman, brother of a local Jewish antique dealer, so I'd have a friend at hand if I needed advice. He still pictured me as constantly in need of advice from my elders. I couldn't go abroad without having a passport, but the manager of the local branch of Cook's was a Rotarian, and he'd tell me how to get one. I'd also need some traveller's cheques. Daddy would arrange for me to collect these from the National Provincial Bank in the Square.

The dates that were finally fixed meant that I'd miss the

beginning of term, but nobody seemed to mind. I was going to be totally free for ten days, to go on holiday alone, to go out of England. When I went back to school, I'd be wearing a university scholar's gown. The new boys would think I was a master, just as I had once wondered why some of the masters looked so terribly young. A new life was beginning. Even the idea of National Service didn't frighten me. After Dunsany Road, the RAF would be like a holiday camp. I'd have been called up at the age of eighteen, but Mr Harding's advice over the telephone had been that I should volunteer early, so as to have my eighteen months over in time to start at Cambridge in October 1951.

On the train from Calais to Paris I was going to eat meat, and after crossing the Channel without being seasick, I was determined not to be one of those Jewish boys who were sick at their first mouthful of non-kosher food. I wasn't going to start with either shellfish or pork, but it wasn't going to be just a matter of setting myself a lower standard of orthodoxy, it was to be a clean break with the religion. I'd still have to play-act in front of Daddy and in front of anyone else who might report my defection to him, but so far as I was privately concerned, I was now an agnostic. The restaurant car was much more attractive than restaurant cars on English trains. The napkin was folded in a special way, and the waiter inspired immediate confidence as a competent, grey-haired professional, seriously interested in the food he was serving. I ordered the vegetable soup, which might or might not have been made from a meat stock. I was glad I didn't have to inquire, especially in French. Then veal, with a thick brown sauce. There was a slight uncertainty in my fingers as I picked up the knife and fork, but they weren't trembling, and none of the people around me could have known I was doing something I hadn't done before. I cut firmly into the meat and included a sauté potato on the first fork-load. It was delicious, and from that moment I enjoyed the meal enormously. The wine was nice, the waiter attentive and the fields outside the window were France.

In another ninety minutes I'd be in Paris, free at last of everything that had held me back. No more *Tefillin* straps, no more headachey fasting. University gowns and RAF uniforms.

One more term of Dunsany Road, but it wouldn't matter now if Aunt Hetty grumbled and Rosalie sulked. Dave could break off the relationship as often as he liked, and if Barry punched me in bed, I'd get up and punch him back.

If London was huge, Paris was incomparably less cramped, with a generous width to the boulevards and avenues that radiated out from the spacious squares. The gardens at Versailles were as big as a small city. I saw the balcony where Louis XVI and Marie Antoinette stood facing the mob from Paris, and I wrote uncertainly in my diary about beauty that served no purpose. If the greatest happiness of the greatest number was the foundation of right and wrong, it must be a mistake to equate Beauty and Truth. The *ancien régime* had caused a lot of misery, but it was impossible to wish that it had never existed while the rhythm of your breathing was being affected by the presence of that baroque palace.

In the Rue de Rivoli I bought an unexpurgated edition of *Lady Chatterley's Lover*. It had been printed in Stockholm and sometimes spelt 'bosom' as 'bossom'. Resisting the idea that every minute of my time in Paris was earmarked for galleries and sightseeing, I stayed in my hotel bedroom, reading greedily. It was a pity that the thrusting of the man's buttocks should look ridiculous to the lady, but it was good that the penis could penetrate so deeply into her consciousness. I wanted to make thrills ripple like a bell inside a beautiful female body, while wild little cries came out of her mouth and her womb clamoured like a sea-anemone for me to come in again and make a fulfilment for her. But if the old England of Squire Winters and Wragby Hall was gone, dead, blotted out, everything I was marvelling at in Paris belonged equally to the past – Versailles, the Luxembourg Palace, Nôtre-Dame, the view from the hill in Montmartre. Was it true that the common people who'd rule the future were only the grey halves of human beings? I didn't want a life with 'utterly no beauty in it, no intuition'.

It was a holiday like no holiday I'd had since the early childhood ones in Swanage, Lyme Regis, Newquay and Broadstairs. There were no mnemonic cards in my pockets, no pressures from adults, no reasons to do anything I didn't want to do. Like a child, I could understand only a part of what everybody else was saying, and like a child, I filled my lungs with the promise that was in the air. The time would come when I too would sit drinking coffee with an elegant lady, her hair tucked neatly into a head-scarf. Later on her high heels would click beside me along the pavement as we walked towards the jeweller that had advertised in last night's theatre programme – a necklace on a bare-shouldered blonde. The goods so tastefully laid out in so many shop windows fed my fantasies as I roamed the streets, revelling in the Frenchness of everything. Was it the way the women moved that was so un-English, or the way they dressed and made up and did their hair? Even the Métro smelt more exciting than the Underground, and there was something French about the smell of the croissants and coffee in the hotel, about the warmth that rose to greet me in the restaurant I kept going back to, and even about the smell of books – new books in bookshops and old books on the stalls in the Quartier Latin. My first glimpse of a nearly naked woman was in the cabaret at the Bal Tabarin, and the next day I saw the Venus de Milo at the Louvre. The beauty of the body and the beauty of the sculpture were indistinguishable. If only there were a chance of writing so well that the prose vanished into the vividness of a description.

Neville Banner was in Paris with a party of twenty students. After meeting at the Café de Paris, we went on to visit the tombs of Rousseau, Voltaire and Jaurès at the Panthéon. I got very little out of it, but two days later I saw Napoleon's hair at the Carnavalet Museum and sat in the chair Béranger had died in. I sent a postcard of it to Mr Harding.

On my last night Mr Goodman took me out to dine in grand style at Wepler. We drank so much wine I could hear myself talking as if an invisible ventriloquist were putting words into my mouth, but instead of feeling sleepy afterwards, I stayed awake till nearly three, and had to get up at seven to catch the 8.15 train from Paris Nord. Daddy met me at Victoria, after missing me at Waterloo, and I talked almost non-stop on the train back to Bournemouth. He was relieved that I'd been all right on my own, but I had to start thinking all over again about how hurt he was going to be when I told him I was an agnostic. Mummy wasn't at the station to meet us because she'd gone to the annual Hoteliers' Ball at the Royal Bath Hotel. After unpacking the presents I'd brought for everybody, I walked down the hill to say hello and give her hers, but Mr Kynaston was with her, so I didn't stay long. In the morning I discovered she was hardly on speaking terms with Daddy. She'd been going out to dinner-dances with Mr Kynaston, and letting him drive her to Brighton and London. During the four leisurely days I spent at the hotel, I made several unsuccessful attempts to patch the quarrel. I travelled back to London on the *Bournemouth Belle*. At Waterloo Teddy was standing at the end of the platform with Uncle Ben.

Lessons seemed extremely dull but there were some interesting lectures at the National Book League. B. Ifor Evans talked about Keats's letters, and Susan Lady Tweedsmuir about Edward Lear. The next morning I had the idea of forming a literary society at school as an offshoot of *The Debater*, which I was still editing. We could have lectures, discussions and poetry readings. The English master was enthusiastic, and the High Master gave his permission. Using *Debater* stationery, I wrote to J. B. Priestley, Louis MacNeice, Stephen Spender, A. P. Herbert, T. S. Eliot, Osbert Sitwell, Sean O'Casey, Harold Nicolson, B. Ifor Evans and Arthur Calder Marshall. As soon as I arrived at school each morning with Teddy, I headed for *The Debater*'s letter-box. Most of the replies were refusals. T. S. Eliot regretted that his schedule was too crowded, and Sean O'Casey's letter was full of friendly chat. He was too old to go round listening to himself talking. The time was out of joint, but we were nearer to Hamlet's age than he was, so we should decide for ourselves how to set it right. The first acceptance came from Harold Nicolson, who agreed to talk about 'English Biography'. He arrived early. He was sixty-two, stout, bluff and quite affable, but he was so keen to start punctually at 4.45 it was quite hard to keep him chatting in the waiting-room till the audience was ready for him. I felt very important when I took the chair. I stood up, clearing my throat as Daddy did when he was about to introduce a speaker. Our second guest was Arthur Calder Marshall, who also looked distinguished, with thick hair slanting down over his forehead. As he was putting his overcoat on at the end, he asked me the question I'd so often been asked before. 'And what are you going to be?' I'd already told quite a lot of people I was going to be a lawyer, but this time, as I said it, I knew that what I really wanted was to be a writer.

The pre-Paris Ronnie would have felt miserable about it for days before broaching the subject ineffectually with Daddy, who'd have said what he'd said before, that security was very important. Why shouldn't I be a barrister and write in my spare time, like Norman Birkett? The agnostic Ronnie went to Mr Harding during break the following morning and said he'd changed his mind about wanting to read Law. How could I arrange to read English instead? All I needed to do, said Mr Harding, was write to the senior tutor.

'Nothing is worse than relaxed religion,' said Erasmus, and I copied the words into my commonplace book among quotations from Huxley, Wilde, Dr Johnson, Bentham, T. S. Eliot, Voltaire, La Rochefoucauld, James Joyce and Jesus Christ, who'd once said: 'Every idle word that men shall speak, they shall give account thereof in the day of judgment. For by thy words shalt thou be justified and by thy words shalt thou be condemned.' I hadn't realized that he cared about words so much, but he had certainly been good at using them. I was avid in collecting definitions of God and formulations of moral principles that appealed to me as phrases which didn't depend on unacceptable premises. I needed a new system of moral values. There was the whole of literature to replace the Old Testament. All the best writing sharpened the reader's consciousness, which improved him morally. He couldn't commit murder unless his imagination was dead to the years of pleasure he was stealing from his victim.

In a diary full of moralizing I wrote that we shouldn't expect life to have a 'meaning' simple enough to translate into a formula, and that we should separate our thirst for certainty from our hunger for a purpose. The thirst could never be satisfied. The hunger could, temporarily, but mine wasn't: now that I'd won the scholarship there was nothing to work for. Having volunteered for early call-up, I wouldn't even be staying on at school long enough to enter for the Truro Essay Competition. This year's subject was 'The Future of Art' and the prize was £28. Then it occurred to me that if I had my essay typed out, Skate could submit it for me under his name. It wouldn't be wrong because it wouldn't harm anyone. It would seem dishonest, but only in the way that lies did when you told them to avoid hurting other people, and it would be no more deceitful than pretending I was still saying my prayers. When Skate agreed, without even wanting a cut of the prize money, I felt I'd at last done something to prove I wasn't a 'teacher's pet', though the taunt had never come from Skate or Lea. It was Fiske and Muley I was still remembering. I started reading and making notes, though the essay didn't have to be finished till July.

9

Into Uniform

The Air Ministry voucher which could be exchanged for a free third-class ticket from Euston to Warrington (Lancs.) was going to deliver me into the grip of a huge deindividualizing machine, inefficient but powerful. An RAF bus collected us from the station. Arriving at the camp, we were given tea, quickly followed by an FFI – a medical to check that we were 'free from infection'. If the university gown had excited me more than any other garment I'd been given to wear since my first two pairs of long trousers, the uniform issued at the RAF Reception Centre, Padgate, made me feel like a convict. We were surrendering our freedom and our identity with our ration book and identity card. In return we were given a number and a rank, AC2, which meant Aircraftsman 2nd Class. We were each issued with a kitbag, a pay book, a thick china mug, a knife, a fork and a spoon, a beret, a greatcoat, two uniforms known as battle-dress and best blue, shirts, underwear, a thick pair of boots, a pair of black shoes, gaiters, blankets, sheets and a metal strip for protecting the clothes when we were polishing our brass buttons.

Twenty-two of us slept in two rows of identical camp-beds in a long wooden hut with a lino floor. The boys were nearly all what Mummy would have called 'common', but they were friendly. The pillows were very hard.

It was a huge camp like a monotonous town with long wooden huts surrounded by small lawns intersected with narrow hedged roads. Reveille was at six o'clock. The best time was the evening, when we could play ping-pong or go to the camp cinema. On the Friday we had to have our hair cut very short and change into our uniform, making parcels of our civvy clothes to send home.

155

After we'd been inspected in our uniform, we paraded for our first week's pay. I sent a pound home to Mummy with a note saying I wanted her to have some of the first money I'd earned. The main topic of conversation all through the week was 'square-bashing', the eight-week course we'd all have to do at one of the recruit training camps. Nobody knew exactly what it was going to be like, but everyone said it was awful.

I was sent to Bridgnorth near Wolverhampton, and here the twenty-four of us in the hut knew that we'd be together for the whole of the eight-week stretch. It was like being in a wartime air-raid shelter: we were all exposed to the same dangers. We hadn't even unpacked when a voice shouted: 'Stand by your beds.' We stood to attention. The sergeant was a short man with a peaked cap low on his forehead, a jutting chin and a loud Scottish voice. He was the NCO in charge of the flight, he told us, and he was going to see to it that our drill was nothing less than perfect. 'I'm a harrd mun,' he warned. When he went, Corporal Bond told us how our kit had to be kept. Our blankets must be made up into a neat pile, each one folded to exactly the same width, with only one fold showing at the front, the sheets tucked in the middle and one blanket framing all the others. The corporal slept in a small room at the end of the hut. Like the other corporals we heard drilling their squads of victims, he seemed to have been trained in the art of using his voice to terrorize. 'At the double!' he screamed, yelling and threatening as we scrambled out of the hut to form ourselves into a three-line squad on the asphalt outside. Then he would talk with a calculated ominous quietness to a selected victim. 'You march like a pregnant penguin. Do you know that, Hayman? Stand to attention when you're talking to me and wipe that stupid grin off your face. What've you got to be pleased about, eh? Listen, laddie, I'm going to be down on you like a ton of bricks if you don't smarten up your ideas. I'm going to make this flight into the smartest flight on the camp, and if you don't change your ideas you're going to wish you'd never been born. I'm going to piss on you from a great height. You're just a pregnant penguin. What are you?' Quite a lot of saliva would be on the victim's face by the time Corporal Bond had finished, but it was dangerous to wipe it off until his back was turned.

When I'd been terrorized at Dunsany Road, I'd been entirely on my own; here I had twenty-three allies, twenty-three friendly boys from all over Britain. Their accents made some of them difficult to understand, but there was no mistaking their goodwill. No one had ever called me 'mate' before, and I liked it. Even the corporal seemed jealous of our togetherness when he sauntered into the hut during off-duty hours, calling us 'lads' and trying to be friendly. Without the peaked cap rammed down on his forehead, his face looked softer, more human, but none of us trusted him except when we were paying him to iron our trousers or polish our boots.

There was a fresh-faced boy from Aberdeen who spoke with the broadest Scottish accent I'd ever heard. Aber, they called him. Many of them had nicknames based on where they came from, Geordie, Taffy, Mac, Scouse, but Bournemouth was no use as a name. At seventeen I was the youngest; the oldest was twenty-two, a ginger-haired Cockney called Ginge. He was the only married man in the hut, and he told us about it. Fucking was bloody marvellous. If we'd only wanked, we didn't know what we were missing. Bloody marvellous, and he'd never had a real proper fuck till he got wed. Bloody funny it was, the way they were both so nervous, both wanting it like mad, but not daring to start, and then, when they did, it was so bloody marvellous they did it three times in a row. Weak as a kitten he was, after. And she was asleep. Then he was asleep too and the next thing he knew – gave him a real turn, it did – this noise and her not beside him any more. Quiet sort of hissing noise like a snake or something. Gave him a real turn. Had to jump out of bed to put the light on and there she was, squatting on top of the sink, having a piss.

I could understand Ginge, but the others all used words that puzzled me. 'Shower' was invariably a word of abuse because it meant 'shower of shit'. 'Bull' or 'bullshit' usually meant polishing or cleaning. 'Shorthouse' turned out to be 'short-arse' and just meant 'short'. One night the rumour went round the hut that there were some regular airmen in the ablutions, pulling the pissers of the National Service recruits. I put off going to the ablutions until the discomfort was unbearable. No one molested me, and a couple of days later, when I heard Ginge asking Aber 'Sure they weren't pulling your pisser?', I realized it was the same as 'taking the piss'.

According to John Ludkin, drill was almost as bad as boxing for killing off brain cells. Each time we stamped our booted feet, the vibrations damaged our brain, which was what they wanted, because the brain was useless to them. What they needed was to short-circuit it, training our arms and legs to respond directly to their commands. They had a big arsenal of punishments at their disposal, from putting us on fatigues to court-martialling us. If you were put on a charge you'd be marched like a prisoner into the squadron leader's office. If the sentence was a reprimand, it was entered in your service documents, like a permanent black mark. Or you might be given several days of jankers, which meant doing extra parades privately and being inspected by the guard commander. One of the commonest threats was that you'd be reflighted – transferred to a junior flight, so that an extra week or two was added to your training period. During my fifth week at Bridgnorth, the flight was inspected before the CO's parade by two sergeants, Sergeant Wallace, the Scotch terrifier, and Sergeant Sullivan, a dangerous, soft-voiced Irishman, who quietly complained that the buckle of my belt wasn't clean. He'd have to reflight me, he said, and told me to fall out, go back to my billet and pack my kit. I'd just finished packing it when Sergeant Wallace came in and told me to unpack it. I was so pleased about not being reflighted that I felt almost grateful for the flow of abuse.

'You're not fit to live among pigs.'

'No, Sergeant.'

Monday night was always 'bullshit night'. We had to stay in the billet, polishing the lino, cleaning the windows, polishing the brass on the fire extinguishers, shining the iron coal buckets and bins. We joked about it, but we accepted that it had to be done, and well done if we were to keep out of trouble.

The drill, the ground combat and the weapon training were physically exhausting. Bayonet practice was the worst, with Corporal Bond yelling at us to make us yell as loudly as we could, rushing towards the sandbag and pretending we were plunging our bayonet into a man's stomach. At the start of each period, we were bullied into scrambling out of the hut like firemen rushing on to a fire-engine, falling in outside under the threat that the last man on parade would be put on fatigues. We never knew what was going to happen next. The corporal knew, but all we could do was make guesses, according to the junction in the asphalt paths. 'Right wheel' would mean that we were going towards the educational huts or the lecture-hall; 'left wheel' would mean yet another hour of drill, thumping the square with our aching feet. But at the end of each period, the words 'Fall out' were like a reprieve, even when it was only for a five-minute smoke. Tea-breaks, lunch-breaks, time off duty in the evening and at the week-end were tremendously welcome. The NAAFI was a haven of repose. The strong milky tea, the Mars bars, the sandwiches, the sticky cakes, the stale, warm atmosphere, the tinkly out-of-tune piano, the companionship – I was amazed at the pleasure they gave me.

The education periods and some of the lectures from officers about the history of the RAF were almost as relaxing as a break, and I was looking forward to the week of fatigues we were to have in the middle of the course, not as a punishment but as an integral part of the training, as if the whole course were intended to crush resistance. I was sent to work in the Salvation Army canteen, and I was scrubbing the floor on my first day there when a warrant officer called me over. 'Laddie, show me your hands.' I held them out, nails towards him, but he turned my hands over, jabbing at the palms. 'I can see you've never done an honest day's work in your life.'

I now had to decide which RAF job to apply for. In the education branch, which was possibly the least boring department to be in, you couldn't be an officer without a university degree, but you could become an education sergeant just by doing a six-week training course at Wellesbourne Mountford, which was only six miles from Stratford-on-Avon, where John Gielgud was in four of the season's five productions.

After eight weeks of square-bashing, the course at Welles-bourne seemed luxuriously unpressured, and I had fantasies of going back to Bridgnorth, wearing my sergeant's stripes, and telling Corporal Bond what I thought of him. Education officers gave us lectures about how to give lectures, and we practised by delivering twenty-minute lecturettes to the other trainees. Non-commissioned officers gave us instruction in how to be a sergeant. We needed to know how to give orders when commanding a squad of men – how to march them about and how to shout such commands as 'Eyes right'. You always needed to ready them for the command that was coming: instead of abruptly shouting 'SHUN', you said, 'SQUAD . . . SHUN.' This seemed simple enough, but it became more complicated when we were taught how to teach drill movements. You called out a man from the squad to demonstrate the movement to the others, and one afternoon I was told to teach a movement that involved me in calling out three men. I told them to stand at ease, but when I wanted to bring them to attention, I needed a word to go before 'SHUN'. I couldn't say 'SQUAD' when there were only three of them. Mustering as much conviction as I could, I shouted: 'DEMONSTRATORS . . . SHUN!' Derisively the flight sergeant sent me back to my place, and for days afterwards he made jokes at my expense about Communist demonstrations.

I'd worked at 'The Future of Art' during fatigue week and I finished my essay at Wellesbourne. Skate was finally a friend. I wrote to him about the absurdities of life in the RAF, and he wrote back about the absurdities of life at school, illustrating his letters with cartoons of Mr Fletcher and Mr Harding. When I went home on a forty-eight-hour pass in the middle week-end of the course, I had the essay typed out in the reception. The blonde telephonist made quite a lot of mistakes, which I couldn't bear to leave, but I did my best to imitate Skate's handwriting when correcting them.

I saw *King Lear* twice, *Julius Caesar*, *Much Ado about Nothing*, *Measure for Measure* and *Henry VIII*. I went with Pat, a tall baby-faced Irish friend from the education course. He claimed to know Barbara Jefford, and I was hoping that after *Measure for Measure* we'd go backstage to congratulate her, but all he said was that she wasn't bad for a nineteen-year-old, so we travelled straight back to camp on the blue-grey RAF bus with every seat full and standing airmen hanging on to the straps. Most of them had spent the evening in Stratford pubs, so the bus was full of

he hotel after the new wing was built.

ft) On holiday with Daddy; (*right*) with Teddy in my garden – the windows of the night
nursery and day nursery are visible in the top right-hand corner.

With Mummy and Teddy after the war

As an adolescent, trying to look studious.

loud talk and raucous singing. The favourite song was about shovelling shit on the Isle of Capri.

With only fifteen weeks behind me, I still had over fourteen months to serve, but at Melksham in Wiltshire it was immediately obvious that time was going to move in a different way. RAF Melksham was a recruit-training camp, like Bridgnorth, and the eighteen-year-old airmen were having to go through the same ordeals of terrorization and physical exertion, but I couldn't use my sergeant's stripes to protect them from the bullying of the drill instructor corporals. I also knew that, for them, education periods could be no more than periods of rest between drill and weapon training.

There were twenty-four periods each week, divided between English, maths and citizenship, which meant lectures on the function of the RAF and the necessity of National Service. After the first few weeks, I didn't have to spend any time on preparation, or more than two hours a week on correcting written work. Each flight was divided up into three classes, so if there had been only three of us in the section, we'd all have had to teach every period, but as there were never less than six of us and sometimes eight, I never had to teach for more than twelve hours a week and sometimes only for eight. If I'd had a room to myself, I could have spent the rest of the time reading, but only the senior education officer had his own office. The other officers and sergeants shared the only other office, and though we all kept books on our desks, most of the time was spent chatting casually about the Korean War and anything else that was being written up in the newspapers, about girls, films and what we were going to do when we got back to Civvy Street. Pilot Officer Libby, a fair-haired, chubby-cheeked, folk-dancing enthusiast, would demonstrate steps on the lino floor between the trestle tables that served as desks, using his corps stick to represent the other dancers.

The train from Chippenham arrived at Cambridge half an hour late, and I arrived for my six o'clock appointment with Mr Doone at one minute past – to find someone else was with him. He wouldn't be free till seven. So I called in on Nigel Firth, who was now at Trinity Hall. His room was narrow but comfortable, with a shabby, well-upholstered suite of furniture. He was so conscious of the marks on his distempered walls that, after going to use his lavatory, I came back to find he'd switched off the overhead light and lit two candles. We went to the first sitting of dinner together. The quick-moving, white-jacketed gyps reached over the rows of gowned shoulders to give us Brown Windsor soup, two slices of corned beef with mashed potato and beetroot, heavy pudding. Within twenty minutes we'd finished eating and wandered over to see Raymond Da Costa in Trinity. In Trinity Street, Nigel pointed up at a red-lit window in a tower, and as soon as we'd knocked at Raymond's door, he was telling me about some American soldiers who'd knocked on his door last week to ask what time the fun began. The main room was bigger and better decorated than Nigel's. One of the highly polished coffee-tables was laden with vases; the other supported a liqueur-bottle table-lamp. Nearly all his conversation with Nigel was about various ways of arranging the furniture.

At seven o'clock I still had to wait ten minutes for Mr Doone to be free, and when I finally went into his large, untidy study, he stared at me interrogatively, obviously with no idea who I was or why I'd come. When I explained, he shook hands and signalled me to sit down on the sofa between a tray and a pile of books. He said I wouldn't be prevented from reading English by the terms of the scholarship.

In the morning I was still in bed when he knocked at the guest-room door and came in to ask how I was doing in the RAF. Before leaving for the station, I went to say hello to Neville Banner, who had let me sleep in his room when I was taking the exams. He was talking to a plump, spectacled boy who spoke with a Midlands accent. Welcoming me warmly, Neville carried straight on with the conversation they were having about a social evening at the Labour Club. They were calculating how many glasses of beer could be got out of a quart bottle, how much to charge, and what to do with the beer left over. Neville said it would be quite an idea to sell potato crisps, because they made people thirsty. When I said I must go and catch my train, Neville said what a pity I couldn't come to the social evening.

As a sergeant I had my own 'bunk' at the end of a hut inhabited by members of the permanent staff. The tannoy relayed the Light Programme all through the evening, and the wall was so thin that I couldn't settle down to any of the reading I'd planned in preparation for Cambridge. In the sergeants' mess it was even noisier. Being a sergeant was quite unlike what I'd imagined when corporals still had power over me, and quite unlike what I'd imagined when I wore the sergeant's uniform in the nursery.

Through my fourteen months at Melksham, my citizenship classes veered further and further away from what I'd been taught to teach. From purveying the official image of the R A F and stonewalling questions that implicitly challenged it, I found myself resorting more often to the phrase 'The official view is . . .' and becoming more forthcoming when they asked: 'But what do you think, Sarge?' Sometimes, like Pilot Officer Libby, I departed altogether from the official programme. Once I went into a classroom and said: 'Well chaps, what shall we talk about today?' Several of the boys shouted 'Women', and for an hour I talked about women.

One morning a fat envelope arrived with Skate's handwriting on it. 'I write under great emotional stress,' the letter began, and I knew we'd been found out. He'd handed the essay in the previous week. Everything had gone well till yesterday, when a letter arrived for his father, addressed in Mr Harding's handwriting. In the evening his mother advised him to withdraw the essay. 'They know all about it,' she told him, but wouldn't say how they'd found out. Certainly Lea wouldn't have reported it, and nobody else in the class knew. 'Well, today I go to Fletcher and put all the cards on the table, omitting your name, and ask if I can withdraw the effort. He, whipping off his glasses as always, said that it was a most heinous crime and very unwise and the HM takes a very dim view of the whole proceeding. I had to reveal your name, as Fletcher said it would be sure to come out later. He was amazed to hear of your being involved in such a slopacious scheme. I am extremely sorry your fine plan should have crashed, especially as the essay was I think of very high quality and sure to have defeated the combined opposition of Messrs Imison and Matthews. Fletcher, although most friendly and I think secretly amused, stressed the serious nature of the offence. How we were discovered I cannot imagine. Must be part of the bad luck which always dogs me.'

Another letter arrived nine days later. 'The actual exposition was due, I must now admit, to a discovery by my parents. Recently I had a row with them over a girl with whom I almost had to enter into holy matrimony, and my mother, thinking your first letter from Wellesbourne to be connected with that matter, took it into her head to read it.' Eleven days later there was a longer letter. 'I was summoned to the presence on Friday, there to meet a most affable HM, far more concerned with the current lack of morality in the school than with our particular offence. He said, however, that the correct course would be for him to inform the governors: that they would insist on my expulsion and – worst of all – would request Trinity Hall to take away your scholarship. But he was unwilling to undergo such a scandal, and no action would therefore be taken. I had expected that to be the end of the matter, but this morning Harding told the form, without mentioning names, briefly what had happened as an example of "intellectual dishonesty and moral defectiveness". He's heartbroken because he feels we're all criminals in some way. He said we were self-centred, anti-social and lazy. He also said he had written to you, forbidding you ever to use his name as a reference.'

He hadn't but he did six days later. 'I have always enjoyed discussing work and filling up real or imagined gaps with my old friends of the Form but for some time yet this in your case could revive memories of something which I trust will die without offspring.' The letter went on to say that he had told me that it was perfectly possible for me to put in an entry for the Truro Essay Prize. I wrote back to say I was quite sure he hadn't. His reply was that I must have been so set on avoiding National Service that I did not hear or take mental note of what he said. 'I hope that you realize I feel badly let down over the whole affair, let alone the crime of drawing back Skate into the kind of actions from which we have been trying to steer him.'

I knew that the whole catastrophe was due to making a secret out of something I could have discussed with Mr Harding, but now I'd go on being secretive about my attempt to deceive; at the same time I'd go on deceiving Daddy by keeping my agnosticism secret.

John Ludkin and I decided to save up all our leave to take a three-week holiday together, hitch-hiking along the Riviera. When I told Mummy, she said I would promise, wouldn't I, to stay with John all the time; when I told Daddy, he said wouldn't I need some of my leave for the Jewish high festivals? No doubt I'd be coming home for them.

Like convicts, National Servicemen talked more about time than anything else. 'Eight months and four days from tomorrow I'll be back in Civvy Street!' 'Roll on demob!' 'Just three more weeks and I've got a week's leave.' 'Two more days and I'm off on a forty-eight.' We had a forty-eight-hour pass over the weekend once a month, and a thirty-six-hour pass every other weekend we weren't on duty. If I could have used the time, I wouldn't have squandered it on looking forward to time that was out of reach, but much as I wanted to avoid upsetting Daddy, I needed the prospect of France too desperately to waste several days of leave on a charade of conformity with grim-faced, headachey Jews, perfunctorily atoning for sins just like the ones they intended to commit in the year ahead. When I wrote to Daddy saying that my application for leave had been refused, he sent a telegram: RING TONIGHT REVERSING CHARGES LOVE DAD.

Friendly at first, his voice soon became agitated. I must appeal to my CO. I must request a personal interview with him, and then explain how important the high festivals were for an orthodox Jew.

The following morning a long letter arrived. I should make it clear to the CO that it was a matter of principle. Every man had duties that were above his duties to King and Country. If I thought a joke was appropriate, I could tell him that God was *his* CO, but it might be better to remain serious.

I let a few days go by before replying that my appeal had been unsuccessful. His next letter said that I must tell the CO quite categorically that I'd be unable to obey him if he ordered me to work either during New Year or the Day of Atonement. I was to telephone home that evening. I told him I was liable to be put on a charge if I disobeyed orders. He said the country wasn't at war, and I should trust him to see that no harm would come to me. He'd enlist help from the Board of Deputies of British Jews. Neville Banner's father had once stayed at the hotel, and if necessary he could ask a question in the House of Commons. Each time I tried to use the three-minute pips as an excuse for ringing off, he said he didn't care how much the call was costing him. I wished I'd rung without reversing the charges. I could have said I was running out of change.

Two days later a typed letter arrived from the senior chaplain to the Jewish forces. There was nothing he would have liked more than to intervene as my father had requested, but he was placed in a difficult position, and did not consider that any useful purpose would be served by his writing to my commanding officer. His advice was that I should appeal once again myself, expressing my willingness to remain on camp, but asking to be excused duties at least during the two days of New Year and on the Day of Atonement.

If he had written to the CO, he'd have found out that I was registered as agnostic and hadn't applied for leave. As it was, his letter gave me the idea of telling Daddy that I'd have to stay on camp, but wouldn't have to work on the vital days. I could pray in my bunk. There were several more letters admonishing me not to make any compromises, and finally a greetings telegram to wish me Happy New Year.

In the mess at Melksham the education sergeants were the only National Servicemen, and we were vastly outnumbered by older regulars. Even with the friendly ones I found myself putting on an act of being more like them than I actually was. Their accents were mixed – Scots, Irish, Welsh, north country, Midlands, Cockney, west country – but they all spoke the same language. I'd got used to words like 'bull' and 'shower', and I realized 'bint' was 'girl', though I wasn't at first sure whether it meant 'bit of cunt'. Uneasy with the words, I was uneasy with the men. If the sergeants, flight sergeants and warrant officers who used the mess were all talking a standardized language, wasn't it because they'd all voluntarily put themselves through a deindividualizing process? The camaraderie of the mess was the camaraderie of men who wore uniform because they wanted to be alike. They were too far gone ever to change, but at least I should warn the recruits against having their language put into uniform. I told them it was dangerous to let words have their meaning eroded: they wouldn't notice how their individuality was being undermined. Were they swearing more than when they joined up? I wasn't against it on moral grounds but, if we really wanted to communicate, we ought to protect the words we used. While 'bloody' would never go back to meaning 'By our Lady', 'bugger' still had a definite meaning, and 'fucking' and 'cunt' were pleasant, full-flavoured Anglo-Saxon words for two of the most enjoyable things in life, so wasn't it a mistake to use both words as terms of abuse? I invented a sentence 'Fuck the fucking fucker fucking fuckly', which was meant to show how swearing debased our verbal currency into meaninglessness. I suggested there might even be a connection between not caring how you used the words 'fucking' and 'cunt' and not caring whose cunt you fucked.

I'd taken to going home almost every week-end. Even on a thirty-six-hour pass it was well worth the journey and, no matter how late I arrived on Saturday afternoon, cold chicken and potato salad would always be waiting for me on the corner table in the dining-room. Mummy would come down to keep me company while I ate.

After a week-end away from it, the camp always felt very cold, and when I caught a chill, I couldn't shake it off. I was coughing a lot, and when my chest started to hurt, I reported sick. The medical officer ordered me not to teach, and to report for treatment every day until Saturday. The treatment seemed to make it worse, and by Thursday of the following week it was becoming difficult to breathe. I was so ill in the evening that I telephoned the hotel, and on Friday afternoon the new garage-man arrived in Mummy's car to drive me home. Teddy was at school, so I was put into bed in the old night nursery, with a temperature of 103. When Dr Waistnedge sounded my chest with his stethoscope, I was almost in tears, not with the pain but the pleasure of being looked after. I had congestion of the lungs, he said, and I was lucky to have escaped pneumonia.

John Ludkin, who came down on a forty-eight-hour pass, kept popping in and out of my bedroom. To go out of England we'd need permission from the Air Ministry, but he was sure we'd get it. As soon as I could breathe comfortably, I enjoyed lying in bed, reading Gide, with Nanny looking after me and putting trays of good food on the old bed-table.

'What a good thing they didn't send you to Egypt or somewhere. Who'd have looked after you there?'

A rich visitor who heard I was ill had a basket of nectarines sent up to me. I lay back on the pillow, nibbling them luxuriously, delighted that life could be full of such contrasts. Since Christmas I hadn't written much in my diary, but now there was a lot I wanted to get down about life in camp. On Saturday morning, when Daddy came in, I had my pen in my hand. Shouting at me, he threw it into the waste-paper basket and stormed out, slamming the door. For several days he didn't come to see me, even to say good-night. Knowing that Mummy was pressuring Dr Waistnedge to stretch the illness out as long as possible, I decided the time had come for a confrontation. I said I hadn't wanted to mention my doubts until I was sure this wasn't just a phase that would soon be over. He immediately said he was quite sure it *was* just a phase that would soon be over. I should have confided in him at the outset. Hadn't it occurred to me that he might have been able to help? I said he could help now by being tolerant and trying to understand my point of view. He said that from any point of view it would be foolish to ignore the dangers of repudiating laws and customs that had proved their importance by surviving over the centuries. If I wasn't careful, I'd destroy something of enormous value. On Friday evening he asked me to pray with him. I said I couldn't pray at the moment. He said I should pray for my faith to be restored. I said there was no point in talking to someone if you didn't believe he was there. In the morning he offered to stay away from Shool to say his prayers at home if I'd join him. When I said I couldn't, he went off alone and barely spoke to me at lunch.

On Wednesday Dr Waistnedge said I was well enough to go back to camp, but I should report immediately to the medical officer, asking to be put on light duties. Mummy offered to drive

me back to Melksham. Daddy was friendlier when we said
goodbye. He promised me some money for the holiday in
France, but his parting words were: 'I'm sure you'll succeed only
as a Jew.'

From Calais it took us two days to hitch-hike to Paris. We had
nine hours there before taking the overnight train to Marseilles.
There were two other men in the carriage, but I curled up on the
hard leather seat, using my mack as a pillow. It was a bit like
being guard commander.

The boulevards of Marseilles were infested with carpet-sellers
and old men who clutched at our arms, offering to act as guides.
We saw Negroes, Americans in white suits, gipsy-like hawkers,
English tourists, beggars, sailors, soldiers, policemen, poor-
looking old women in black, rich-looking young girls sauntering
sexily, two men handcuffed together. The bus to Cassis took us
through the outskirts of Marseilles, past attractively misshapen
houses dotted about among the lower foothills of the Alps. The
road wound round the mountain, and on one side we saw massive
crags and green shrubbery. Then, beyond a steep cliff, I had my
first glimpse of the sea whose name I'd heard so often in wartime
news bulletins. The Mediterranean was purple and azure and
silver under the clouds, but persistent rain was falling on
it.

The youth hostel was outside the town. We started to walk,
but just as we were passing a quarry in one of the valleys, a
thunderstorm broke. Seeing some shacks ahead of us, we ran to
the nearest. When we knocked, a woman's voice shouted
'Entrez, entrez'. In the darkish space inside we saw a bed, a
table, a stove, some chairs and a bench, with two young children
and a baby playing on the floor amid the shambles of clothes and
saucepans. A moment later the father ran in through the open
door behind us, drenched, carrying a bag he transferred to his
left hand as he offered us his right. They looked like gipsies, but
he said they were Portuguese. The woman was preparing food,
and when the man invited us to eat with them, John accepted
immediately. I wished he hadn't. First the man and the children
were served. Then came the unmistakable sound of the woman

spitting into the pan to clean it. The man produced a bottle of red wine. She gave us meat, not sitting down to eat with us. We made conversation with him. By the time we finished eating, the rain had stopped. Giving him some money, we started our long climb up to the hostel, enthusing about the scenery until the rain started again.

Finally we found ourselves in a long dark room with a tiled floor, a stone fireplace and gaudy amateurish murals. A low-wattage bulb hung from the beamed ceiling; a half-open door revealed an empty kitchen. Exploring, we found dormitories with clumsy wooden bunks and straw mattresses. We'd been there, gloomily, for about half an hour when a girl came in. Under the shock of blonde hair was a freckled face with wide eyes and vermilioned lips. She'd been a telephonist in Stockport, she told us, but after saving up sixty pounds she'd come to stay for four months in France, living in youth hostels. Her dad hadn't wanted her to. None of the family would ever speak to her again, but she was glad she'd made the break. She talked about her figure and the shape of her legs. She told us about the men she'd met and the meals they'd bought her. She knew it was cadging, she said, living off her looks, but so what? By the end of the day we were both sitting with our arms round her. Marie, she was called.

In the next few days I spent a lot of time wishing John would have the tact to go away and leave her alone with me, knowing that he was wishing I'd go away and leave her alone with him. To be so accessible to both of us was to be accessible to neither. The three of us went to Cassis for our lunch, buying meat, cheese, bread and fruit for supper and breakfast. John cooked our steaks, ruining the delicious-looking meat, but he wasn't used to cooking on a stove like this one, he said.

He teased me for days about eating shellfish. Now that we were on the Riviera, I wasn't going to procrastinate any longer, was I? Marie was going out on her own tomorrow, so why didn't we share a bouillabaisse? 'The bouillabaisse a many-splendoured dish is,' he declaimed. 'Full of noble and delicious fishes.'

'What's that from?'

'Byron wrote it in collaboration with Han Suyin.'

There were crayfish, prawns, mussels and a lot of fish I

couldn't identify in a rich, steamy, aromatic soup. I knew at once there was no danger of our being sick.

On our last day in Cassis, John burnt himself in the sun and felt too ill to cook. I'd never cooked meat, but he said he could tell me exactly what to do. I fried the two steaks, the four eggs and the potatoes, surprised at how easy it was. The results tasted very good, I thought, but as soon as he'd finished eating, he clapped his hand to his mouth and rushed towards the lavatory. He sounded quite weak when he announced that he ought to have an early night.

I was sitting alone by the fire when Marie came in. She'd drunk too much wine, she said, teasing me for being sober. The room was darkening as we sat by the fire talking very seriously, then joking, then being serious again.

'I must have a pee,' she said, standing up unsteadily, and giving me her handbag to hold. I wandered out into the moonlight, listening to the crickets. When she came back, I kissed her hard on the mouth.

'Let's go and sit on my bed,' she whispered.

My heart was bouncing against my ribs as I followed her. First we sat, and then I pulled her gently downwards, clinging close, annoyed to find I was trembling. I couldn't control it, so I tried to conceal it by holding on very tight.

'You don't have to be afraid of me,' she murmured.

'It's not that, I don't know what it is.'

'You're a child,' she said.

We didn't talk for a while. I caressed her arms, her breasts and then hugged her whole body to me, pressing my mouth against the side of her neck. We shifted position. My fingers explored her hips, her stomach, the coarse hair at the bottom of it. Suddenly she was pushing them away.

'You're getting a bit audacious, aren't you?'

'Am I . . . Didn't you mean that?'

'Grief, no! I just wanted to kiss you goodbye. My legs were a bit shaky, and the bed was the first solid thing I could think of.'

I started to get up.

'But look, you don't think I wanted to take you for a ride? You don't think I brought you here to make a fool of you, do you? No, wait. Come back a minute.'

When I moved my body off hers we were both holding each other as close as we could, but again she moved my hand away when it came to the thick pubic hair.

'I wish you weren't going away tomorrow.'

'We want to hitch-hike all along the Riviera to Nice. Why don't you come with us?'

'I don't like your friend.'

If only I'd known that earlier.

'Hush,' she said suddenly. 'Listen.'

She turned her back on me to lean up on one elbow, peering out of the small window. 'I thought I heard Pierre. He knows I'm here alone. At least he thinks I'm here alone. I thought he might have decided to pay me a visit.' Pierre was the boy in charge of the hostel. He slept in a hut at the bottom of the garden. 'It's all right. It isn't him. It's nothing. Where are you going?'

'I'm a bit tired. Good-night, Marie.'

'Look, I wouldn't have let him. I didn't mean that. I just thought he might have fancied a try.'

I tiptoed into the men's dormitory, hoping John was asleep. I didn't write the episode up in my diary till the following evening. I headed it *Incident for a Novel*, describing it all in the third person, showing my contempt for people who lacked courage when a quick decision needed to be followed by quick action. I knew I was trying to warn myself against making the same mistake again. How much longer would it take me to win the success that Skate and Lea had won years ago? I could so easily have offered to stay in Cassis instead of leaving with John.

When the holiday was over, I had less than four months of National Service ahead of me, and never stayed in camp over the week-end unless it was my turn in the rota to be either guard commander or orderly sergeant. I often went to London for the week-end, usually staying with the Ludkins, sometimes with friends from St Paul's and once at the Union Jack Club in Waterloo Road. I was going to the theatre a lot, and to concerts, operas and films, greedy for each opportunity to be lifted out of the grey routine of camp and the routine interruptions of hotel luxury. Daddy was still asking whether I wouldn't like to join him for prayers, and on forty-eight-hour passes I had to sit through the grace after meals without joining in. If I didn't conform to the point of putting on a paper Kappul, I'd be the only bare-headed male in the room, sitting in isolated embarrassment, with the mirror behind my head adding to the chances that I'd be spotted.

The girls at the hotel dances were all prim in comparison with Marie. Most of them liked to dance cheek-to-cheek, and some of them liked kissing, but none of them talked about their legs with the same frankness. Week-end friendships often began in the ballroom, but unless I took Teddy, who was even shyer than I was, Mummy didn't like it when I left the family table to sit with a girl or a group of young people. Sometimes she'd grumble about me so loudly that every word was audible half-way down the room. 'We don't mean anything to him any more. All he does is run up bills at Austin Reed's. He doesn't care what happens to us. Teddy's never been like that.' But if I went back to give her a dance, I could count on her being quieter afterwards.

Daddy, who now wore a corset, was no longer dancing, but Teddy was dancing with her quite a lot, hunching his tall body forward in the style of Mr Kynaston, who was teaching him. Daddy nearly always seemed tired and moody, worried about the shop, the hotel and most of all, my 'drifting'. He was still unfailingly good-tempered when visitors came over to our table, but, like Mummy, he switched the smile off too abruptly afterwards. Instead of radiating goodwill, as they intended to, they both glared around the room to spot inefficiency among the waiters, shouting to Tonks when they did. 'Mrs Freeman's been waiting ten minutes for her sweet.' 'Who's supposed to be looking after Mr and Mrs Kahn?' Torn between wanting them to be better at what they were doing and not wanting them to do it at all, I tried to turn my mind on to automatic pilot; sensing a withdrawal, they'd accuse me of feeling superior and would bring the conversation back to religion, the ground on which they felt most secure. They both took the view that my former orthodoxy implied a commitment I had no right to shirk. Mummy kept saying how arrogant I was to think I knew better than people who'd had so much more experience of life than I had. Daddy kept repeating that if I wasn't careful, I'd find I'd destroyed something very valuable.

One week-end I was approached by a rich Oxford Street furrier, a short, wide-shouldered man, who came regularly to the hotel with his sleek, chic, silver-haired wife, and their frail, dark-haired daughter.

'I'd like you to be my son-in-law,' he said. 'I want you for my Muriel.'

I thought it was a joke. His wife tried to stop him. 'You're embarrassing the boy.'

He took no notice of her. 'I mean it,' he said, and in the morning he repeated the proposal. 'You go ahead and get qualified, and in five years time we'll see if you'll come into the firm.'

I told Nanny about it. She said that as a small boy I'd always been frightened of him. When I went up to say good-night to Grannie in her bedroom, she offered me a cheque for thirty pounds to buy clothes for Cambridge at Austin Reed. I was in the middle of thanking her when she said: 'I don't want you to break away from us. You must go on thinking like we do. Don't be led away and different from us. If you stay being Jewish, it'll bring you luck.'

I could remember the impatience I'd felt for childhood to be over, but ten years after my first trolleybus ride to Hailey I still wasn't free to do what I wanted. I couldn't even recount a conversation I'd had without being told what I should have said. I could talk freely to Nanny, but my diary was the only place I could go into detail about what was going on in my mind, the way I used to when I was praying silently in English, offering up my thoughts. But if the diary was a prayer, who was I worshipping?

I knew that with the religion I'd lost my main incentive to self-improvement and my sense of belonging to a community. 'We don't need a community,' John used to say. 'You and I belong to the future.' I came closest to sharing his optimism when I went with him to the Festival of Britain Exhibition. Within a few hundred yards of the rusty, baroque Victorianism of Waterloo

Station, we were transported into a new world of bright colours and extravagantly modernistic shapes: flights of triangular steps, unpredictable fountains, tall emaciated constructions with sections that revolved or rotated functionlessly, networks of triangular flags at zanily obtuse angles, coloured circles and blocks, and the magnificently futile Skylon towering above the admiring crowds like an idle exclamation mark. Even the waste-paper bins were streamlined.

On the day I was demobbed, Mummy came to collect me from camp in her new green Jaguar, which had the registration MUM 952.

'I love my Mum,' she said. 'Don't you think Mum's beautiful?' And she went on talking about driving. 'I should be half the person I am without a car. Driving is the one thing I can do as well as the next person. As well as any man, and better than some.'

Her passion for ballroom dancing must stem from the same need to feel she was conquering her lameness, which was something I didn't like thinking about and therefore forgot. I should try to be more understanding in future.

A week before the Cambridge term began I had to go with Daddy to visit Aunt Hetty, who was in hospital and still hadn't recovered, after three days, from the shock of regaining consciousness to find that her breasts had been amputated. All the surgeon had told her was that he was going to remove a swelling. She gave us the story in detail. How she hadn't wanted to bother the doctor about it because there wasn't any pain. How she'd fallen over in the street when she was carrying two shopping bags for the Friday night meal. The agony in her wrist and the realization she'd broken it. The gratitude to God for sending an accident to save her life, because otherwise she'd never have gone to hospital. The astonishment when she found out what the surgeon had done. Daddy tried to console her by saying 'It doesn't matter.' He'd brought her a box of grapes. I wondered what it was like for Teddy in her absence at Dunsany Road.

10

Freshman at Cambridge

I'd been too excited by the idea of going to Cambridge for the actuality to be anything but an anti-climax. I was given a small bedroom and a large, airy living-room full of shabby furniture. There were several pages of resolutions in my diary about not working too hard. The danger, I'd thought, was that I'd swing automatically back into the same disciplined efficiency that Mr Fletcher had inspired. But at Dunsany Road there'd been nothing to do in the evenings except work; here, within the radius of a two-minute walk or bicycle ride, there were hundreds of friendly undergraduates. An invitation to coffee after dinner in hall could lead to squandering the evening on conversation. The lectures were all in the mornings, and there was no check on attendances; the only equivalent to homework was one weekly essay. How we used the time was entirely up to us, and sitting about in the office at the education section had been more habit-forming than I'd realized.

John's rooms were in the main court at Trinity, but against this background his affectations were less likeable. One Sunday he invited six of us to a lunch he cooked in his rooms. At the end of the meal he asked us to pay. 'It would have cost you far more in a restaurant, and you couldn't have had real Turkish coffee.'

The food in hall was hardly better than in the sergeants' mess. I'd escaped from family arguments about religion, but I dreamt one night that Daddy had found out about something I'd eaten and decided to disinherit me. On Monday evenings I regularly telephoned home, reversing the charges, and I went back to the Hammersmith routine of writing a weekly letter, timed to arrive by the first post on Saturday morning. Daddy wrote to me fairly often and, as before, Mummy regularly every week. I also went on sending a weekly parcel of dirty laundry to Nanny.

Towards the end of my second term Mummy came up to see me. The college porter knocked at my door to deliver a telephone message: she'd arrived at the Blue Boar Hotel. After spending three more minutes on an essay about *The Duchess of Malfi* I cycled quickly over. In the entrance-hall she bore down on me tearfully. Why had I been such a long time? She'd had to ring twice and she'd been there twenty-five minutes. Why hadn't her booking been confirmed? They said they couldn't put her up for more than a night. Didn't I even care enough about her to make sure of her accommodation?

The receptionist had told me the room had already been confirmed.

In that case why hadn't I gone along in the morning to take in a sixpenny bunch of dandelions, even? I shouldn't have invited her if I hadn't got the time to attend to her properly. She'd go straight back to Bournemouth tomorrow morning. No, she didn't want to move to another hotel. She was sorry she'd come at all. She'd come only because she'd forgotten I was the wrong sort of person.

Luckily, somebody cancelled a single room for Friday and Saturday, and by accepting in silence a good deal of blame, I persuaded her to stay. She kept telling me I could go back and get on with my essay. She didn't want to be a nuisance to me. Finally she agreed to come out for a light meal. Over the omelette she became quite communicative about charity evenings she'd arranged at the hotel, and a victory she'd achieved by arranging for the chairman of the T.B. Seals Sales Committee to speak at a Rotary lunch.

She admired King's College Chapel from the outside but didn't want to go in, and she complained about the under-graduates – how untidy their hair was; how wrong it was for them to be here if they were all taking life so irresponsibly; how noisy they were in restaurants. She wanted to sit as far away from them as possible. In the Whim I spilt a glass of water over the table. She stood up, shouting 'Miss' to the waitress, who brought a cloth and helped to dab at the drops on her skirt. Three men from Trinity Hall were sitting at the table behind, and I was so embarrassed I didn't even apologize until she was sitting down again.

'I don't know how it happened,' I said quietly.

'I don't know either, but I felt it all right.'

One evening six of us were walking past King's, wearing gowns, as we had to after dark. We'd been drinking Merrydown cider. Giles Bedford, a tall, good-looking, ex-public-school boy, announced that he needed a pee and was going to use a telephone box. We watched, laughing. He came out with his flies undone and his cock hanging loose. He wrapped his gown around himself like a dressing-gown, and, all the way down King's Parade, drew it open at each bunch of passing undergraduates. At the corner of Trinity Lane he said: 'Think I need a bit of sex. Anyone coming? I'll pay.' I didn't know whether he was joking or whether he knew a brothel. The others, taking him seriously, one by one said no. I was the last to answer. There was nothing I wanted more than to lose my virginity, but there was the risk of VD, and besides, I might make a fool of myself by not knowing how to behave with the girls or what to say to the Madam.

'What about you, Ronnie?'

I said no, and regretted it as soon as he was out of sight.

My closest friendship was with Larry Best, a tall, spectacled boy from Malvern, who'd come up without doing National Service. He was no more self-confident than I was. 'I wish I were like you or Eccles,' he said. 'But I'm only a child. No one ever listens to me or quotes my opinions to other people.' Softened immediately, I'd reassure him with an invented instance of when I'd quoted his opinion.

'And how was it taken?'

He wrote sonnets in which he intoxicated himself with his own rhythms, alliterations and assonances, though he did write one Apollinairish line that stuck in my memory:

A tall, cool girl, lit by a music hand.

He was also working on a novel about schoolboy love. Called *The Years of Colour*, it was mainly about an affair he'd had at Malvern. 'Homosensuousness' was his word for kissing and touching. Mutual masturbation was OK, but he didn't believe in going the whole hog into buggery. His sonnets were full of lips, and bronzed Panic bodies. He was unhappily in love with a boy called Derek, who came to supervisions with me. 'Oh, if only I were beautiful! If I had a thinner face and interesting bones!' He read me extracts from his diary. 'I could never kiss Jane again. All my love is for Derek and possibly for other beautiful males.' When he came to stay at the hotel, he described Mummy in the diary as 'a beautiful Jewess'.

Grannie had bought Uncle Phil a farm in Cornwall, and when an invitation arrived from him to help for a week on the hay-harvest, bringing a friend with me, Larry was the one I asked. On the long drive to Launceston he was more responsive than I was to scenery. I preferred the sprawling tors and tussocky fields to the characterless proliferation of hotels in Bournemouth, but I couldn't join in his enthusiastic commentary on the landscapes that streaked past as he turned from one car-window to another. I was more interested in the outstanding white pyramid of a china-clay works.

I didn't like the smells on the farm, especially in the pigsties. Warm, breezeless air, animality and shit – the three seemed inseparable. But haymaking was different. The smell reminded me of mown grass when I'd had my own garden, but now I wasn't playing. Nothing could be more real than forking hay rhythmically on to a stack. Larry's and my forkfuls were shamingly small in comparison with Jack's, Frank's and Robin's, but it was real work. On the parade-ground my mind had protested impotently against the movements my body had to make; here everything was in harmony – the smell of hay, the bright sunlight, the birdsong, the heat, the muscular effort, the consciousness of a gradually accumulating thirst that would soon be slaked with cider.

After breakfast on the third day we saw two pigs copulating in the distance, and it gave me an erection. 'It's not the shape of their bottoms that's exciting,' Larry said, consolingly, 'only the colour. And if you weren't sex-starved, it wouldn't affect you. I feel quite sorry for you heteros with only two colleges of girls for all those boys.'

Of the three labourers on the farm, only Jack and Frank were called 'workmen'. Strong, gnarled, weather-beaten men, they lived with their families on the edge of Uncle Phil's land. After presenting themselves early each morning in the farmhouse kitchen for him to brief them, they worked unsupervised till late in the evening. Robin, who was nineteen, lived in the farmhouse. He was going to be married in October. At first he was untalkative, but one evening, when Larry and I went out with him to shut up the chickens, he told us the names of all the fields on the farm. 'This un's Bales Meadow.' He talked about the local dialect, with its *we'm* and *us'm*, and explained words like 'hog' (a first-year lamb), '*entyre*' (stallion) and '*eaver*' (thin, bodiless hay). "Eaver. I donno how to spell it, so it's no use askin' me. It's thin grass. It's not thick. Eaver's what farmers around 'ere call it.'

It was odd to see East Cliff Court crockery and cutlery on the rough kitchen table, but after a long day's work in the fields we tremendously enjoyed the food that was served up by Mary, the housekeeper. She had a birdlike little body, with almost no neck, and a broad, round, flat face like a soft doll's. Her hair was straight and greyish blonde. She treated us with the same quiet concern as the sheepdog. 'And didn't they speak to you, eh?'

Since the fatigue week at Bridgnorth I'd forgotten what it was like to be exhausted from physical labour, and I was ashamed of the blisters on my hands. Uncle Phil's were already hardened by three years of farming. I couldn't imagine how he'd picked up the knowledge he needed to begin with. Sometimes he asked advice from Jack and Frank, who'd farmed all their lives, but mostly he seemed to be in control, able to command their respect and to get on with the neighbouring farmers. It was strange to see his fat body chasing chickens, but he looked more at home here than at the hotel. We sat around the table all evening, with the sky darkening outside the low, square, uncurtained window. The conversation was interspersed with long bouts of brooding silence. Mary talked in bursts, reverting to her newspapers in between. Phil read a bit, spending more of the time doodling and playing with his cigarettes, building them

up into a triangular pile inside his silver cigarette case, letting
them tumble back, and starting all over again. He also doodled
with his pencil on his newspaper, filling in all the spaces inside
the letters of the headlines, and then doodling on the wooden
table. At his end, every hole in the wood was coated with pencil
lead.

Country life had sharpened his powers of observation, he
claimed. From watching for weather signs and for what
neighbouring farmers were doing with their fields, he'd learned
to look at people more carefully. In big towns nobody had time
to be interested in other people. Certainly I felt more interested
in him than I had before. I'd taken him for granted – a fat uncle;
now I was beginning to know him, a man who'd been hurt. I
could talk more freely with him than with Daddy, partly
because he'd never liked the religion, partly because he seemed
genuinely interested in what was going on inside my head,
without wanting to pressure me into being more like him,
though obviously, as he'd never had a son, he'd have liked to
leave his mark on someone. He said the farm had brought him a
feeling of freedom. I could come whenever I wanted to, and stay
as long as I liked. Orthodox Jews were always narrow-minded.
The family had forced him to divorce his wife, just because she
wasn't Jewish, and if he married out of the faith again, it would
kill Grannie. Literally. If he married a Jewish girl, the interest
she'd take in the kids might keep her alive for another ten years,
but he'd never found a Jewish girl, and he wasn't really the type
to look, though she still nagged him to go down for week-ends in
the hope that he might meet someone in the ballroom. It was
bad enough having to interrupt harvesting to go there for the
festivals. Even at the farm he couldn't feel completely free,
because East Cliff Court Ltd had a mortgage on it, and he was
undercapitalized because Mummy and Daddy were keeping
Grannie short of money. She'd have liked to give him much
more, but they didn't understand anything about the farm except
the value of its produce to their business. 'I'm not in it for the
money, but tell me, Ron, honestly, which do you think has more
value to the world – a farm that breeds livestock or a Jewish hotel?'

He wanted to tell me about his early life. After leaving school
he'd been apprenticed to a dentist, travelled in gowns, won a

scholarship to the Bournemouth School of Music and studied
the cello for three years. He'd played in a dance band and
worked as a motor mechanic until Grannie bought him the
garage, but it wasn't till three years ago that he'd found
something he could care about. The important thing was to find
out what you really wanted to do and then have a good shot at
doing it. If I still wanted to write when I finished at Cambridge, I
could come and live rent free at the farm. In the meantime he
gave me two pounds for my week's work, and Larry got the
same.

11

Too Many Deaths

'I'm looking forward to meeting Ronnie the man,' Aunt Val had written. Uncle Dan couldn't come on this visit, but she was bringing Marian. I was looking forward to seeing Aunt Val again, though I hadn't thought about her much on the farm, where the immediate experience had, for once, crowded out the daydreams.

In retrospect I was worried about Uncle Phil's relationship with Mary. At the time, I'd felt I was understanding him, but I still didn't know for sure whether he slept with her. She had her own bedroom, but he certainly didn't sleep with anybody else, and it seemed very unfair that ever since his divorce he'd been deprived of the animal pleasure that had been at Uncle Dan's disposal ever since he'd refused to marry Mummy and married Aunt Val instead. Having seen no photographs of the aunt that Uncle Phil had wanted to bring into the family, I pictured a cuddly blonde crooner with a slightly Midland accent, hair like Betty Grable's, lips like Hedy Lamarr's and breasts like Rita Hayworth's.

Both in bed at night and at the bureau in the Oak Room, when I was supposed to be working, I spent a lot of time making mental composites of beautiful women I'd never seen in the flesh, trying to imagine what it would be like to make love to them. But next week, when Aunt Valerie arrived, at least there'd be one beautiful woman I could touch. I could dance with her and kiss her good-night every night. I remembered her velvety voice more clearly than her face or her body, which were mixed up in my memory with colour photographs of her and Marian in bikinis. Marian's plump young body made Aunt

Valerie's look even shapelier, and the smile was partly a smile of superiority.

What took me by surprise, after she'd arrived, was the way other men were magnetized, almost as if something in her eyes were signalling that her husband was a long way away. When Teddy and I took her and Marian down to the beach, a ginger-haired man who was sunbathing behind us kept staring at her, stroking his moustache and rubbing his hairy chest as if to send invisible sparks flying to her through the warm air. She glanced at him a couple of times, pleased with herself.

According to Aunt Hetty, Uncle Dan would never have had the courage to propose if Aunt Valerie hadn't made it easy for him. As a young girl, when she still had both eyes, she was showing him some photographs of herself, hoping he'd ask to keep one. When he didn't, she dropped them on the floor. As he stooped to pick them up, she said: 'Don't bother. I don't really want them.'

Dancing with her was very nice. She pressed her body towards mine just as much as I pressed mine towards hers. When I was kissing her good-night, I found myself holding her the same way I had on the dance floor. 'That's nice,' she said, and when I kissed her on the mouth, 'Mmmm. Ronnie the man.' I went on kissing her. Tasting her tongue. Breathing her scent. My hand cupping her springy curls. When she spoke, the sound might have come from inside my own head.

'Last night I nearly came to your room.'

'Why didn't you?'

'I wasn't sure whether you'd be pleased.'

'Come tonight. Come now.'

Because the hotel was full, I was once again sleeping in the housekeeper's office. In the narrow space between the wall and the edge of the bed, our bodies kept touching as we took our clothes off. 'Ronnie the man,' she said. 'Dear, you have done this before?' I hesitated and admitted I hadn't. 'Oh well,' she said. 'Never mind.'

After all my dry experiments, I was surprised by the moisture inside her, and I hadn't expected her to move so much. She taught me to put my hands on her waist, but the harder I tried to hold her still, the more the soft, sucking flesh seemed to move.

'Nearly,' I said, thinking she was impatient for the climax to come as quickly as possible. 'I won't be a minute.' Afterwards I could tell that she wouldn't have minded starting all over again, but I didn't want to appear greedy. I hadn't understood what I'd read about the gamekeeper's heroic efforts to keep going inside Lady Chatterley. When she'd put her clothes on, her parting words were: 'Dear, now I'll always have you inside me.' I hoped she wasn't going to meet anyone in the corridor.

All I wrote in my diary the next day was: 'Sex is really very trivial. It's foolish to pay much attention to it. Love is what counts. Sex is a condiment to it. To be drugged by it is like being addicted to eating pepper. I don't like pepper.'

I didn't see her at breakfast. When she came into the Oak Room, I was at my bureau, with my back towards the door. I stood up, but didn't look her in the eye. We asked each other how we were and both said we were all right. As soon as the door had closed behind her, I knew that the habit of secretiveness had blighted an important opportunity. It didn't matter that we were never going to make love again; what mattered was that there could have been a sort of togetherness. Couldn't we have had a frank conversation? Why hadn't I looked her in the eye? In all the fantasies I'd had about losing my virginity, making love to a beautiful woman was the beginning of a long partnership, and after looking forward for so long to that moment, I'd felt entitled to the desperate step I'd taken, but instead of solving the problem of partnership, which had dogged me ever since the first chemistry classes, I'd made things still worse for myself. Surely, if Skate and Lea found it easy to get on with girls, it was because they got on with each other: they knew how to relax with a partner. Once I'd nearly had a partnership with Dave, but it had turned into enmity, and if I couldn't have a relaxed conversation now with such a friendly woman, how would I ever be able to talk frankly to the next woman who said 'Dear, have you done this before?' I'd lumbered myself with yet another secret, a secret I'd want to destroy, like the letters Mummy and Daddy tore up, but it would always lurk there shamefully inside the waste-paper basket of my consciousness. This was it. This was the moment I'd looked forward to so much. Yes, I'd finally lost my virginity to a beautiful woman. But why did the beautiful woman have to be a one-eyed aunt? Whoever would have expected a Barmitzvah boy who read two *Sedras* to lurch into manhood like this? Half the imaginary audience was booing, and the other half was clapping derisively.

Two nights later I had a dream which I recorded in detail. I was in love with a queen, tall and beautiful, with a soft, young, clear-cut face and hair swept upwards into a wavy confusion. She wasn't yet crowned in the first part of the dream. She loved me, but our love was unconsummated. After the coronation the atmosphere changed into stale debauchery. Ennui and corruption. She's in bed, I'm one of three men in the room with her. Suddenly in a bored, passionless voice, almost peevishly, she beckons me over. 'You may as well slip in for half an hour.'

I comply and we copulate. Somehow we are both on the floor. The men go on talking, not noticing. I can see myself as if I were someone else. Then the others start watching.

'The Queen is wrestling with the Earl of Earlham,' says one.

'The Earl?' The other sounds as though he's about to confiscate my title as punishment.

'Thank you, stranger,' I say. 'That's my title.'

The conversation has not interrupted the copulation, but no sensation accompanies it. Bored with it now, and aware that I'm dreaming, I wake up.

The next day I was in the Oak Room, trying to work, when Mummy burst into the room, sobbing, handkerchief in hand. I stood up miserably, not knowing what to say in self-defence.

'We've had bad news,' she gulped. 'Dad's got to go up to London. Dave's gone.'

The sense of relief that flooded over my brain made it slow to take in what she meant. How could Dave be dead? Anyway, what mattered was that my secret was still undiscovered.

I went up with her to the flat. Daddy was in his dressing-room, half-crying as he fumbled in the wardrobe for his black suit. She put her arm around his shoulder, weeping in sympathy. 'Oh, Jack!' It was the first sign of affection between them I could remember seeing. Grannie came in. 'It's unbelievable,' she said. 'Shockin'. Shockin'.'

Aunt Valerie and Marian were going to travel up with Daddy on the *Bournemouth Belle* to be with Aunt Hetty. Apparently Dave had been knocked off his bike by a lorry. We had a hurried tea together before Mummy drove the three of them to the station. Most of the time I avoided Aunt Valerie's eye.

Mummy, Teddy and I went up for the funeral. The coffin was in the front room. A lot of people were standing about awkwardly, as if they thought there was something they ought to be doing. Relations were there who hadn't been on speaking terms with the Hatters for years. Quarrels were forgotten, and the air was thick with compassionate goodwill. Revd Lazarus was talking in his loud, shaky voice about the mysteriousness of God's ways. Aunt Hetty was in an armchair with Rosalie holding on to her, and Daddy at her side, talking not so much to her as for her. 'Poor Hetty! What a terrible tragedy! I suppose it had to be. What a brilliant future he might have had!'

I kissed her damp cheek. She wasn't hysterical or wailing but talking non-stop in a low, wronged, urgent voice. 'Oh, why did they have to take my Dave away from me? Haven't I suffered enough? Is that Ronnie? Go back to your religion, Ronnie. Pray for Dave. Is that Teddy? Teddy loved Dave. He used to go up every evening and talk to him before he went to bed. They had so much in common. Oh, they don't need to say prayers for him. He's in heaven. He was an angel, so good and pure. He was just given to me for a short time, and now they've taken him away. I don't want to go on living. They tell me he'd have wanted me to, but there's nothing left for me now. What I have got to live for? Haven't I suffered enough? I don't want to go on. You know how he used to work, Ronnie. He had a paper in the accountancy exam marked one hundred per cent. Did they tell you? And look at this letter of Clive's. He says he'll try to be much better than he is, just to be one tenth as good a person as Dave was, but he knows he'll never do it. Pray for him. And don't tell Grannie about it. She loved Dave and it would break her heart. I don't say there's no God in Heaven, but couldn't He have left me my Dave? I made them take the lid off the coffin to see his face. It was so peaceful, except his eyes were red, and they never used to be. Oh, he was a saint. Everybody loved him.'

Aunt Valerie came up behind her to put a hand on her shoulder.

'You've saved my life, Val. If it hadn't been for you, I'd have gone with Dave. I would, really.'

'Now *dear*,' said Aunt Valerie, 'you've got to live. You know that. You're a wonderful person, and you've still got Ben and Barry and Rosalie. What about them? They still need you.'

'I'm not interested in them. But you're coming to live over here, aren't you? You promised.'

I looked at Aunt Valerie, and the real eye winked. But she knew how to handle Aunt Hetty, who had hysterics when they took the coffin out. Only the men went to the funeral. Uncle Ben and Barry travelled in the Rolls-Royce hearse. Daddy, Revd Lazarus, Teddy and I in the Rolls-Royce behind it. I wondered whether Dave had ever travelled in a Rolls-Royce when he was alive.

Revd Lazarus was enjoying himself. 'I can tell you this, Jack. In all my experience I never came across a better type. And that he should be taken, when so many worthless young men carry on! He was a truly lovely boy. Such a tragedy, a terrible tragedy! It had to be, but we can't expect to understand. And how's Mrs Morris been keeping? I wish Fanny and I could come to Bournemouth for the New Year.'

He was eager for all the details Daddy could provide about the accident. On Monday Dave had his last singing lesson. Hetty had asked him not to go on his bike because the roads were slippery, but he would have been late if he'd walked. Yes, said Revd Lazarus, so much better to be a little late in this world than early in the next. No, said Daddy, it hadn't happened till he was on his way home. When he stopped at some traffic lights, a bus pulled up on his right. A shooting-brake stopped on the other side, signalling that it wanted to turn right. When the lights went green, the driver cut in ahead of the traffic from the opposite direction. He cleared the bus, but he hadn't seen Dave. He didn't seem to be badly hurt. He was put into a taxi, but, not wanting Aunt Hetty to be worried, he asked to be taken home, not to a hospital. Later, after being taken to Hammersmith Hospital for an X-ray, he'd been told he'd broken his collar-bone. They bandaged it, telling him to come back tomorrow for it to be put into a plaster cast. At home he joked about it; with a bit of luck he might get his National Service deferred for another six months. But during the night he was in so much pain he couldn't lie down. The family doctor came over and gave him a sleeping tablet. Early in the morning he woke up in great pain. At seven o'clock Uncle Ben rang for an ambulance, only to be told that they couldn't send one without permission from the hospital. It arrived at ten past eight, but it was nine o'clock before a doctor examined him. By then he was breathing with great difficulty and his pulse was weak. The lung specialist saw there had been a lot of internal bleeding, and said it might be necessary to operate. He was given permission to go ahead, but a splinter from the collar-bone had perforated Dave's chest wall, and he died about half-past twelve of a haemorrhage.

Daddy was almost in tears by the time he came to talk about the inquest. The solicitor had defied the coroner, continuing with his statement after being told to sit down. He said that Dave's life could have been saved if his chest had been X-rayed when he was first taken to the hospital. Another hearing had been arranged for 1 September.

I couldn't help glancing at the hearse ahead as if a different turn in the story Daddy was telling could bring Dave back to life. As the cars drove slowly onwards, I watched the expressions on both men's faces. Daddy was deeply upset, but completely deceived by Revd Lazarus's display of emotion. If birth, copulation and death were the three elemental realities, circumcisions, weddings and funerals were the three occasions that made believers turn to ceremony and ministers of religion, not to reveal reality but to dress it up. For Daddy and Aunt Hetty, Dave's death was tolerable only if it belonged to a meaningful pattern whose meaning eluded them. It must be assumed that God had his reasons for not making the driver of the shooting-brake see Dave in time, not stopping the collar-bone from splintering and not putting someone a bit more competent on duty at the casualty ward. Could Revd Lazarus genuinely believe that? It was conceivable, perhaps that God was punishing Dave for some sin I didn't know about, but how could he have done anything worse than I had? In biblical times, people were stoned to death just for ordinary adultery.

Daddy was telling Revd Lazarus about Aunt Hetty. For two days she'd been in bed, drugged, delirious, refusing to eat. No one could do anything with her except Valerie. Daddy hadn't wanted the coffin to be brought from the mortuary to the house, but Aunt Hetty had insisted. He shouldn't have let them unscrew the lid for her, he said. She'd spent the rest of the morning stroking the coffin and talking to Dave.

When we arrived at the cemetery the coffin was carried into the hall for the funeral service, which was conducted by Revd Lazarus. They hadn't wanted Revd Kleinmann. The coffin was wheeled out of the hall on a trolley. A small man dressed in a top hat, black bow-tie, black jacket and striped trousers was telling everyone what to do. 'Will you all stand behind the coffin? Leave your books here.' Asked to be one of the bearers, I had to walk behind Barry as we carried the coffin from the trolley to the freshly dug grave. With the weight pressing down on my shoulder, I felt an irresistible impulse, connected somehow with the loud chirruping of the crickets, to tap on the bottom of the coffin in case Dave could hear. Afterwards I wished I hadn't done it. I was thinking about his face (freckled), his hair (always carefully brylcreemed and neatly brushed diagonally back) and the feel of the skin I had so often tickled when he was still my friend. I felt guilty because I was only pretending to be sorry he was dead. I was no more responsible for his death than for the deaths of my prep school headmasters, but I'd probably have sentenced him to death at the moment when Mummy came bursting into the Oak Room if I'd had to answer the exam question: 'Your mother is in tears EITHER because she has discovered your secret OR because your cousin has been killed. Give reasons for your choice.' I had reasons. He'd turned into a deadly enemy whose smooth hypocrisy deceived everyone in the family. He had betrayed me; I hadn't betrayed him. I'd never told them about him. But hadn't I betrayed them? All of them. Mummy and Daddy, Aunt Valerie, Uncle Dan. I'd put horns on the bald head of an uncle with a strong resemblance to my father, an uncle who'd turned down the chance of marrying my mother, and therefore deserved to be punished. Aunt Hetty should never have told me, and she deserved to be punished, but not quite so severely.

We lowered the coffin on to two planks spanning the narrow grave, while the ropes were looped around the big wooden lozenge. As it was moving into the earth, I heard Uncle Ben murmuring: 'Goodbye Dave. My poor boy.' The ropes were jerked roughly free, and the earth was piled in. The men all filed past Uncle Ben and Barry, shaking hands and saying: 'I wish you long life.'

A man I didn't know said 'That's that', and asked me whether he could smoke. Overhearing, the small man in the top hat said he couldn't until he left the grounds. After that he could do as he pleased. In the car with us on the way back to Dunsany Road there was a very wrinkled old man with dusty skin. He said he'd been to Daddy's father's funeral.

In the front room Aunt Hetty was still talking in her quiet, reasonable, wronged voice. 'They've taken him such a long way away. It's a day's ride if you want to visit him.'

'Dear,' said Aunt Valerie, 'we'll go together.'

Without quite forbidding me to dance with Berna, Daddy made his disapproval clear. 'You do realize that girl isn't Jewish?' Mr and Mrs Spiegelberg had brought her to look after their children, but she didn't wear a nanny's uniform, and they let her come down to the ballroom with them. She had short, fragrant, light brown hair, dreamy green eyes and a lilting Irish accent that made me think of the girls in *Dubliners*. She used words like 'choosed', but everything she said about her life in London had the quality of fiction. 'Berna has what amounts to a genius', I wrote in my diary, 'for treading delicately and attractively between half truths, so nimbly that I'm at once left uncertain and satisfied. And when too much truth obstreperously reveals itself, she'll confidently bend the stem of what she's said to perfume the new fact with the flower. She responds to personal questions with incredible protestations either of innocence or of affection for me, both answerable only with a kiss.' I desperately wanted to believe she was telling the truth about not having a boyfriend in London, but what about all that dancing she'd done? Oh, she always went out in a foursome. Otherwise she only had a pen-pal in Canada, and she didn't want to meet him. Not ever.

It wouldn't have occurred to me that I could invade the night-time privacy of the Jewish girls I danced with, however closely we'd held each other, but Berna was different, and she was sleeping in a single room overlooking the tennis-court. I'd often climbed on to the flat roof outside the window to retrieve tennis-balls from the gutter. The main danger was the night porter. Usually he started his round of shoe-cleaning at about one o'clock, so if I waited until I heard him outside my door, and then allowed five minutes or so for him to finish the other shoes in the corridor, I could get to the door of the fire-escape without being seen, and if I wore my tennis-shoes, no one would hear my footsteps on the iron. It would be all right as long as nobody happened to be awake and looking out towards the tennis-court.

Her window was open, and I climbed in without waking her. Her face was turned towards the wall. Bending over her, I thought for a moment that I was in the wrong bedroom, that it was another woman in the bed, who'd wake up and scream. But the fragrant hair reassured me. I kissed her ear.

'Oh, Ron, you did give me a start.' Scarcely seeming startled at all. 'I wasn't expecting you.'

Kissing her on the mouth, I felt her hands behind my neck, pulling me closer. Soon I was lying on top of her, and enjoying it so much I could hardly bear to let go for long enough to take my clothes off. When I finally did wrench myself away, I was so impatient to be holding her again, I got into bed without taking my pants off. We kissed and cuddled and I thought I'd never been so happy. I told her she had lovely, fresh, creamy skin and I adored the feel of her body.

'I haven't got very much here,' she said, touching her breasts.

'Never mind. You've got just the right amount here,' I answered, caressing her thighs and fumbling to get my pants off.

'Oh no, Ron, don't. Something terrible might happen.'

We went on kissing, cuddling, caressing each other, and it didn't seem to matter all that much if we couldn't make love properly. If she hadn't got whatever contraceptive equipment Aunt Valerie had, it was all the more likely to be true that she hadn't got a boy-friend in London. Even if I'd had a French letter in my possession, it would have been unromantic to climb through her window with it all ready in my pocket. All the same, it was a nuisance that I still had my pants on. But on the following evening, when I climbed in through the window with every intention of taking them off, I was again in too much of a hurry to get into bed with her. And the next day she went back to London.

My second year at Cambridge was equally full of abortive relationships with girls and unfulfilling friendships with boys who seemed to have something I lacked but couldn't acquire by chatting with them about intimate relationships. In conversation with Larry I was constantly amazed by the freedom he enjoyed from the shame that was clogging my own responses to physical needs. Was it really all as simple and wholesome as he made it seem, or did it get simplified and ennobled as he described it? Sometimes I looked down on him for apparently being incapable of doing, feeling, or saying anything he wouldn't afterwards be able to talk about; but he was still so likeable that I disliked myself for looking down on him. Who was I, with all my secrets, to feel superior?

He was constantly in need of reassurance. 'You do think I'm a worthwhile person, don't you?' 'I know you don't think much of my poetry, but you do think I've got it in me to write worthwhile stuff one day, don't you?' He was childish, yes, but Cocteau said the artist was the man who'd kept the child inside himself alive. Or was that what was wrong with Cocteau? Larry admired him enormously, but Larry's opinions about literature were annoying. He said *The Waves* was the greatest novel of the century. James Joyce was 'too sordid and too all-inclusive to be significant'. His own literary ambitions were considerable, but his greatest ambition in life was to kiss Derek.

Learning to apply stringent standards of criticism to literature, I wanted to be equally critical of my friends and myself. Determined to reject everything that wasn't 'worthwhile', I was afraid of being left with nothing. It had been ridiculous to expect Cambridge to lift me, like a magic carpet, above the values, habits and people that seemed middle class and mediocre. It had been easy enough to disapprove of Mummy's disapproval of the leisurely, coffee-drinking conversations, but could I be sure that

what we said in them was less mediocre or less middle class than
her attitudes? Reviewing Aldous Huxley's *The Devils of Loudun*
for a literary magazine called *Mandrake*, I felt very much under
attack when I read his description of the trivialities that occupied
most minds for most of the time: 'a bobbing scum of
miscellaneous memories, notions, and imaginings – childhood
recollections of one's grandmother's Skye terrier, the French
name for henbane, a white Knightish scheme for. . . .' In fact
his examples of triviality sounded rather less trivial than most of
our sprawling conversations about love affairs and the lack of
love affairs, about the current production at the ADC, the
current film at the Rex or the Regal, the current issues of *Granta*
and *Varsity*, about lectures and undergraduate actresses. But
Huxley's interest in diabolical possession seemed to have
developed out of a long-standing revulsion for the 'unregenerate'
self that fed on this scummy consciousness. 'A great man differs
from ordinary men in being, as it were, possessed by more than
human spirits,' he'd written, going on to describe the meta-
phorical 'devils' in Clemenceau. His new book explained the
possession of the Loudun nuns as a 'downward escape' from the
self, parallel to the upward escape of 'dying to self', as saints and
mystics had. Unvarying in its essence, the human mind was
perpetually faced with the alternatives of unregeneracy and
enlightenment, self-assertion and self-transcendence. Either you
remained one of the 'ordinary, nice, unregenerate people' who
were so very much alike, or you tried to achieve 'one-
pointedness of being' by striving towards communion with the
'divine ground' in the soul. Most of the book was about the
nature of the self that he condemned and about escape routes
that led downwards.

I could see that it was just as much of a simplification to
pretend that the escape routes were outside the self as it was to
make ego, super ego and id sound like three separate entities;
but the phrase 'one-pointedness of being' seemed apt: something
sharp inside my brain could either become a strong tool or a
dangerous weapon. I wanted to sharpen it, but then it would
stab at everything I disapproved of, including myself. By
January I'd been thinking seriously of leaving Cambridge
without a degree, but I wouldn't succeed better anywhere else

when I didn't even know what sort of success I wanted. I couldn't bear the idea of just being ordinary, nice and unregenerate, but I felt like the green shell round a conker, with clumsy blunt spikes pointing in all directions. How could I transcend mediocrity without a transcendental faith?

Daddy never gave up hope that I'd return to my religion, and when I wouldn't go to London with him for Dave's tombstone setting, his reaction was: 'You might do well to pay less attention to your principles.' He'd stopped standing for re-election as president of the synagogue, and his successor, Henry Gideon, ruled that the hotel must pay compensation for the business it was taking away from the synagogue by holding morning services in the ballroom during Passover. Daddy was furious, but advised Mummy not to refuse payment: Mr Gideon had threatened to cut off the supply of Passover milk.

In the summer I'd thought of going back to the farm for at least a week in every vac, but when it came to the point, I didn't want to, though I could have talked to Uncle Phil more openly than with Daddy, Mummy or Teddy. The conversations I most enjoyed were with Nanny, whose function had shifted to looking after all of us generally, and in particular Grannie, who'd had a stroke and could no longer control her bladder. There was a new, unpleasant smell in her room, mixing with the scent of Wintergreen and the eau-de-Cologne Nanny sprayed everywhere.

Nanny had been with us for twenty years, and it was unthinkable she should ever leave. If I recorded Daddy's remarks in my diary to prove how unrealistic he was, and Mummy's to show how her philosophy of altruism masked an incapacity for empathizing, the quotations from Nanny showed how much she was having to put up with. 'Hazel says to me: "I don't know how you can stand there washing and ironing on a Sunday. Why don't you go to church?" And I say to her: "I'm quite happy as I am. I can listen to the service on the wireless, and I've got to get this work done sometime." But she's a Baptist, and she says there's enough things in the world without worldly things. She lives a good life, mind, doing work for the church and that sort of thing, but she wouldn't sit with you if you were ill. Grannie is a bit trying, though. With the dressmaker the

other day she had the new dress pinned round her, and I was
going to take out the pins, and she said: "You go away. You
don't know anything." But she couldn't sit down with her pins
in her, and she had to let me take them out. I never go against
her, though. If she gets too bad, I just stop talking for a bit, and
that's the worst punishment for her. It's the same with your
mother. I'd do anything to keep the peace.'

At mealtimes now Grannie still sat at the head of the table,
with Mummy on her left, but the balance of power had shifted,
and it was largely her fear of being told off that made Grannie so
silent. In June, on the day Mummy was due to leave for a
fortnight at a health farm near Bristol, Grannie asked at lunch:
'Where are you going?' Mummy explained again, her patience
pulled taut. When Nanny took Grannie's tea up on a tray, she
said: 'I'm glad it's not you that's going.' At about 4.45 she
wanted to get up. Nanny tried to persuade her to stay in bed for
a bit longer. She'd have nothing to do till dinner-time. She
insisted, and Nanny began helping her to dress. Sitting at the
dressing-table in her underclothes, she cried out with pain. Her
chest was hurting. Suddenly the right side of her body seized up
with paralysis. Almost taking her full weight, Nanny helped her
from the stool to the wicker chair and from that to the armchair.
She asked for a brandy, but instead Nanny gave her one of the
powders Dr Waistnedge had left for the emergency of a heart
attack. She was gasping 'Don't leave me' and clinging to Nanny
like a desperate child.

'I'm only going to the phone,' Nanny said.

It was on the bedside table. First she tried to ring the doctor
and then rang me in the Oak Room. I found Grannie in the
armchair, leaning forward and over to the right, choking and
sickly spluttering into a handkerchief. 'Gran's very bad,' Nanny
said, with a hard strain in her voice. 'See if you can get the
doctor.'

I picked up the receiver from the bed and jiggled the silver
button but got no reply.

'I'll go down to the office,' I said.

'Come back quickly,' said Nanny as I closed the door on the
sick sound of choking.

Leaning over the counter of the reception, I talked over the

switchboard telephone to Dr Waistnedge's secretary. He was
due back in the surgery any minute, and she'd send him as soon
as he arrived. Dr Winner, his partner, was out too. I started
ringing round all the nearby doctors listed on the telephone pad,
but I hadn't found one in when Nanny rang down again from
Grannie's room. She said something I couldn't catch. 'Get any
doctor. It's urgent,' I told Miss Black, and rushed back to the
bedroom.

She was lying back in the armchair, her head on a pillow and
her eyes closed. Her body was slumped over to the right, and her
breathing was incredibly noisy. Each breath was a moaning
grunt, loud as a shout, and inhuman, as if some merciless
machine had taken possession of her. It was pumping her lungs
without permission and making the rough noise out of her
mouth.

'She's going,' Nanny said.

I wanted the noise to stop, but I was panic-stricken to realize
we were both standing there not doing anything to save her.

'Could we give her brandy?'

'No. Not for the heart.'

It seemed ridiculous that when so many Bournemouth
doctors spent so much time with patients who weren't even ill,
we couldn't get one now we needed him. I hadn't expected
dying to be like this. I'd pictured a family grouped round a bed,
a face ennobled with suffering, eyes red with weeping, a sad,
brave, deathbed voice, and memorable last words. Instead there
was this undignified mess of once-loved flesh in the armchair
and this raucous, impersonal grunting, as if non-existence were
battering its way into her body. We waited for it to enter.

We telephoned Daddy at the shop. 'Come straight away.'
And we went on waiting. Nanny talked in a normal voice about
death. 'It's my third. There was my mother, then Mrs Tanchan
and now this. It's the first time for you, isn't it? I could tell she
was going from the greyness in the fingernails and the eyes. It's
just like Mrs Tanchan. She was breathing this way, and I had to
hold her in a chair for half an hour. I do wish your mother hadn't
gone away though.'

'The hands are still warm,' I said, aware we were talking as if
the parts of her body were things that didn't belong to her. The

hand was more tepid than warm, with a stiffness of movement that made it seem clammy, though it was quite dry and not really stiff. But lifeless. And her face was stiff and stained with grey. The word 'corpse' came into my head.

I could no longer be certain of anything. I thought I noticed a lengthening of the intervals between the noisy breaths. The machine was running down. The power that pumped the lungs and made the inhuman rasping noise was going to leave her alone. I wasn't aware of the last breath. Only that the breathing had stopped. But I still didn't think of her as dead. Spasmodically there was a faint fluttering of the lips on one side of her mouth, like a subdued breathing.

'She's going very peacefully if she's going.'

So Nanny wasn't sure either. But soon the fluttering stopped. A few minutes later, I thought I could see faint movements of breathing, but nothing was happening.

At 5.50, half an hour since I'd come into the room, and twenty minutes since I'd told Miss Black to get any doctor, no doctor had arrived. Then we heard the gates of the lift clicking shut, and Daddy came in, overcoat on, hat in hand, very flustered. 'Mater,' he said in a loud anxious voice, 'Mater'. He strode across to the armchair and went round behind it to grab her shoulders, shaking them, letting his hat fall to the floor.

'Mater! Can you hear me? Mater!'

The head let itself be jolted unresponsively. I didn't want him to speak to her or to shake her.

'How long has she been like this?'

Then Dr Cookman arrived, dapper in a dark suit, carrying a bowler hat and business-like case. Fifteen minutes earlier, the arrival of a doctor would have been exciting, like a climax in a suspense film, when you don't know whether the police are going to be too late. The body failed to disturb his spruce smoothness. Nothing he did had any urgency about it. He looked at her, felt her pulse, took his stethoscope from his bag and began sounding her chest as if all she had was a cold. Nanny cut the strap of her bodice to allow him free access, and the silk fell to expose a large, sagging breast. Dr Cookman continued unhurriedly with his sounding. Carefully putting the stethoscope on the table, he gripped her ribs with his white, manicured hands, pushing at the body below the breasts in a dignified effort at artificial respiration. Looking up, he shook his head like a salesman refusing to haggle.

'Is there nothing you can do, Doctor?' Daddy asked respectfully.

He shook his head again. 'I'm afraid not.'

In the silence I was aware of the doctor's professional patience, Daddy's agonized reluctance to believe she was dead, Nanny's resignation.

'There's nothing at all you could do?' Helplessly, knowing the answer would be no.

'I'm sorry,' Dr Cookman said.

A few minutes later Dr Waistnedge arrived. Daddy and I went out of the room with him. He made Daddy concede that the end could have been very much worse. When we went back into the bedroom, Dr Winner was there with Nanny.

After the three doctors had left, we moved the body to the floor. Daddy held her under the left shoulder, I held her under the right. When we lifted her, the head flopped sleepily forwards. Nanny pulled the chair away from behind as we lowered the body gradually but ignominiously to the floor. The stumpy right leg straightened out in a graceless, almost obscene kick. To see the short fat body prostrate in pink underclothes with one naked breast and short arms spreadeagled was to see her degraded as death had no right to degrade her. People would come up to me after the funeral to say what a wonderful woman my grandmother was; I'd remember what she looked like now. The mouth fell open. We tied a towel round her head to keep it closed. Then we put a pillow under her head. I wanted to lift her back on to the bed, but Daddy said we must leave her on the floor. Nanny and I stripped the bed, covering the body with the top sheet. Nanny and Daddy went around the room, locking away valuables before the woman arrived from the synagogue to watch by the corpse. Daddy told me to take the rings off her fingers. A jade ring and a wedding-ring. I felt I was undoing the marriage that had given birth to Mummy, and I kept having to remind myself that I wasn't hurting the dead hand as I pulled the flesh back, pinching it above the knuckle to slide the rings off. The jade came easily, but I had to struggle

with the wedding-ring. Then I tucked the arm back under the
sheet, thinking of the amputated hand in *The Duchess of Malfi*,
but gently, because it was still human. We locked the bedroom
door behind us, leaving the body to stiffen under the sheet.

Uncle Phil and I were woken at 5.30 on Sunday morning to
drive in the Rover to break the news to Mummy at the health
farm. Mrs Ellyott, the owner, told her we'd arrived but not why
we'd come. She was sitting up in bed, trembling violently.

'What's it all about? Who?'

I faltered with the phrase I'd thought up as the kindest preparation. 'It's the worst news you could possibly have expected.'

'Who? Tell me quickly.'

'Grannie.'

A sharp intake of breath, almost a sob. 'Gone?'

I couldn't answer, and Uncle Phil confirmed it.

'When?'

I hesitated again, quailing before her voracious urgency. He
said, 'Friday'.

She was crying now.

She drove me back to Bournemouth in the Jaguar while Uncle
Phil followed us in the Rover. She told me the reason she didn't
seem more upset was that in some respects Grannie had been
dead ever since the first stroke. She hadn't been herself. Not the
woman she used to be.

The three-hour drive was going to give us the longest
conversation we'd had since her visit to Cambridge. It
meandered between death and trivialities, until suddenly she
was saying: 'I don't know whether there's any way of verifying
it with statistics, but it's my theory that whenever one soul dies,
another one is born.'

'You mean you think the old soul from the dead body goes
into a baby?'

'I don't know exactly. It's only a theory. But it must be
something like that, or there'd never be room in Heaven for all
the souls that there are.'

She said that when she was a young girl, Grannie had kept
pinching the bridge of her nose. 'I want you to look beautiful

when you grow up.' When I was a baby she kept interfering.
'You'd never have had acidosis if she hadn't given you such rich
food.' Worst of all she'd made Mummy feel that I didn't belong
to her. 'You were only a baby, but you made it very clear to me
that you didn't need me. So when Teddy was born I made up
my mind: "This time I'm going to keep him for myself."'

In the hotel the visitors still didn't know that she was dead. In
the dining-room they would come over to our table, gravely
solicitous. 'How's Mrs Morris?' 'Is she any better?' Mummy and
Daddy would shake their heads as if to indicate there was not
much hope or would answer evasively. Seething with disapproval I kept silent. Why were they always so secretive? Why
should they want to keep the death to themselves? The visitors
surely had a right to know about it, or was death bad for
business?

Mrs Evansky, who moved in the highest of Anglo-Jewish
circles, came down to Bournemouth so that she could be with
Mummy while the men went with the coffin to the cemetery.
Almost as soon as she arrived, Mrs Evansky showed how adept
she was at comforting the bereaved. She talked about experi-
ences she'd shared with Grannie, sounding as if she had felt
privileged. Mummy told her how Grannie had spent a whole
day watching the Coronation on television. Mrs Evansky
nodded, saying how wonderful it must have been to see it all on
television. Then she told us how she had spent the day. Her
daughter was married to a lawyer who was orbiting towards
eminence. 'Beryl and Victor had seats in the Abbey, you know,
and they asked for the loan of the car and the chauffeur for the
day. I said they could have them, but I thought I may as well see
something of it. So I went with them as a lady's maid. I dressed
in black and sat in front with the chauffeur.' She was naïvely
proud of having humiliated herself. Could this have something
to do with Jewishness? There was the same naïveté in the *pièce
de résistance* of her solace. 'I don't know whether you know this,
but it's supposed to be a great *Mitzvah* to die on *Erev Shabbos*
(Friday, the eve of the Sabbath).' *Mitzvah* literally means
'commandment' but the sense can be extended to the privilege

of being allowed to fulfil a commandment, though otherwise it can hardly mean a privilege. 'My mother passed away on a Friday too,' she added happily.

From saying he'd have to go back to the farm after the funeral, Uncle Phil resigned himself to staying for the *Shiva*, the regulation week of mourning, when the bereaved sit on special low chairs provided by the synagogue. For details of correct procedure Daddy kept consulting Volume 2 of *The Laws and Customs of Israel*. Mummy said the *Shiva* chairs looked greasy. When Daddy said she needn't sit on one, she seated herself in a low leather armchair.

'Is this chair too comfortable?'

After considering it, he shook his head.

'I'm not allowed to sew, am I?'

'No. You can read or write, but you mustn't do anything you enjoy.'

The next day a wreath arrived. Daddy stared at it balefully. 'That's what I was afraid of. We should have put "No Flowers" in the *Echo*.'

'Isn't it silly?' Mummy said.

I checked the impulse to say we had no right to expect everyone to know that flowers were against Jewish custom.

'Who's it from?' Daddy asked.

Mummy looked at the note. 'I'd rather not say. I'd rather just tear it up without saying anything. It's so silly. Do you mind, Jack?'

Evidently he didn't mind. Tearing the letter and the envelope into small pieces, she limped across to let them flutter into the waste-paper basket. The florist's card was still on the table. Daddy tore it up. Nanny was told to undo the wreath and send the flowers to the sanatorium. Later Mummy told me it was from Mr Kynaston.

In the dining-room Grannie's place at the head of the table remained empty all through the *Shiva* and for several days afterwards. Then, coming down to lunch, I found Mummy sitting in it, eating her grapefruit a little tensely. Teddy's place was laid in the middle of the side he'd been sharing with her. Nanny still shared my side at lunch-time, eating her dinner upstairs. In the evening, a smaller table was prepared for us, just big enough for four, with Mummy in Grannie's place. At neither meal did anyone comment on the new seating arrangements.

Six weeks went by before they let Uncle Phil see the will. Daddy was in London for a tombstone setting. With the stiff brown envelope in his hand, Uncle Phil sat down on the sofa in the Oak Room to pull out the legal parchment. I saw his hands tremble as he read. Then he folded it up again to put it back in the envelope. His voice was quite steady. 'Well, that's that. I've wasted my life. I might just as well have married.'

'If you'd known what the will was, you'd have got married again?' It hadn't occurred to me that what had been stopping him were his expectations.

For a moment he sounded almost jovial, relishing the idea of the opportunity he'd missed. 'I'd have said: "Thank you very much, I'm off." I had lots of chances, you know, two of them were really good. Real smashers. You know one of them very well.'

'Clarice?'

'Yes, Clarice would've had me. Do you think, Ron, do you really think my future wasn't worth more to me than thirty bob a week?'

He'd been left the interest on £3,000 for the rest of his life or until such time as he married a woman not of the Jewish faith. On his death the £3,000 was to go to his son if that son was brought up in the Jewish faith, or to his wife. If he died unmarried, it was to be added to the residual estate.

He was bitter and incredulous. 'She said it to me so often. "You'll be all right, Phil. You'll be all right when I'm gone. The farm'll be yours, and no one'll be able to take it away from you." That's what she used to say. "You'll be all right, Phil. I've seen to it." Ron, do you know what I wish? I wish she hadn't any money. Then I couldn't have kidded myself there was anything worth waiting for.'

If it was true that he could have married Clarice, it seemed silly to have given up the chance just for money. There he was on the sofa, fat, bald and fifty, with nothing left to look forward to. But he went on taking me so frankly into his confidence that I went on liking him, in spite of wanting to be as unlike him as possible. Daddy would disinherit me if I married out of the faith, but I wasn't going to waste my life waiting for a legacy. Phil was blowing his nose now, on the edge of tears – not mourning his mother, but the son he'd never had. He'd always wanted one and now he needed one. 'To help me with the farm and take over when I'm gone. But I couldn't do it. She'd have fretted like anything. It was bad enough with Isadore. You should have seen how she carried on.'

I asked him about his marriage. It hadn't lasted long, he said, and it happened only because Maggie kidded him into believing she was pregnant. As soon as he knew she wasn't, he let the family buy her into giving him a divorce. After that, Grannie had bought him the garage and gone on giving him money for the other business ventures. All his advice to me had been based on his own failure. I must find out what I really wanted and fight free of the family. But I knew I mustn't let him see how weak I thought he'd been. 'Would you like to hear my new record of Sibelius's Fifth Symphony?'

'Yes, it'll steady my nerves.'

He seemed to be listening attentively, but I could imagine what was going on in his mind. He'd spent several week-ends at the hotel since the funeral, and each time he'd waited till 6.45 to say mourner's *Kaddish* at the service Daddy had arranged for him in the Card Room. Today at six o'clock he looked at his watch. 'Well, I must be off.'

'Aren't you going to wait for the service?'

'Not today. It's a long journey back, you know.'

'If I haven't succeeded yet,' said the hero of a play I was writing, 'I haven't failed yet either.' Time was still on my side, but I still wasn't questioning my compulsive drive to distinguish myself, though I knew it would become less compulsive if only I could succeed in making myself matter to a girl who mattered to me. At school it had seemed natural to work very hard for good reports and prizes to take home. It was less important now to win prizes and get firsts in the tripos than to be talked about and written about in *Granta*. If, most of the time, I couldn't think favourably of myself, it was all the more important that other people should know me by name, read what I wrote and vote for me. I was editor of a literary magazine, president of the college dramatic society, secretary of the English Club and vice-president of the Young Writers' Group, but if this was 'success' I wasn't the only one who was uncertain whether I deserved it. 'What is all this about Ronnie Hayman?' asked Derek, late one night, when a dozen of us were huddled blearily together on the lawn after the drink had run out at a bottle-party. 'What do people see in him?'

I was no longer thinking so much about 'self-transcendence' and 'one-pointedness of being' as about Gerard Manley Hopkins's phrase 'selfyeast of spirit'. Selfyeast of spirit was what I most hated lacking, but unlike him, I couldn't believe it was God's decree that I should wake up every morning to the taste of myself; and if I didn't enjoy that taste, how could I hope to find a girl who would enjoy it enough to let me enjoy the taste of her? The best moments were when I could forget myself by punting along the river or lying on the grass near the bridge at King's, gazing up at the overhanging trees, studying the infinitely intricate pattern of sunlight on leaves and branches, green, brown, greeny brown and browny green, shifting slightly in the light breeze. But most of the time I was too depressed to look at what I saw. It was there, and it was beautiful, but it didn't help me. It wasn't the work of a Creator I could pray to.

The worst depression came in January, when I bought a tube of toothpaste at the chemist's from a girl who looked like Berna. Walking down Trinity Lane afterwards, I suddenly wanted the tall walls to close in on the narrow roadway as if the perspective had risen out of a picture. I wanted them to topple and squash me into a pulp with the metal and the saddles of all the bicycles parked along the kerb. Life couldn't go on the way it was, and the sooner it stopped, the better. 'Sometimes I sit in my chair', says one diary entry, 'with a book open in front of me, but behind the silence in my mind, I'm listening to the nerves and pulses ticking away and waiting for myself to explode.'

Not knowing how to value myself, and not knowing what people saw in me, I was liable to miss opportunities through lack of self-confidence. After reviewing John Whiting's play *Marching Song* in a duplicated magazine, *Broadsheet*, I got to know him, and later on to know the actress who was playing Dido Morgen. Full of excitement I visited her in her West End dressing-room and in her Chelsea flat. One day she asked: 'Are you going to the May Ball?' 'I don't know,' I said. 'Are you?' 'Only with you.' But we didn't end up going to it together. I was still the boy I'd been at Hailey when I knew I'd won the hundred yards but didn't believe it.

That I was debilitated by incredulity became painfully apparent one afternoon when I was walking along a pathway in King's on my way to visit a friend. Suddenly a first-floor window was thrown open, and a voice said: 'Ronnie, would you come up?' The list of names at the foot of the stairs showed that the rooms on the first floor belonged to the most fêted of all the undergraduates. I'd met him once in hall, when he'd been there as the guest of Giles Bedford, who afterwards reported that he'd said he liked me. There was no reason to disbelieve that I'd been summoned into the presence, but I couldn't believe it. How could I take the risk of going up to knock on his door? What if he opened it and looked at me blankly? How could I say: 'Somehow I had the impression that somebody called me out of your window?' Reluctantly I went away, and told my friend what had happened. It was a relief to talk about it, but I couldn't explain why I hadn't gone up. A few days later I saw a letter in *Varsity* signed by the star undergraduate and a great many others. I'd gladly have added my name to the list, but it was too late.

The first words I heard Caroline say were 'Are you the man I'm looking for?' I was casting a college production of Cocteau's *Bacchus*, and hearing that there was this professional actress in Cambridge who'd completed her training at the Guildhall, I'd written a postcard to ask whether she'd be interested to come round for a chat about the production. She had short, reddish hair and a blue plastic mackintosh. Within minutes she was telling me she'd just broken off her engagement, so she'd love to be in the play if I thought she was suitable. It would take her mind off her boy-friend. Everything about her seemed taut – her voice, the freckled skin over the prominent cheekbones, the sweater over the prominent breasts.

When we were kissing, I knew what life was going to be like: full of endless-seeming stretches of dreariness, and then suddenly a knock at the door, a new face, the taste of a new tongue. From probing into my vertebrae, her strong fingers moved to my erection, massaging to make it even bigger. She knew exactly how hard to press, how fast to move her hand. She was kneeling on the floor now, and I was looking anxiously through the uncurtained ground-floor window. Fortunately the courtyard was empty except for two gowned figures walking in the opposite direction.

I was very happy during rehearsals. One of my secret fears had been that, if I did find a girl, I'd want so much physical contact that she'd get fed up with being kissed and cuddled so much, but Caroline wanted no less of it than I did. At first I wasn't much good at feeling her up, but she was a good-humoured teacher. 'A gentleman must keep his nails cut very short if he wants to please his lady.' I got better at it, but somehow we kept putting off the moment of making love properly. Several times she said: 'I'll stay all night if you want me to'; but I'd be sent down without a degree if they found out I'd had a girl in my rooms all night, and I still hadn't bought any French letters. Not wanting to borrow one from Giles, I made up my mind one afternoon to get some at the chemist's. But when I came to the shop, I walked past it. Miserably I walked up and down on the pavement, each time intending to go in through the glass door. What was I going to ask for? How did one word it? Could I ask to be served by the man? Would he grin at me? In the end I went back to my room without any. When Caroline arrived in the evening I hated myself for my cowardice as much as I loved her for her sexiness. We felt each other up, and she left before midnight.

The production was having a lot of publicity because it was the English première of the play, and there had been a possibility that Cocteau would come to Cambridge for it. But a few days before the opening I got an anonymous letter from someone who said that though he hadn't read the play, he understood it was anti-religious, and therefore unsuitable for production in college. He advised me not to go ahead.

On the first night I was backstage during the interval, and when the curtain went up again I had to go outside the building to make my way back to the auditorium. I heard a huge burst of laughter when there shouldn't have been any, and, hurrying into the back of the hall, I couldn't help laughing myself. A duck was waddling behind the Duke, who was pacing and nodding his head, so the bobbing head of the duck seemed to be mimicking his. Its wings must have been clipped, and each time it looked as though it were going to walk off-stage, it turned back. With so many people standing at the back of the hall, it was impossible for me to get anywhere near the stage. I thought of shouting for the curtain to be dropped, but there ought to be a less drastic solution. Eventually the duck waddled into the prompt corner, where the stage manager must have caught it.

Mummy and Daddy had come up to Cambridge for the performance. It was Daddy's first visit. I'd organized a party in Giles's room, which was bigger than mine. The actors were all coming, and about forty other people, including the translator, a BBC producer and an actor. It was a beautiful evening. Standing in the courtyard, Daddy admired the skyline. Mummy said they'd decided not to come to the party because they were tired after the train journey. When I tried to persuade them, she said: 'You don't really want us to come. You've got your friends. You don't want us.' I told her I wanted her and Daddy to meet my friends, looking at him for support.

'I'm a bit tired,' he said uncertainly. 'Why don't you come and have breakfast with us at the hotel in the morning?'

I knew they would come if I tried hard enough to persuade them, and I did try, but not hard enough. I was tired, upset about the duck, uncertain whether my production had been any good. I needed reassurance too much to be able to give any.

'Do come,' I said. 'Or would you really rather not?'

When they still demurred, I said OK, I'd meet them for breakfast.

'We did enjoy the play,' Daddy said as I kissed them good-night.

Guiltily I moved away towards the party, wishing I hadn't organized one, wanting just to be alone with Caroline. The room was full. She was the only girl in the play, and as the boys came in, one or two at a time, all looking smaller in their own clothes, I kept asking did she know where to come? Oh yes, she was still taking her make-up off. Or putting more make-up on. You know what women are. I had a premonition that she wasn't going to come, but I didn't altogether give up hope until nearly midnight.

On the way back from breakfast at the hotel I telephoned her house. She was going to be out all day, her mother said, but I'd see her at the performance in the evening. I started waiting in the dressing room an hour before she was due. She arrived ten minutes late, and by then the boys were making up on the other side of the curtain.

'I'll explain later. Don't talk to me now or I'll get the make-up all wrong.'

There was nothing for it but to sit down and wait for the curtain to go up. Somebody had told me at the party that the so-called professional actress was giving the only amateurish performance; I still desired her too much to be objective about it. Afterwards I stood behind her while she took her make-up off. We couldn't talk till the last of the boys had gone from behind the curtain. When she told me, it was as if I'd known all along. Her ex-fiancé had come to the performance and had taken her home with him on the pillion of his motor bike. The engagement was on again. A few days later she wrote to say she was very happy. She hoped I didn't feel too used.

In the Easter vac it seemed incredible that my Cambridge career was nearly over. If Mummy and Daddy still believed they'd made sacrifices to send me here, their resentment focused on the mistake they'd made in letting me give up the idea of reading Law. It wasn't just English literature I'd learnt to criticize, but them and the religion. Fortunately Teddy, who was also due for a university education, had no ambition to

write. Somebody would have to earn some money, he said, to
support Ronnie. When his first attempt at an Oxford scholarship failed, Daddy said: 'Perhaps he was fated to go to
Cambridge.' But Mummy believed it was partly my fault. 'I
can't help thinking you could have been more helpful on the
phone before the oral. It was the oral he fell down on.' Later she
added: 'Perhaps religion had something to do with it too.'

She accused me of wanting to forget that we were business
people, and of thinking myself superior to the sons and
daughters of the business people who came to the hotel. 'If only
you'd make friends with them, you'd like them.' Often I tried
quite hard. I was too shy to edge my way into conversations the
way they did by saying 'Mind if I join you?', but I'd go into the
lounge after dinner and sit down in an armchair, waiting for
them. Even when I had a circle of them sitting round me, I found
it hard to join in the conversation. I'd stick it out as long as I
could, knowing that sooner or later I'd hear myself murmuring
some excuse for retreating to the Oak Room.

Mummy and Daddy usually made it over to me, though not
always without reluctance.

'Where are you having your appointment?'

'In the small office so as not to disturb Ronnie.'

They all came to have tea there, and one Sunday, when Barry
was staying for the week-end, he and Daddy sat on at the table,
talking about the family. After I'd retreated to the card table I
used as a desk, Daddy turned round. 'You won't be offended if I
go, will you?'

I knew that as soon as the exams and the last May Ball were
over, I'd have to go away. 'Living with them', I wrote, 'is like
living at close quarters with people who speak a different
language, and it's a strain to keep it up. Either they talk
unnaturally, or I do. It would be better to live abroad, where I'd
be entitled to outsider status. Perhaps I could get a part-time job
somewhere, plugging myself in at the same time to the European
tradition.'

My latest writer-hero was Arthur Koestler, who was saying
that most of the novels written in England since the war could
equally well have been written before the war. The Cambridge
atmosphere was so special and the Bournemouth atmosphere so

stuffy that I thought I'd stand a better chance of developing into a worthwhile writer in a country where it was impossible to pretend the war hadn't happened. Germany would be best of all, but Daddy would feel deeply hurt if I went to live there.

One of the speakers at a Union debate had called university life 'three years of premature retirement'. It was this that was coming to an end. Never again would I have so many friends within such a small radius, never again so much leisure for chatting and comparing notes. But the freedom had come to feel like an unlicensed extension of my childhood right to non-commitment. Now I'd be responsible to myself for what I did, even if I didn't get a job. Grannie had left me £1,000, but if I went abroad, I could take only £50 with me. Unlike my friends who were taking Civil Service exams or applying for interviews with the BBC, I wanted to remain independent of the big institutions. I was counting on myself to work harder than I had at Cambridge, and before taking any other decision I wanted to see what the results would be.

On the Monday before my final exams started, Daddy had a coronary thrombosis. I wasn't to worry, Mummy said, and the doctor's advice was that I shouldn't come home any earlier than I'd been planning to. It would only alarm him. He was comfortable and doing nicely. I didn't know exactly what a coronary thrombosis was, so I asked the boy-friend of an ADC actress who was a doctor. He said they varied enormously in their seriousness, but one's expectation of life wasn't necessarily reduced, provided one took things easily. What could have caused it? I asked. Possibly strain, physical or mental. Did he worry a lot?

My telephone calls home increased in frequency. He was still in bed, with a full-time nurse, but the news was consistently good. The doctor was still saying I should stick to my original plans. I'd been intending to go down on the day after the May Ball. I'd be up all night, and then, after a few hours of half-dressed sleep, finish off my packing and say goodbye to everybody.

There was more luggage than I'd expected – three bulging
Revelation suitcases, my portable typewriter, my umbrella, my
swordstick from Daddy's shop, my tennis-racket, my overcoat,
my mackintosh, two improvised parcels and the loose books that
wouldn't fit in anywhere.

It would have been impossible to carry it all if my friend
Alfred, the editor of a London-based magazine, hadn't been in
Cambridge for the day.

We arrived at the station with five minutes to spare, but there
was no porter, and it didn't occur to us until after we'd missed
the train that we could have got on to it without buying tickets.
The next train to London was the 6.12, which wouldn't arrive in
time for me to catch the 7.30 from Waterloo, and the next train
to Bournemouth after that was the 10.30, a stopping train that
arrived at 2.14 a.m. We adjourned to the waiting-room to
discuss what to do. I could go back to spend another night at
Trinity Hall, I could stay at Alfred's flat in London, or go on
with the journey. I decided to go on, but accepted his invitation
to a meal in between the two trains. It was from his flat that I
telephoned the hotel to say what time I'd be arriving. Miss Black
answered: 'There's bad news, I'm afraid. Your brother's been
sent for.'

I went into the kitchen, where Alfred was frying sausages and
eggs.

'Bad news. I think my father must be dying.'

That he was already dead was a possibility which had occurred
to me, but which I dismissed; and if he was dying, well at least
he was still alive, and if he was still alive, he might go on living
for a bit. There was nothing I could do to get myself down to
Bournemouth any faster, but why hadn't I asked Miss Black
what the bad news was? Just because she sounded as though she
didn't want to tell me? The more I talked to Alfred, the further
the possibility of death receded, and there was no point in not
eating. Soon we were slicing bread to go into the toaster and
drinking tea at the kitchen table, chatting and joking as if
nothing had happened. But in the taxi to Waterloo, I
remembered that the last words I'd spoken to him were: 'It's
strange – my own body feels quite well.'

In the uncomfortable railway carriage I thought about the

fantasies I used to have about Daddy's death. The imaginary camera had favoured me.

Newsbearer (*apologetically*): I'm afraid your father's passed away.
Self (*matter-of-factly*): Died, you mean?

Then the manly comforting arm around Mummy's shaking shoulders, the strong, silent, understanding exchange of glances with Teddy, the quiet assumption of adult initiative that impresses even the undertaker. There'd been no serious possibility that he'd die, so there was no danger in thinking about it. Now I did believe he was going to die, though not that he was dead. The light would be on in his bedroom, a small group round the bedside, and I'd walk quickly in to grasp his dying hand. I'd send the others to bed and stay in the room all night, sitting on the floor if necessary to keep myself awake. But I was so sleepy already that I nodded off into a comfortable dream to wake up, jolted back into uneasiness as the train braked to a halt at a station with no visible name. Raindrops outside the window were invisible until they touched the glass. Not even midnight yet. Still another three hours in the dry, stale heat of the carriage before I'd hear what the bad news was. If only I'd asked Miss Black 'How is he?'

What if I had the choice now of shortening my own life to add a year to his? Would I? Why should I? It's my life. Yes, but he gave it to me. Am I going to refuse him one year when he gave me so many?

For all the discomfort of ideas like that, the reality of my drowsiness was more immediate, and I knew I had years stretching ahead of me in which I could slide comfortably between sleeping and waking. Whatever else happened, I could go on writing, and he wouldn't be able to take the pen out of my hand if I wrote on Shabbos.

It was still raining when the train arrived at Bournemouth Central. Uncle Phil was standing at the ticket-barrier in his old mackintosh.

'What's happened?'
'He's gone.'

'When?'

'Six o'clock.'

I'd been drinking coffee in the station waiting-room. Gone. A fact. All over.

Home is where you should never have to confront anything unfamiliar; on a night like this your own family consists of strangers. In the old nursery Mummy was sitting oddly erect in Nanny's old chair, speechless and almost paralysed with weeping. 'I'm sorry,' I said, and went on about missing the train, and how I could have come down earlier if only I'd known there was any danger. It sounded stupid as I said it. How could you have a heart attack and not be in danger? I'd simply done what I was told, like a child. 'I was so surprised,' I said. She blurted out a few facts of what had happened, but soon broke into choked weeping. Teddy, already practised at comforting her, moved his tall body to the side of the armchair, stooping to rest his large hands on her shoulders. 'Ronnie's here now. Ronnie's here. Why don't you go to bed? You can't stay up all night.'

Wanting to see him, I hesitated outside the bedroom door like a small boy who has to knock. I heard Teddy behind me. 'I was waiting for you. I thought you'd want to see him.' I pushed at the door. The thin body of an old man from the synagogue levered itself out of a chair. The watcher by the dead. 'I want to see him,' I said. The coffin was standing on trestles, draped with black silk. Daddy's bed was already stripped; a memorial candle was burning on his bedside table. The old man was holding out an open prayer book to me, pointing at Hebrew print. When I repeated 'I want to see him', he moved over to the coffin. How had they made it and put him into it so quickly? Twenty-four hours ago I'd been at the May Ball, dancing with Madeleine.

The thin old man slid back the lid of the coffin. Crooking his arm round the dead neck to raise the body, he started to unwind the linen winding-sheet from around Daddy's face. But it wasn't. It was the face of a corpse, with features that looked like Aunt Hetty's. So remote, so unbeautiful, so dark, so smooth, so indisputably cancelled as a living entity. I'd pictured myself holding his dead hand and kissing his dead face; the face was untouchable. I turned away. Teddy's inexpressively sad gaze made me turn back, trying to see something more. I wished the old man wasn't there, but didn't feel entitled to send him out of the room. I stood staring at the face till I was no longer seeing it. I didn't even put my hand to his cheek. Then the old man skilfully lifted the stiff, sheeted body just enough to wind the winding-sheet back. As he finally let go of it, there was a faint thud.

On the day before the funeral I was alone in the room, relieving the watcher. I wanted to have another last look at the face I'd kissed so often. I'd been reading Gide's *Strait Is the Gate*, and my eyes kept switching between the lines of print and the unvarnished wood under the black, weighted silk. I'd have to lift the stiff body myself, unwind the winding-cloth and wind it back afterwards. What if someone came in? All the same, I pushed the black silk out of the way and tugged at the wooden lid. It didn't move. They'd screwed it down already, and there was a faint smell of putrefaction.

Mummy wanted Revd Lazarus to come down from London to take the funeral service, and I had to meet him at the station. He kissed me on both cheeks.

'Ronnie, my dear, I wish you long life. I never wanted to be alive to see this day. I loved him like my own son. I gave him Hebrew lessons, he was a Barmitzvah boy in my Shool, I married him, I was there when you were circumcised, and Teddy was circumcised, and now I've got to bury him. Ronnie, my dear, promise me that you'll always remember one thing. I know you didn't always see eye to eye with him, but what son does with his father? Tell me that, eh? Perhaps I shouldn't say this to you, but I'm an old man, and I'm going to. He talked to me a lot about you, and I want you to know that his love for you was something very special. Something really rather rare. Now tell me, how's poor Sadie taken it? It's so soon after your poor dear grandmama passed away, God rest her soul.'

As soon as we were inside the hotel, Mr Gideon stepped forward. Shaking hands with us both, he asked to have a word with Revd Lazarus. 'No, don't go away, Ronnie, we'll need you in a minute.'

They disappeared into the Lisle Lounge, and I played with the cat until I saw Mr Gideon beckoning me to go in.

'I understand from your brother that you're not intending to say *Kaddish* at the funeral.'

I couldn't say any prayers, I told him.

'Now listen to me, Ronnie. I want to say this to you in front of Revd Lazarus, who's known your father since he was younger than you are now. All his life he was a good Jew, sincere, upstanding, a worker for the community, a fine example to us all. The Bournemouth congregation owes more to him than to anyone, and for my part I consider it an honour to follow in his footsteps as president. Now I want to ask you something, Ronnie, and I know you'll give me an honest answer. Does a man like your father deserve to be publicly insulted at his own funeral by his own eldest son refusing to pray for the salvation of his soul?'

I said it wasn't intended as an insult. If we had souls, my father's would be judged according to his actions, not mine.

'Believe me, Ronnie, I've been to a lot of funerals since I've been president, and what you privately believe is a matter for your own conscience, but never in my whole life have I heard of a Jewish boy refusing to say *Kaddish* for his own father. Whatever you believe now, you were brought up the right way, and that's what should matter to you this afternoon. You've got your whole life in front of you to do what you like with, but today it's *his* funeral, and he needs you to play your part in it. It's a nice day and I'm sure we're going to get a very good turn-out. And I don't mind telling you, Ronnie, if all these people see you leaving it to your younger brother to pay your father his last respects, well, I'm afraid you're not going to be very popular in the community. You may not intend it as a public insult, but that's how it'll be taken. It's my duty as president to warn you.'

'Ronnie, my dear,' Revd Lazarus began, 'try to look at it like this. We don't know what happens to us when we pass away. Different people have different opinions, but nobody knows for sure whether the souls of the dear departed can look down from Heaven and see what's happening on earth. Perhaps my poor old friend Jack can hear every word we're saying in this room at this minute. Just try to imagine that he's listening. He can't speak to us, only hear us. Just imagine that, can you? Now if you wanted to hurt him, can you think of any way you could hurt him more deeply, more grievously than by refusing to pray for his soul's salvation?'

I said there couldn't be any value in prayers said without belief, and that I couldn't behave hypocritically at a time like this. I had no choice.

'You not only have a choice, my dear, you cannot escape making it. The choice is between hurting yourself by going against what you think you believe, and hurting everyone else by what they'll regard as childish stubbornness, even if you know and I know that you're trying to be sincere. You'll be hurting your dear mother, hurting Teddy, who doesn't want to feel isolated at such a vital minute, and hurting the whole community, which doesn't want to see a man like Jack dishonoured at his own funeral. Believe me, Ronnie, I know it isn't going to be an easy decision for you to make. Mr Gideon, I think you and I should leave Ronnie alone to give him time to think.'

I said I didn't need time to think.

'Does it occur to you', asked Mr Gideon, 'that you're being rather selfish?'

'Ronnie, my dear, I'm going to be absolutely frank with you. I'm a minister of religion, and I'm seventy years old. For sixty years I've prayed every day, and for nearly fifty I've been doing it professionally, which means I've been paid to do it. Now do you think that in fifty times 365 days there's never a time when your heart isn't fully in it? Sometimes the act of praying brings one's faith back, which is what might happen with you today, if you give it the chance. But in any event, if I were a young man like you today – and I'm not saying this lightly, I assure you – I would go to this funeral with an open mind. I would try not to decide in advance. And when the moment comes, I would try not to harden my heart. I would just ask myself one simple question: "Can I better express my love for this man who loved me by remaining silent or by offering up a prayer for his soul – a prayer which may or may not be heard, may or may not make any difference?" How does God judge us? By the results of our teaching on those we leave behind? How can we know? All we can do is hope and pray. Now forgive me. I'm an old man and it's been a long journey for me. I must wash my hands before the service.'

There was no denying the reality of the tears that were rolling down his cheeks.

The funeral seemed intolerably similar to other funerals. Why should they behave differently, just because it was my father in the box? I stood with my knees touching the coffin as they said the usual Hebrew words, and Revd Lazarus made a speech in English fulsome with praise. Afterwards he got into the hearse with Teddy and me. I didn't feel entitled to say we wanted to be alone with the coffin. A large crowd of men in hats surrounded the car as it halted in the burial ground. I was aware of the eyes on Teddy and me when we got out. Like a self-conscious actor, I was aware of my dragging pace as I followed the coffin, and the long pause, spade poised in the air, before I dropped the first earth on top of the raw wood that hid him from the eyes of all these people. Most of the men shook hands with both of us, some only with Teddy.

When a wreath arrived, I didn't ask who it was from. During the next ten days, Teddy and I both did our best to make Mummy less miserable. We both went to the services with her. I wore a hat and I stood up and sat down when the others did but my lips stayed shut. Teddy's voice was alone in the *Kaddish*. We sat in the Oak Room all day for the *Shiva*, while visitors to the hotel and people from the town called in to condole with us. Most of them started by saying 'There's nothing anyone can say but. . . .' Mummy said the same sentences over and over again: 'Only a year and four days since my mother died.' 'Yes, I've had the most wonderful letters. So many people knew him and liked him. And they all say how kind he was.' 'Yes, everybody says how kind he was. He loved to be of help. There's a barber in this town he helped when he was trying to get started, and now he's manager of a shop in the Arcade.'

After a week of it, Teddy and I persuaded her to come away with us for three days at Southsea. A lot of what she said to us was what she'd said already to other people, but we listened and sympathized, neither of us trying to tell her what we were feeling.

One night after we'd got her off to bed, Teddy and I went for a walk along the promenade. The season hadn't begun yet, and not many of the lights were on in the hotel bedrooms. It was windy. The sea threw itself uselessly against the beach.

I knew I wanted to make a sort of apology to him. He was the only one who hadn't seemed to be blaming me for refusing to pray, and he was the one who'd had the burden of it. From the moment of my early morning arrival at the hotel, he'd revealed a quiet strength I hadn't expected of him. But I'd never really tried to find out what could be expected of him. The rivalry had been too intense. He was obviously her favourite, and she'd fought so hard to make me spend more time with him that I'd fought back by spending hardly any. I was also feeling guilty towards him because I knew that the sooner I went away from Bournemouth, the more difficult it would be for him when he came home on holiday from Oxford.

We left long lines of footprints behind us on the damp sand. He said he was having doubts about the religion. I said I'd had them for a long time before deciding to break, and made the decision a long time before I stopped conforming. But I couldn't have pretended at the funeral. It hadn't even been a matter of deciding not to.

'I think that's right,' he said. 'Morally right.'

I wondered whether Aunt Hetty had told him about Daddy and Grannie. The idea of a relationship between them was all the more repulsive now that they were both dead, and if he'd really wanted Uncle Dan to marry Mummy, we had that much less right to be alive. But if Teddy didn't know, so much the better, and without telling him there was no way of finding out whether he knew.

He was as puzzled as I was about how the coffin had been made so quickly, but he said it was definitely better not to upset Mummy by asking questions. The 'definitely' might have been picked up from Aunt Hetty; the concern about upsetting Mummy had been characteristic of him for a long time. His experience had been the same as mine. He'd arrived too late to see Daddy alive because he'd been told not to come home until the end of term, and when he arrived, Mummy seemed to feel that he ought to have come sooner. But there was no point in arguing about it now. What good would it do? Better to keep the peace.

'Do you want to go back?' I asked.

He was turning up his coat collar against the wind. 'No, let's go on.'

We walked mostly in silence. I thought of asking whether he knew any more than I did about Mr Kynaston, but there was nothing we could have done about it. His face looked very young. When visitors to the hotel had said that we looked alike, I'd always resented it, but in the dark, with the coat collar half hiding his cheek, I saw something that looked like me, only more vulnerable. There was so much I could have warned him against, but I'd given him too much advice in the past. Or not enough love to stop the advice from seeming patronizing. If I stayed in Bournemouth, perhaps the relationship could improve, but how could I stay in Bournemouth?

'Let's go back now,' I said, eventually.

The day after we arrived back at the hotel, Tonks gave notice. When Mummy went down to breakfast at eight o'clock, there were no waiters in the dining-room. She complained to the manager, who pounced on Tonks in his changing-room. 'You're supposed to be on duty at eight. Mrs Hayman's been sitting there for ten minutes, and there's no one to look after her.' After giving notice on the spot, Tonks came into the dining-room shouting 'Another week and I'll have none of this to worry about.' Then he served her breakfast.

Not wanting him to go, she asked me to have a word with him. He sat down on the other side of the oak table. I tried to think what Daddy would have said. I told him we'd be sorry to lose him after all these years. At first he was reluctant to talk, but soon the grievances came pouring out. A large and troublesome family had stayed for a fortnight and left without giving him a tip. Chef was refusing to start serving dinner before seven. The visitors grumbled, and the manager was bad-tempered. 'I haven't told anyone what I'm telling you, haven't told Mrs Hayman, and I haven't even told my wife, but I'm scared. I really am scared in this place, as I've never been in my life before. And I've been through a lot in the war. I was at Arnhem, you know, and honestly, sometimes I come here in the morning and feel I'd rather go through all that again than another day here.'

I felt quite guilty at persuading him, especially when he agreed to stay. 'But if it gets bad again in the future, I'll come to you.'

'Yes, you do that, Tonks.'

I thought Mummy would be delighted when I reported my success, but instead she started trying to convince herself it was better for him to stay.

'He does well enough for money, too. One family may go away without giving him anything, but another will give him five pounds, and his salary's gone up from five pounds ten to eight pounds ten.'

Miss Emily Swayne, head of the British Centre at Wuppertal-Elberfeld, was looking for someone to work four hours a day in the library. She'd written to the librarian of the German faculty library at Cambridge. I'd been looking for a book in the English faculty library when the German librarian wandered in, with her letter in his hand, to chat to the English librarian, who knew I wanted a part-time job abroad. Miss Swayne presumably needed someone with a degree in German, but there was nothing to be lost by applying. When I was eventually offered the job, Mummy said: 'I only want you to do what's right.' Surely the right thing was to stay in Bournemouth with her for a year. She'd given up her whole life to looking after her mother. Surely she didn't deserve to lose her elder son just after losing her husband and her mother.

I was making an effort to be consistently nice to her, but I knew I was in danger of becoming a professional son, awarding myself marks for my attentiveness. When I heard my voice persuading her to have an early night or not to ask for a smaller portion of sole, I reminded myself of her as she'd been when she took charge of Grannie's diet and resting routine. When we went out for walks, the pressure of her hand on my arm, heavier as she stepped on her lame leg, reminded me of Mrs Feather and her son. And when Uncle Phil discovered an unsigned will of Grannie's, leaving a quarter of her estate to him, I found myself taking Mummy's side against him.

They sat shouting at each other from the two leather armchairs on either side of the Oak Room fireplace. I sat on an upright chair in the middle, trying to arbitrate, but they wouldn't listen to each other, let alone me. The solicitor had

seen both wills, and though the unsigned one had a later date on
it, there was no doubt which one was legally valid.

'But Mother must have thought she'd signed it.'

'I'd be a pauper if she had. What did you say to her to make
her draw it up? What did you tell her about me?'

'She intended to sign it. She told me she had. I can prove it.'

'That's what you'd like, isn't it? I've had the burden of her all
these years while you went off and had yourself a good time. You
wanted me to lose everything I've worked for.'

'Just a minute. Didn't you open her letters?'

'If she had signed it, I'd have to sell the hotel. Do you realize
that? How else would I be able to raise the money for you?'

'You did. I know you did. So when the draft will came from
the solicitor, I bet you didn't even show it to her. That's why she
thought she'd signed it.'

'I suppose you went to the solicitor's office with her to have it
drawn up. I know it's your work. It couldn't be clearer if it was in
your handwriting.'

'You knew her memory wasn't good towards the end, so you
took advantage.'

'You're the one who took advantage. No one in her right
mind would draw up a will like that.'

There was nothing I could do except listen. Eventually their
voices quietened. Uncle Phil asked could he please have the
£3,000 in cash instead of just the interest on it. She said she'd
think it over, and in the morning she arranged it for him. A few
weeks later he wanted to borrow £1,000 to buy livestock and
machinery. She gave it to him, telling me Grannie would have
wanted her to. Two months later he wanted to borrow another
£500 because he was still undercapitalized. I advised her to say
no.

He then enlisted the help of a thin solicitor I'd sometimes seen
in Shool on the Day of Atonement. We all went to his office
and sat round a table covered with a green baize cloth. Morris
Muskin had only one lung. He coughed incessantly, spitting into
a silver box which he kept in his waistcoat pocket. I tried to keep
my eyes averted each time he spat, but he was sitting in a shaft of
sunlight, and the silver box glinted as it shuttled in and out of his
stained waistcoat pocket. He talked about the respect he'd

always felt for Grannie and Daddy. Between bouts of coughing he said that it wouldn't have been their wish for the family to be torn by dissension. Surely some compromise could be made. I said he was deliberately confusing emotional and legal issues, but when Mummy started to argue back emotionally, I knew we'd end by compromising. The wet noise of the coughing made me picture the oozing yellow mucus inside his one lung, and the glinting silver box was like a swinging silver disc in the hands of a hypnotist.

I was using the word 'Mummy' less and less, but I didn't want to call her 'Mother'. When I wrote to her, the letters started 'Dear M'; when I talked to her I didn't call her anything. But I was still being mainly a son. Whether I gave in to her or opposed her, danced with her or went out for long, stubborn, solitary walks in the pouring rain, the only choice was between being dutiful and being rebellious. In the end I went to Germany.

A friend once told me: 'If you had to be a Jew, your father should have been an East End tailor, very poor, with a strong Lithuanian accent. Then you could have learnt how to fight your way to the top.' To dislike your childhood is to dislike yourself, and though I went through a period of envying the people who had been less deprived of privation, I'm glad to have so many recollections of sun, sand, sea and space. I remember the pre-war period as one long seaside holiday in a warm climate.

Having grown up in a hotel, eating regularly in the restaurant, I have been left with an incurable need for holidays, hotels and restaurants. As a child I never had to clean my shoes, do the washing-up or cook; I still hate cleaning my shoes and washing up. I enjoy cooking, but I cooked my first chicken when I was in my thirties and my first joint after my wife and I separated. I still spend more than I earn, which may mean that I still assume that the hotel is there in the background, an inexhaustible source of necessities and luxuries.

What do I regret most about my childhood? The secrets, the habit of secretiveness, the failure of the initiatives that might have liberated me from a habit which is even more pernicious than it seems: when you are not open with other people, you are not open with yourself. Liberated from it, the crown prince might have found out sooner that the throne was just an armchair, dangerously soft.

I have no regrets about losing my faith: I found a substitute for it by building myself a religion of consciousness. I believed in the capacity of the human mind and in my capacity for making mine function rigorously. I believed in honesty and in the artist's imagination. With a notion (taken mainly from D. H. Lawrence) of self-realization, I believed that the closer a writer could approximate to it, the more he could help other people towards a fuller life. I knew that even if I succeeded in writing good books, they wouldn't be read by people like the Hatters, but the underlying aim was to fight imaginatively against the only evil I recognized – stupidity, insensitivity, ignorance about what causes suffering.